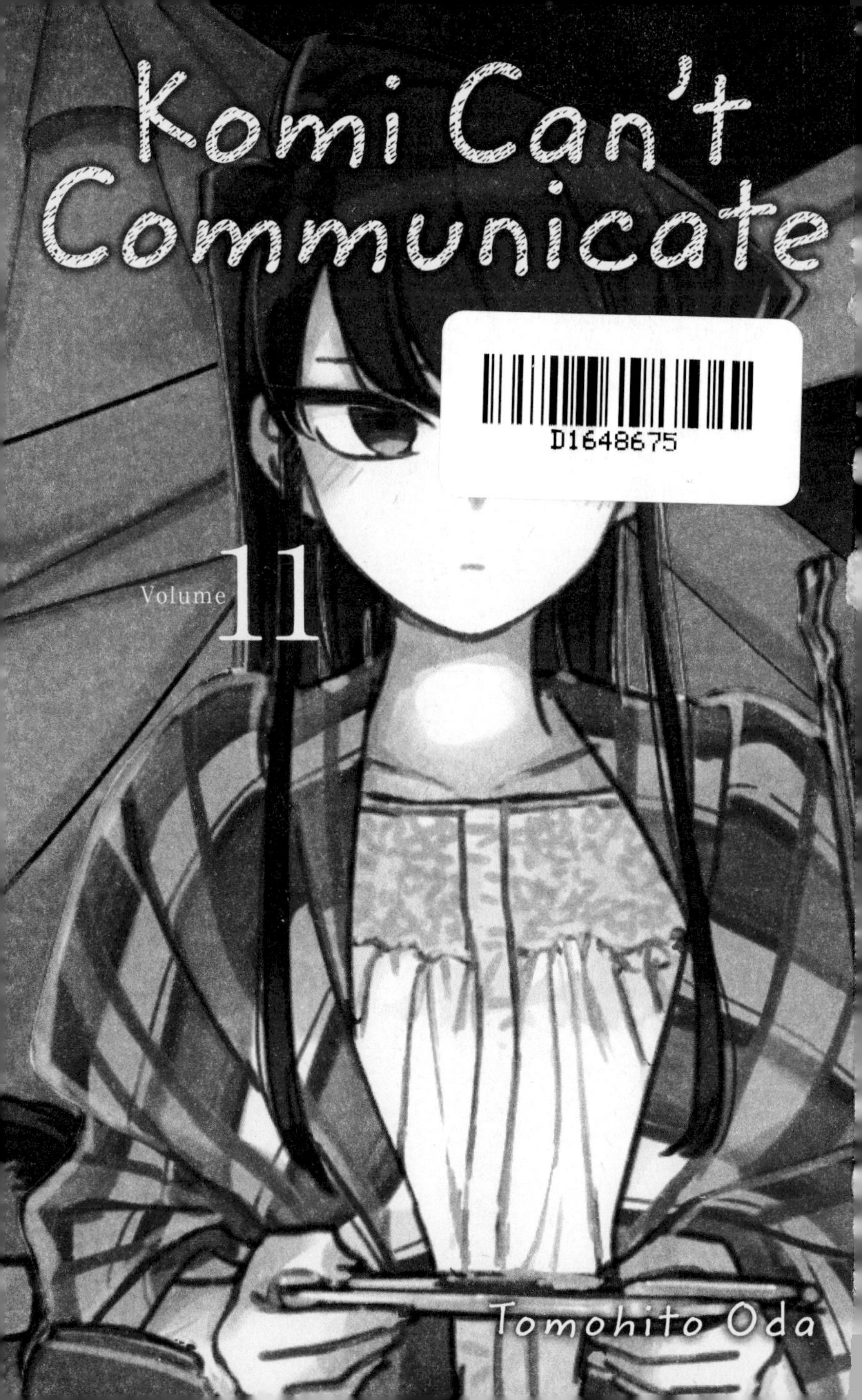
Komi Can't Communicate
Volume 11
Tomohito Oda

Contents

Komi Can't Communicate

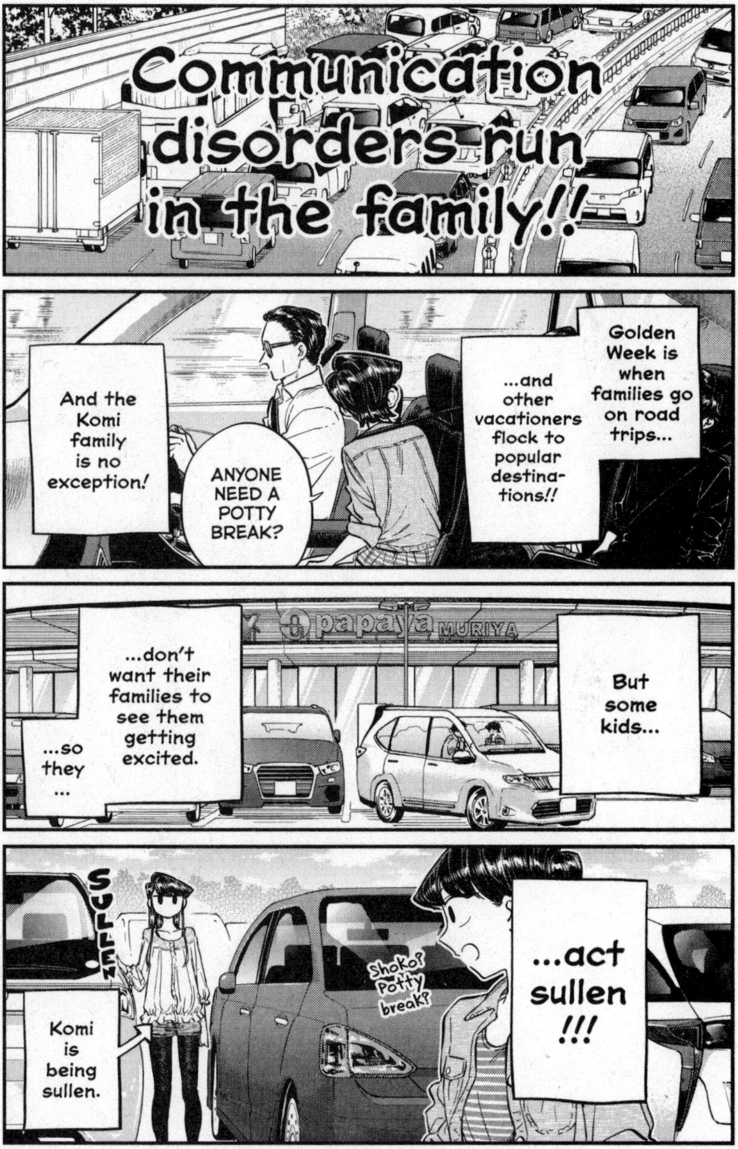
Communication disorders run in the family!!
Golden Week is when families go on road trips...
...and other vacationers flock to popular destina-tions!!
ANYONE NEED A POTTY BREAK?
And the Komi family is no exception!
papaya MURIYA
But some kids...
...don't want their families to see them getting excited.
...so they ...
...act sullen!!!
Shoko? Potty break?
SULLEN
Komi is being sullen.

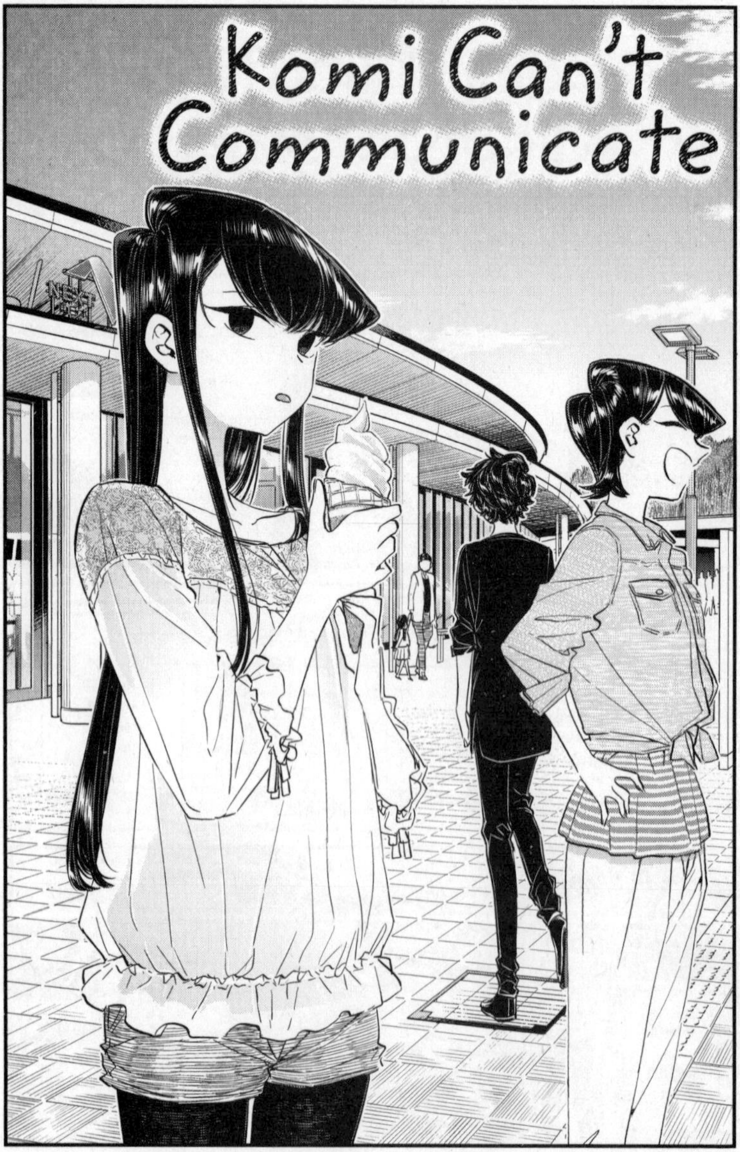
Komi Can't Communicate

Communication 143: Athletic

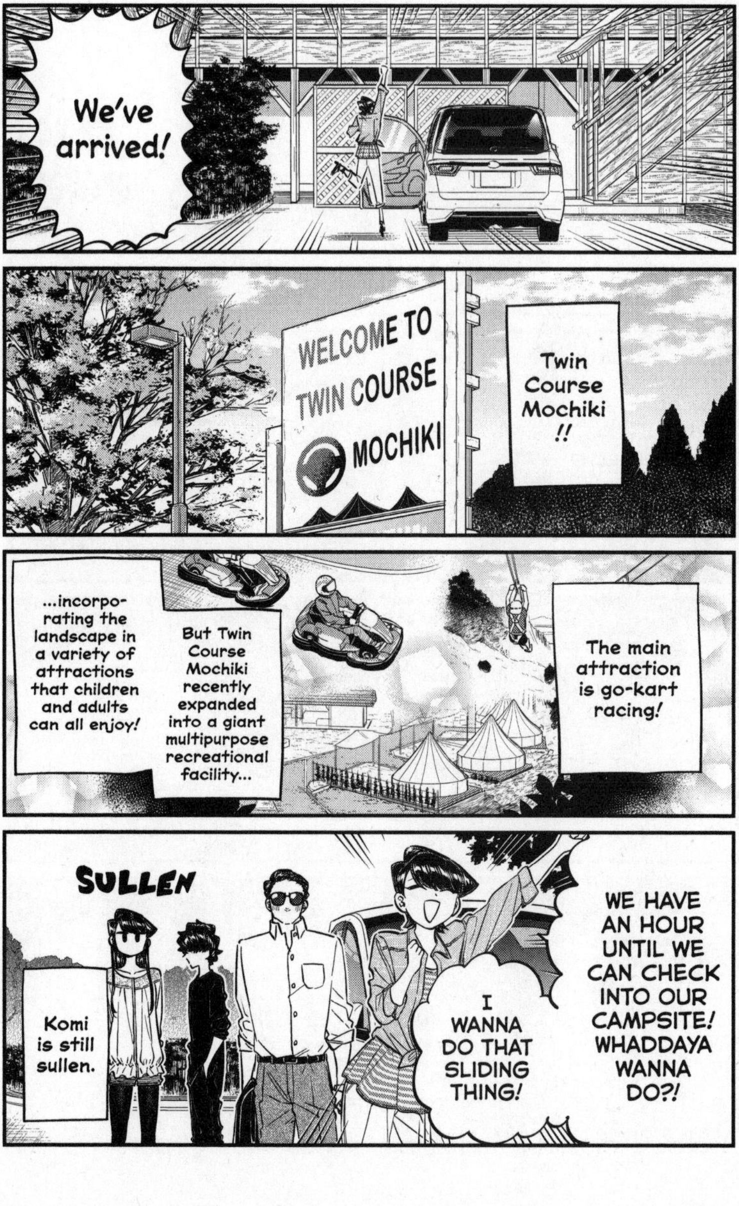
We've arrived!
Twin Course Mochiki !!
WELCOME TO TWIN COURSE MOCHIKI
The main attraction is go-kart racing!
But Twin Course Mochiki recently expanded into a giant multipurpose recreational facility...
...incorporating the landscape in a variety of attractions that children and adults can all enjoy!
WE HAVE AN HOUR UNTIL WE CAN CHECK INTO OUR CAMPSITE! WHADDAYA WANNA DO?!
I WANNA DO THAT SLIDING THING!
SULLEN
Komi is still sullen.

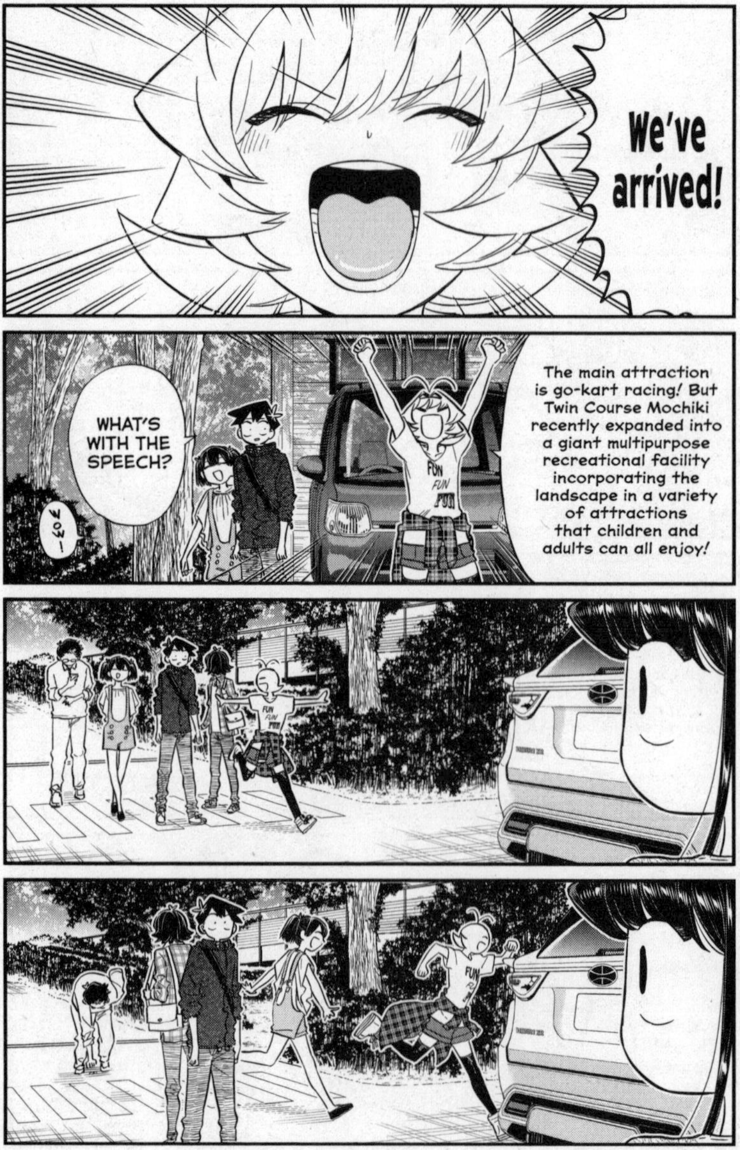
We've arrived!
The main attraction is go-kart racing! But Twin Course Mochiki recently expanded into a giant multipurpose recreational facility incorporating the landscape in a variety of attractions that children and adults can all enjoy!
WHAT'S WITH THE SPEECH?
WOW!

?!
KOMI?!
Komi family
OH, IT'S HITOHITO'S FAMILY!
THANK YOU FOR BEING SUCH A GOOD FRIEND TO SHOKO!
...
Tadano family
NO, THANK YOU!! NOW THAT OUR SON IS CLASSMATES WITH SUCH A BEAUTIFUL GIRL, WE FINALLY FEEL LIKE HE'S WORTH SOMETHING!! PLEASE, PUT HIM TO WORK AS A MAID OR SOMETHING!!!
Dad
Mom
Son
DON'T OVERDO IT, GUYS...
?!
DEEP BOW

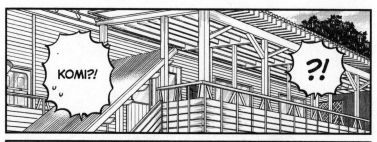

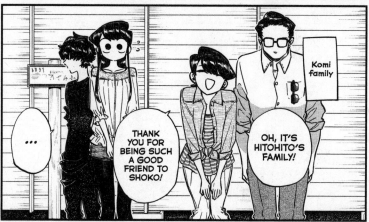

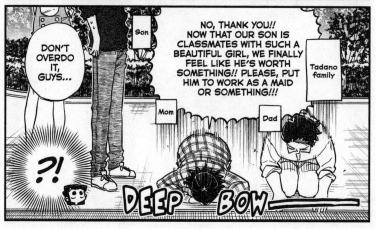

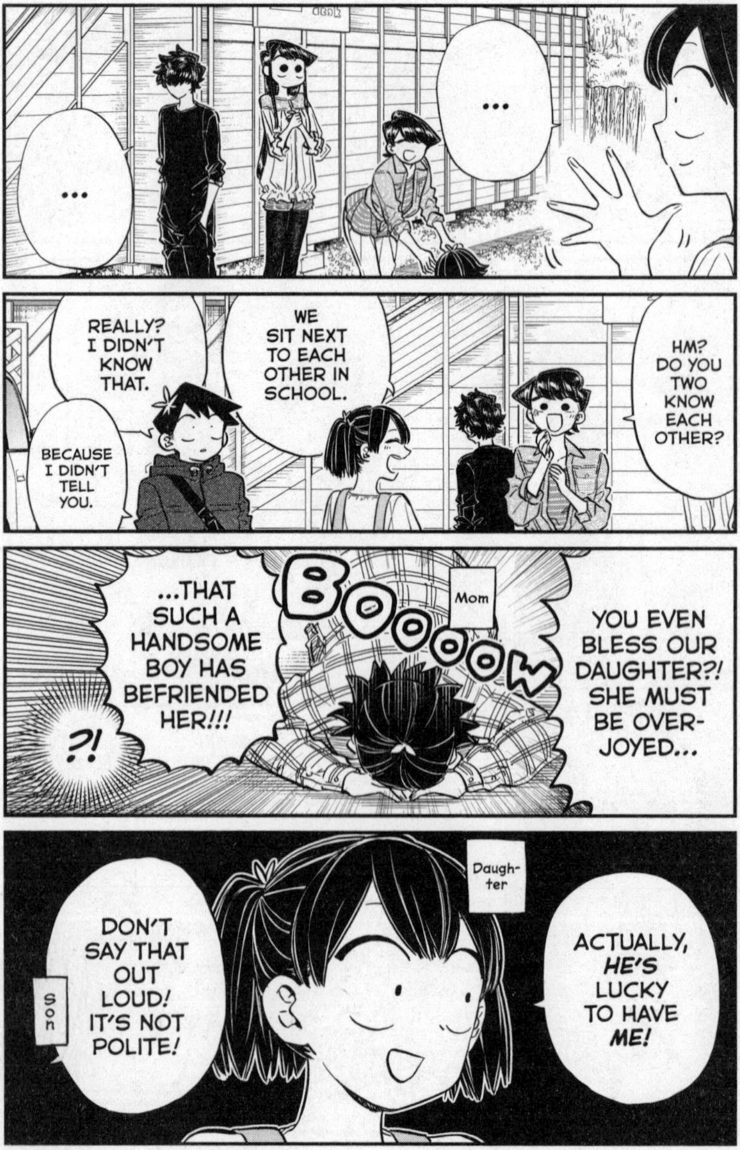
...
...
HM? DO YOU TWO KNOW EACH OTHER?
WE SIT NEXT TO EACH OTHER IN SCHOOL.
REALLY? I DIDN'T KNOW THAT.
BECAUSE I DIDN'T TELL YOU.
YOU EVEN BLESS OUR DAUGHTER?! SHE MUST BE OVER-JOYED...
Mom
BOOOOOW
...THAT SUCH A HANDSOME BOY HAS BEFRIENDED HER!!!
?!
Daugh-ter
ACTUALLY, *HE'S* LUCKY TO HAVE *ME!*
Son
DON'T SAY THAT OUT LOUD! IT'S NOT POLITE!

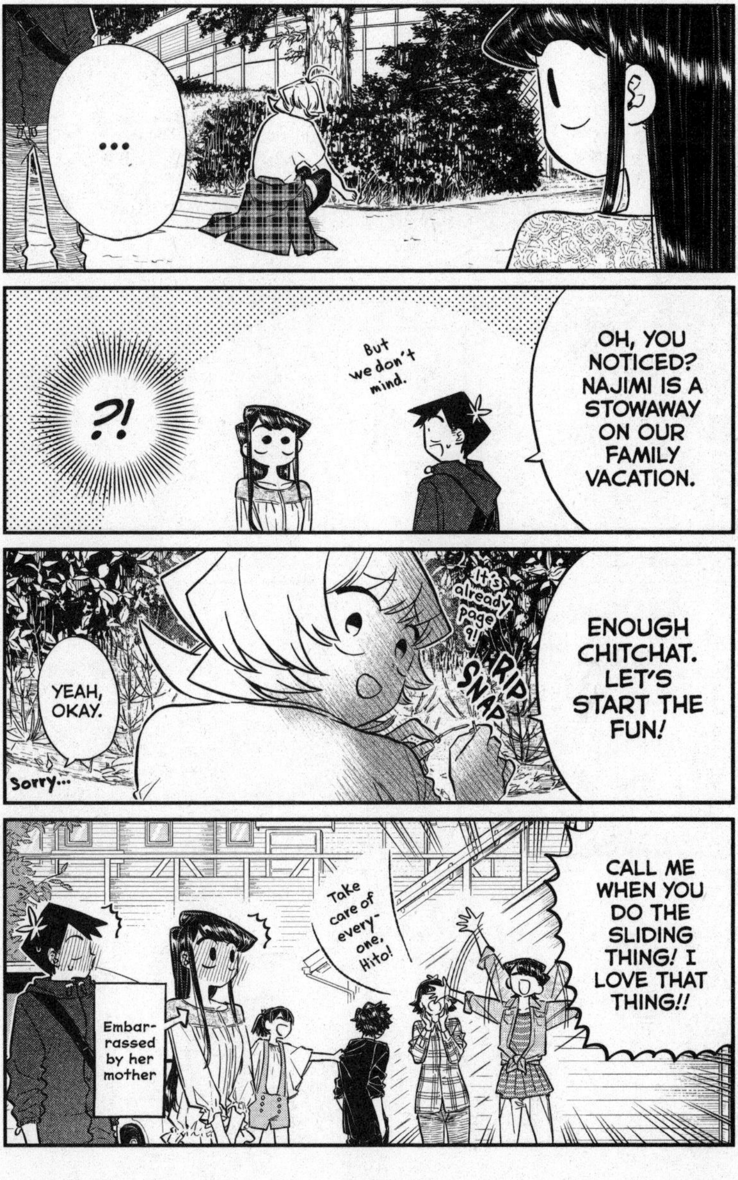
...
OH, YOU NOTICED? NAJIMI IS A STOWAWAY ON OUR FAMILY VACATION.
But we don't mind.
?!
ENOUGH CHITCHAT. LET'S START THE FUN!
It's already page 9!
RIP SNAP
YEAH, OKAY.
Sorry...
CALL ME WHEN YOU DO THE SLIDING THING! I LOVE THAT THING!!
Take care of every-one, Hito!
Embar-rassed by her mother

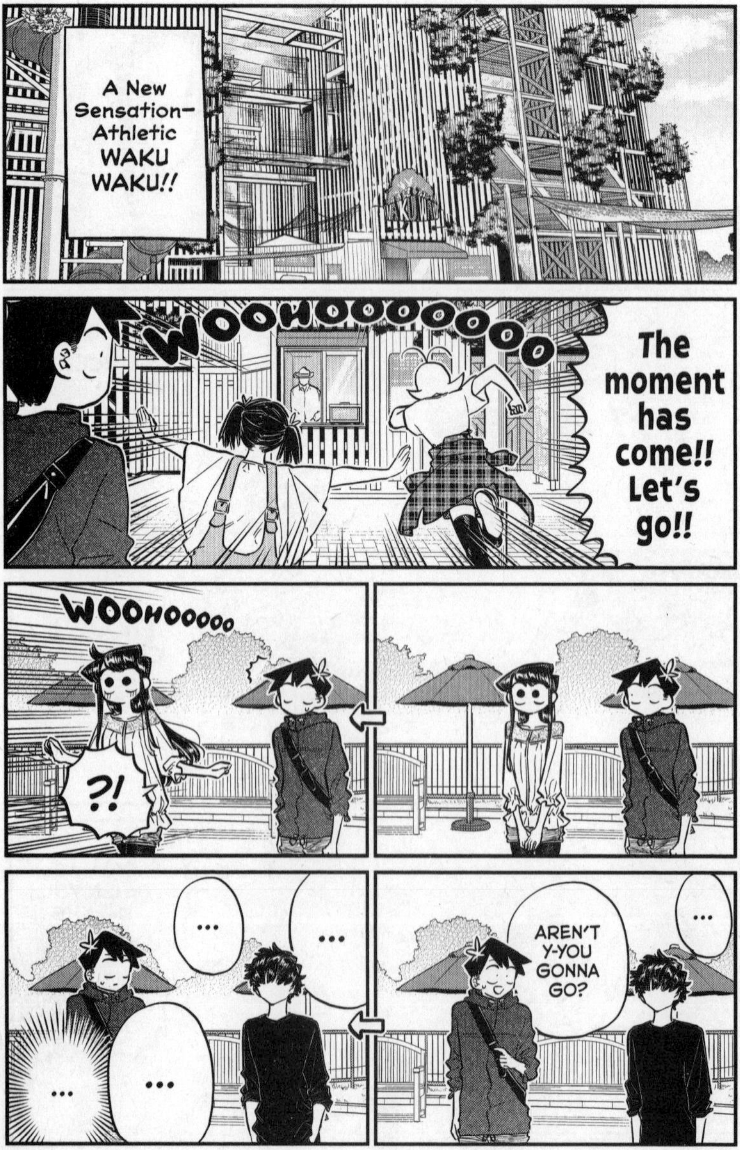
A New Sensation—Athletic WAKU WAKU!!
The moment has come!! Let's go!!
WOOHOOOOOOOOO
WOOHOOOOOO
?!
...
AREN'T Y-YOU GONNA GO?
...
...
...
...

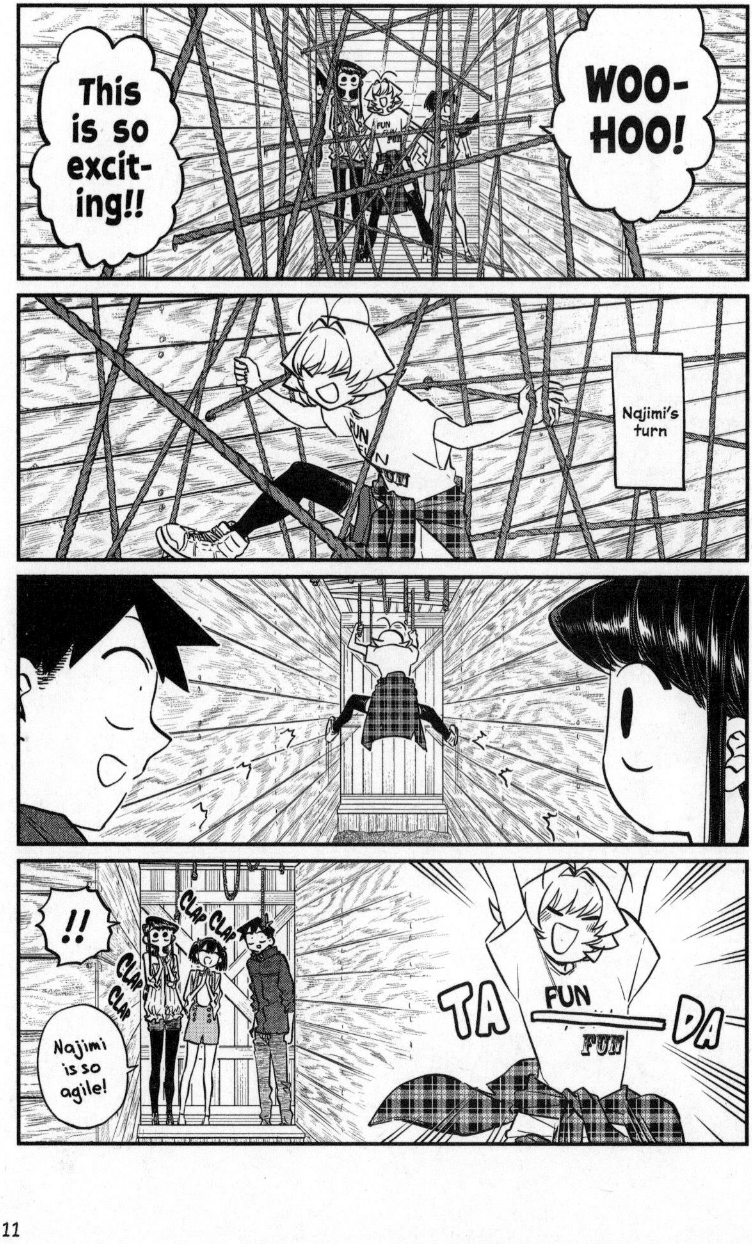
WOO-HOO!
This is so excit-ing!!
Najimi's turn
TA FUN DA
FUN
!!
CLAP CLAP
CLAP CLAP
Najimi is so agile!

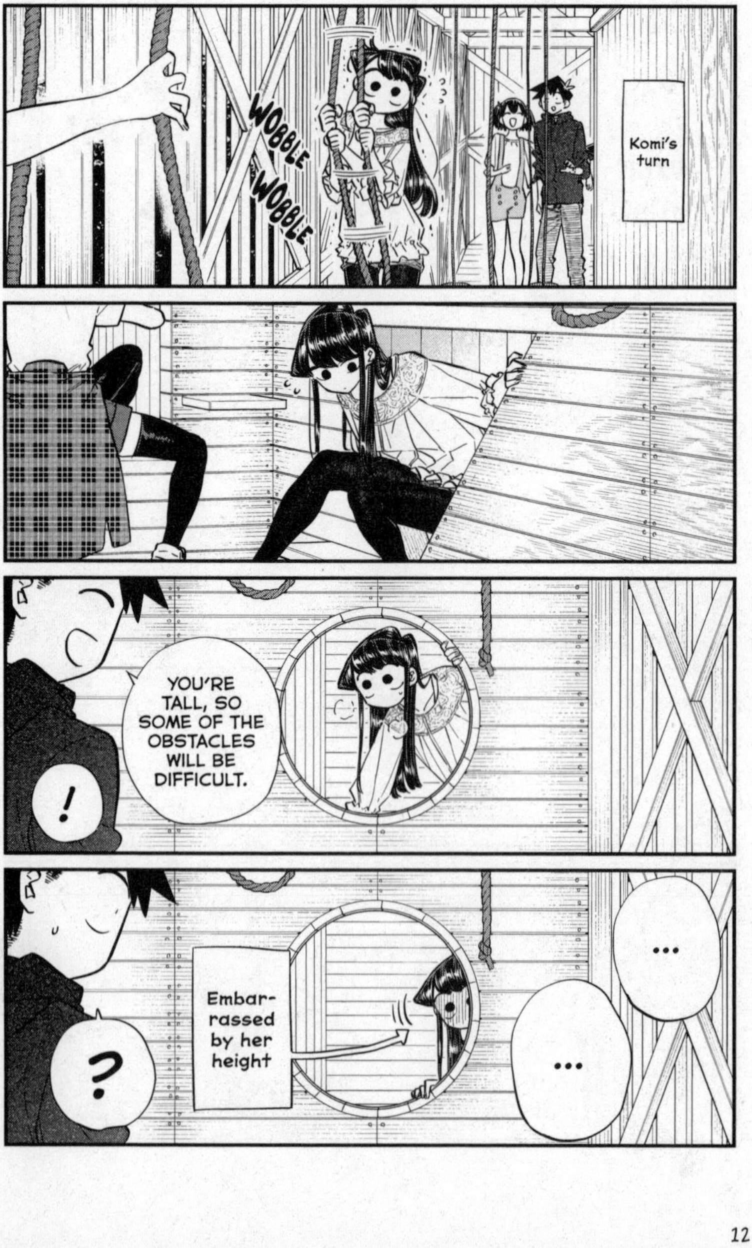
Komi's turn
WOBBLE WOBBLE
YOU'RE TALL, SO SOME OF THE OBSTACLES WILL BE DIFFICULT.
!
...
...
Embar-rassed by her height
?

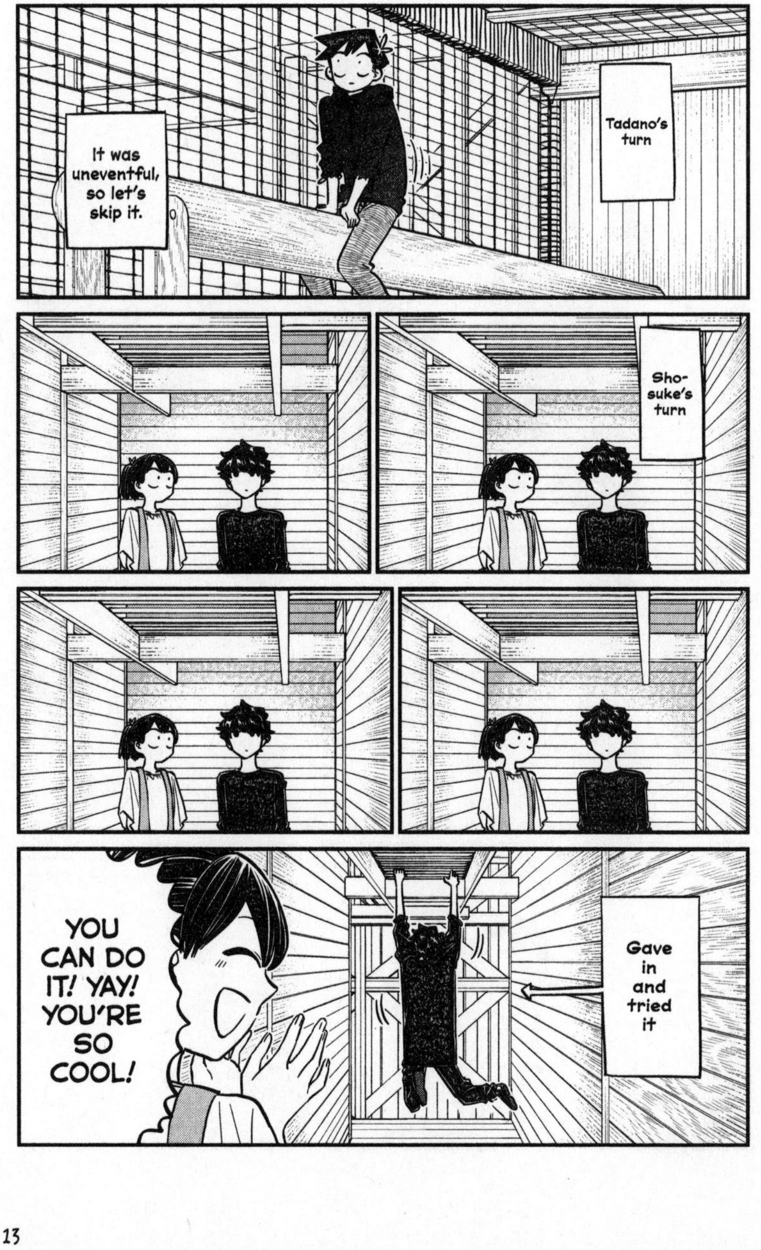
Tadano's turn
It was uneventful, so let's skip it.
Sho-suke's turn
Gave in and tried it
YOU CAN DO IT! YAY! YOU'RE SO COOL!

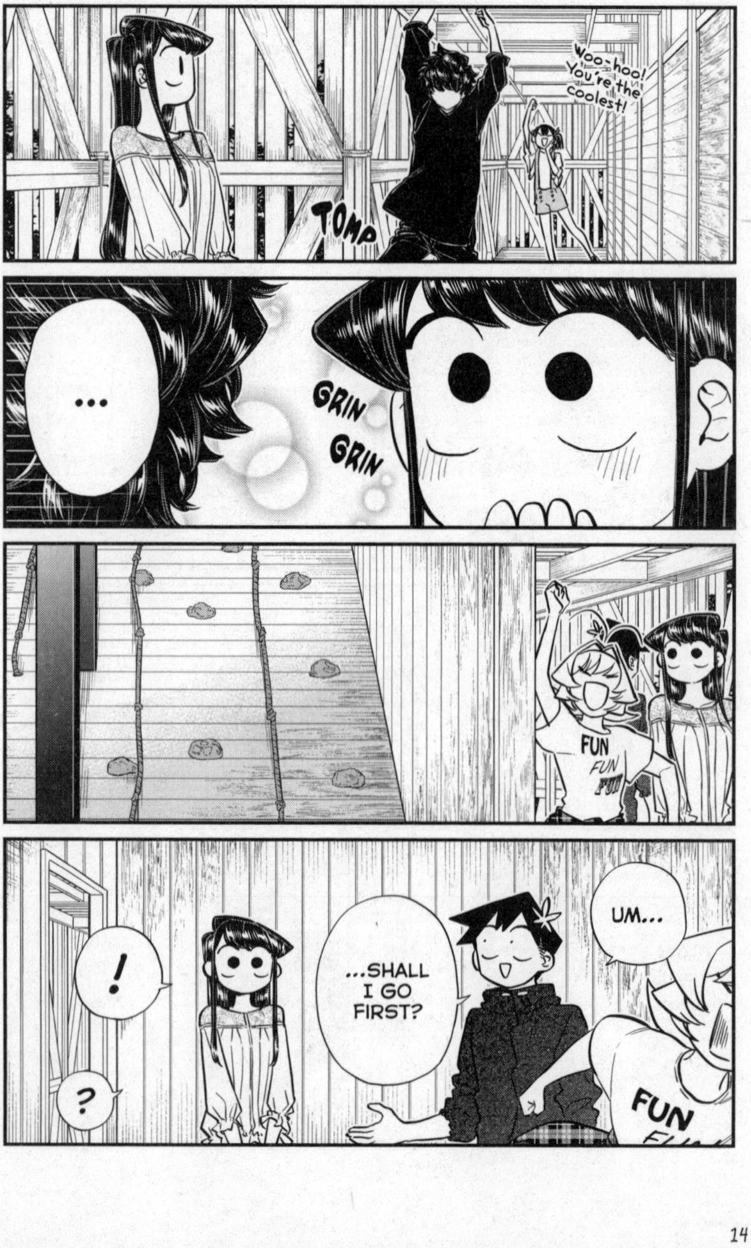
Woo-hoo! You're the coolest!
TOMP
GRIN GRIN
...
FUN FUN FUN
UM...
...SHALL I GO FIRST?
FUN
!
?

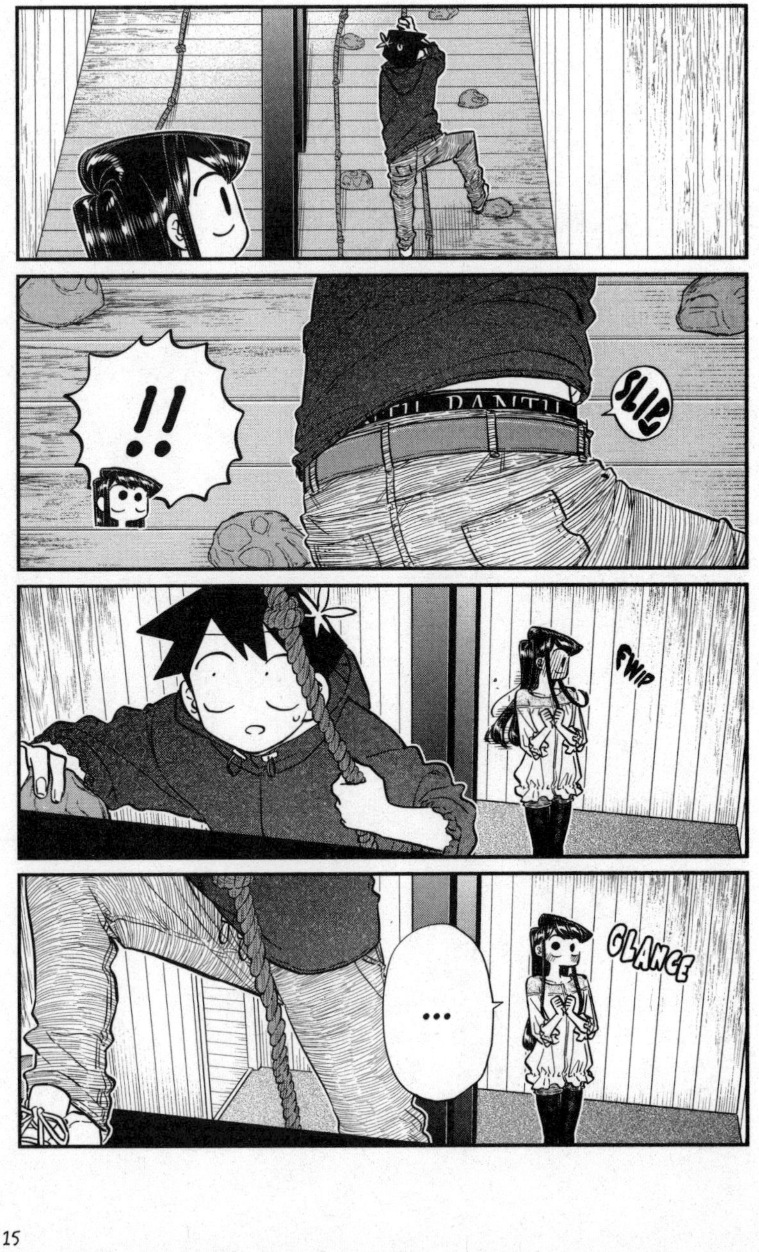
SLIP
!!
FWIP
GLANCE
...

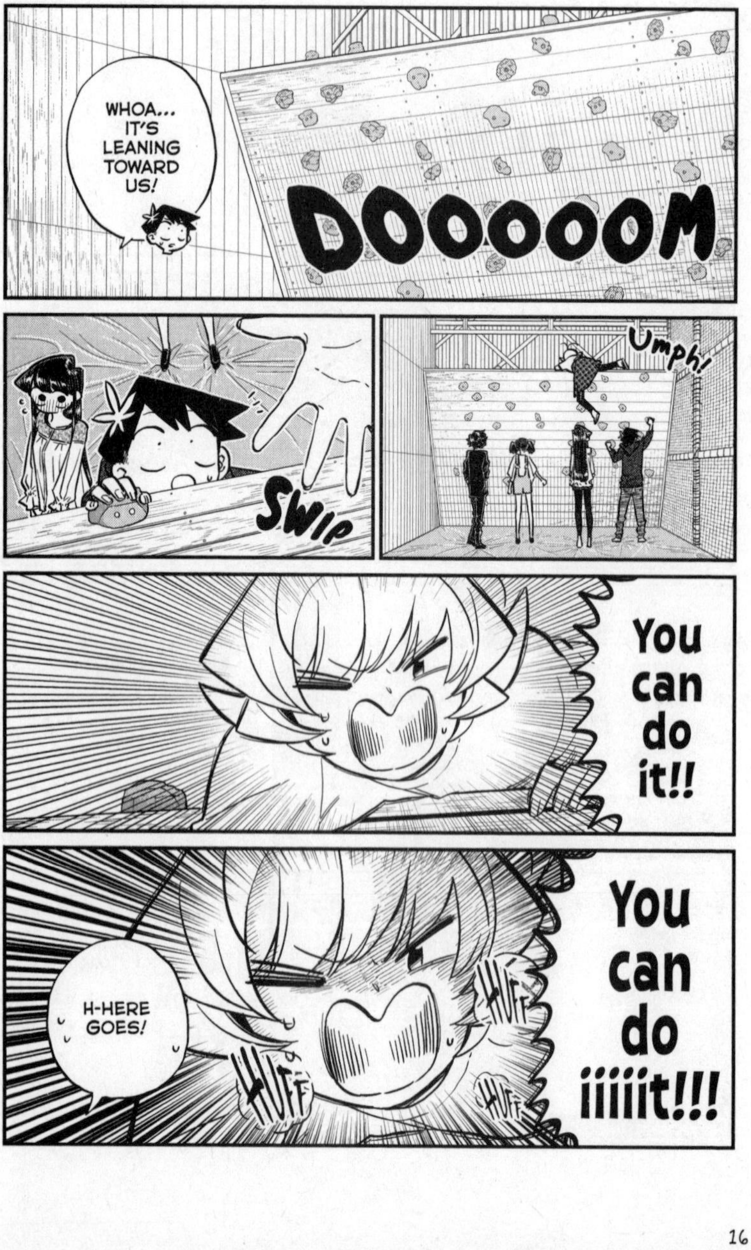
DOOOOOM
WHOA... IT'S LEANING TOWARD US!
Umph!
SWIP
You can do it!!
You can do iiiiit!!!
HUFF
HUFF
HUFF
H-HERE GOES!

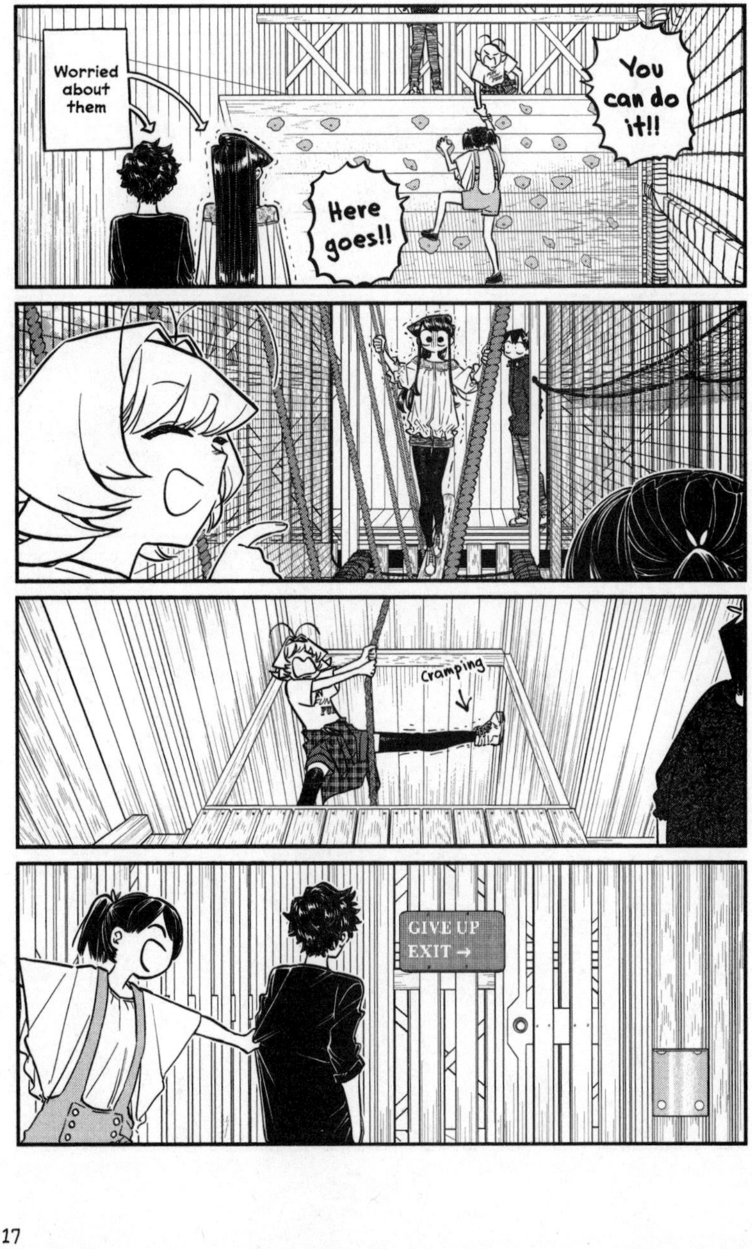
You can do it!!
Here goes!!
Worried about them
Cramping
GIVE UP
EXIT →

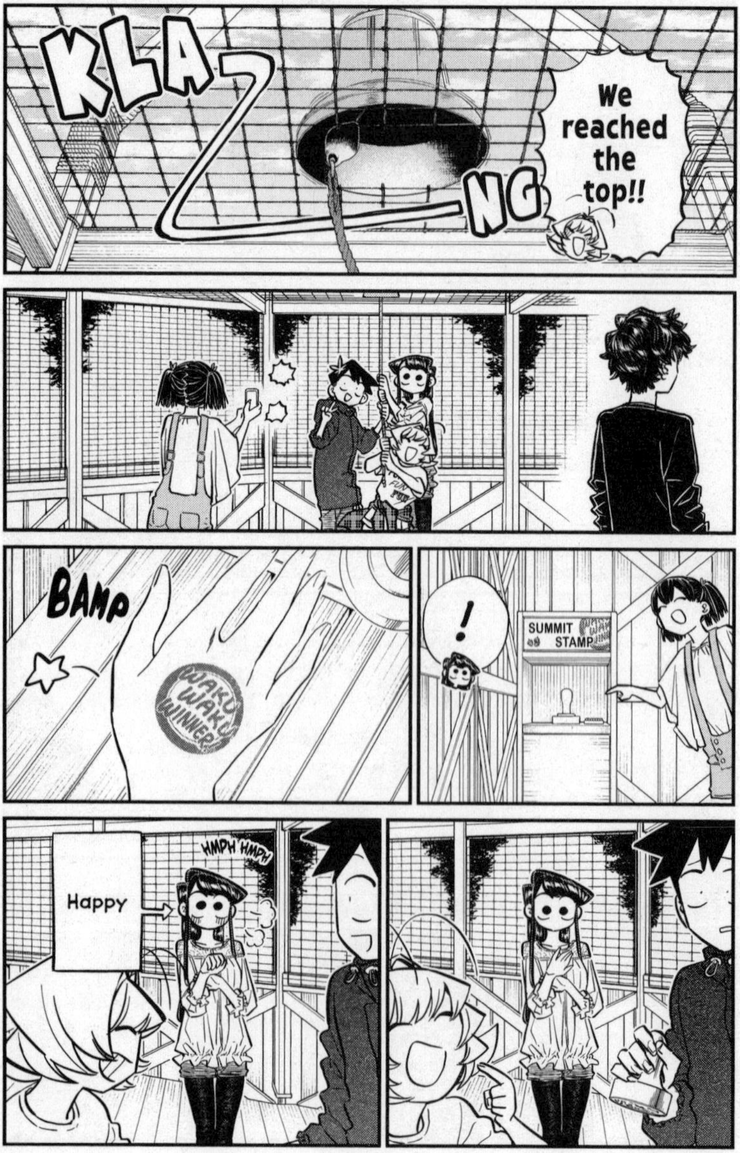
We reached the top!!
KLANG
!
SUMMIT STAMP
BAMP
WAKU WAKU WINNER!
HMPH HMPH
Happy

THEY'RE SO SULLEN IN HIGH SCHOOL.
I KNOW!!
THEY'RE NO FUN AT ALL!
The mothers are getting along.
They won't wear the clothes I buy!!
And they suddenly clean their rooms!
OUR CHILDREN ARE GROWING UP...
...BUT I HOPE THEY'RE HAVING FUN TODAY.
I'm baaack!

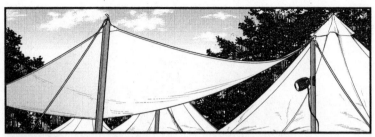

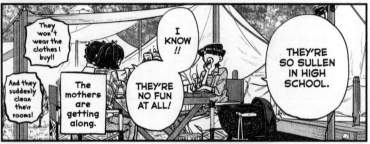

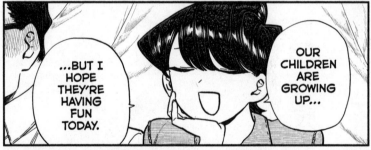

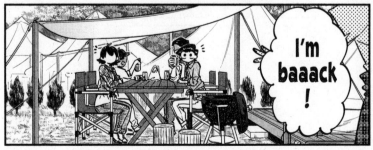

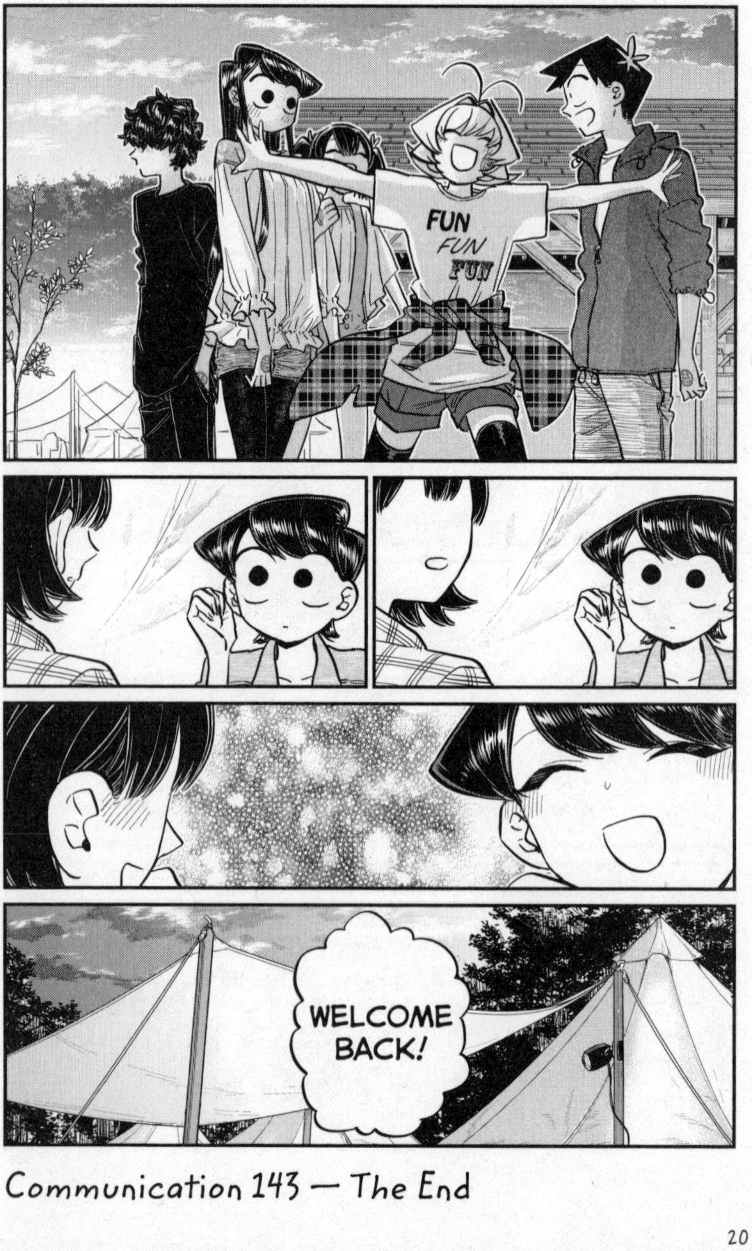
FUN
FUN
FUN
WELCOME BACK!

Communication 143 — The End

• Deleted Panel

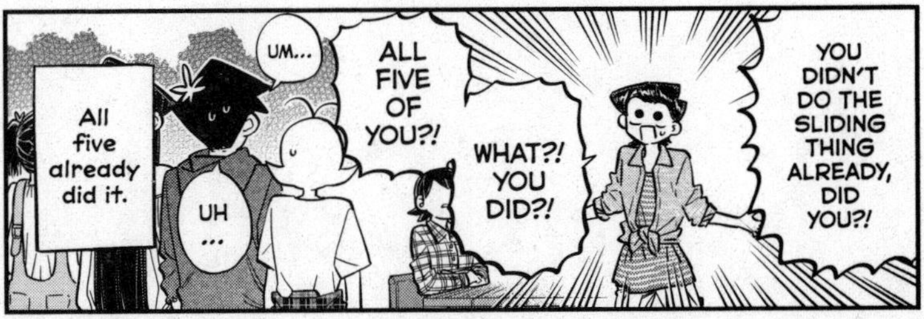
YOU DIDN'T DO THE SLIDING THING ALREADY, DID YOU?!
WHAT?! YOU DID?!
ALL FIVE OF YOU?!
UM...
UH ...
All five already did it.

Komi Can't
Communicate

Komi Can't Communicate

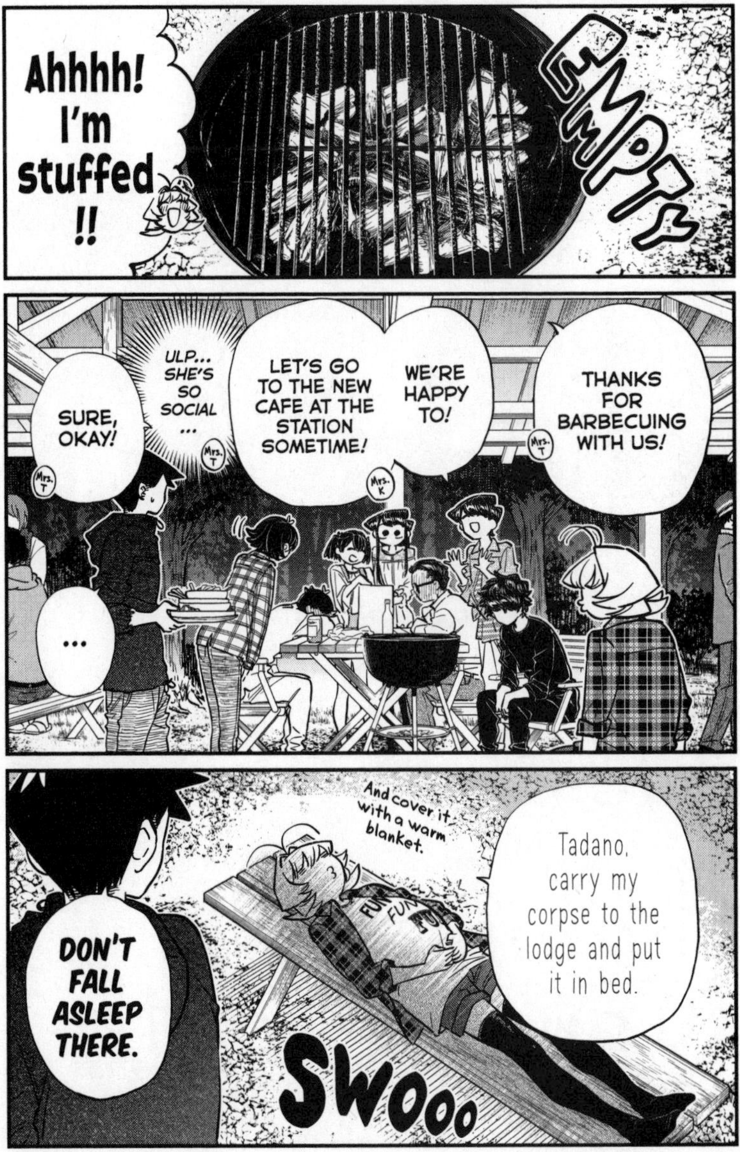

EMPTY
Ahhhh! I'm stuffed!!
THANKS FOR BARBECUING WITH US!
WE'RE HAPPY TO!
LET'S GO TO THE NEW CAFE AT THE STATION SOMETIME!
ULP... SHE'S SO SOCIAL...
SURE, OKAY!
...
Tadano, carry my corpse to the lodge and put it in bed.
And cover it with a warm blanket.
DON'T FALL ASLEEP THERE.
SWOOO

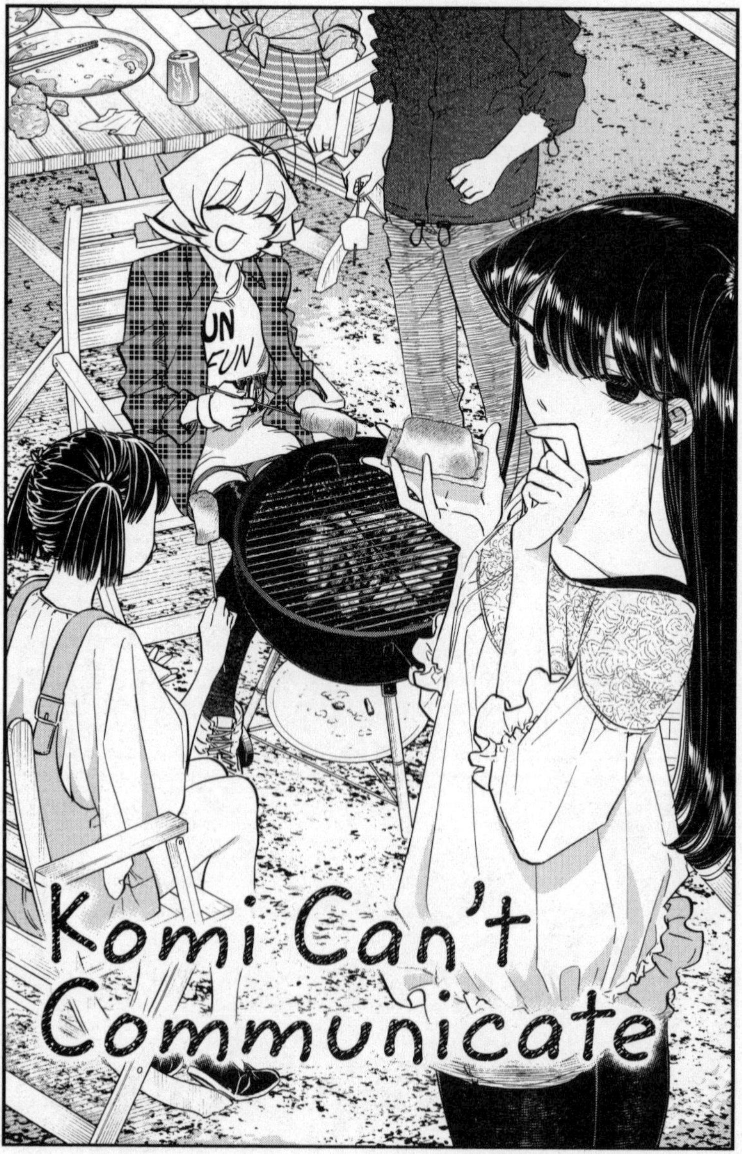
Komi Can't
Communicate

Communication 144: Stars

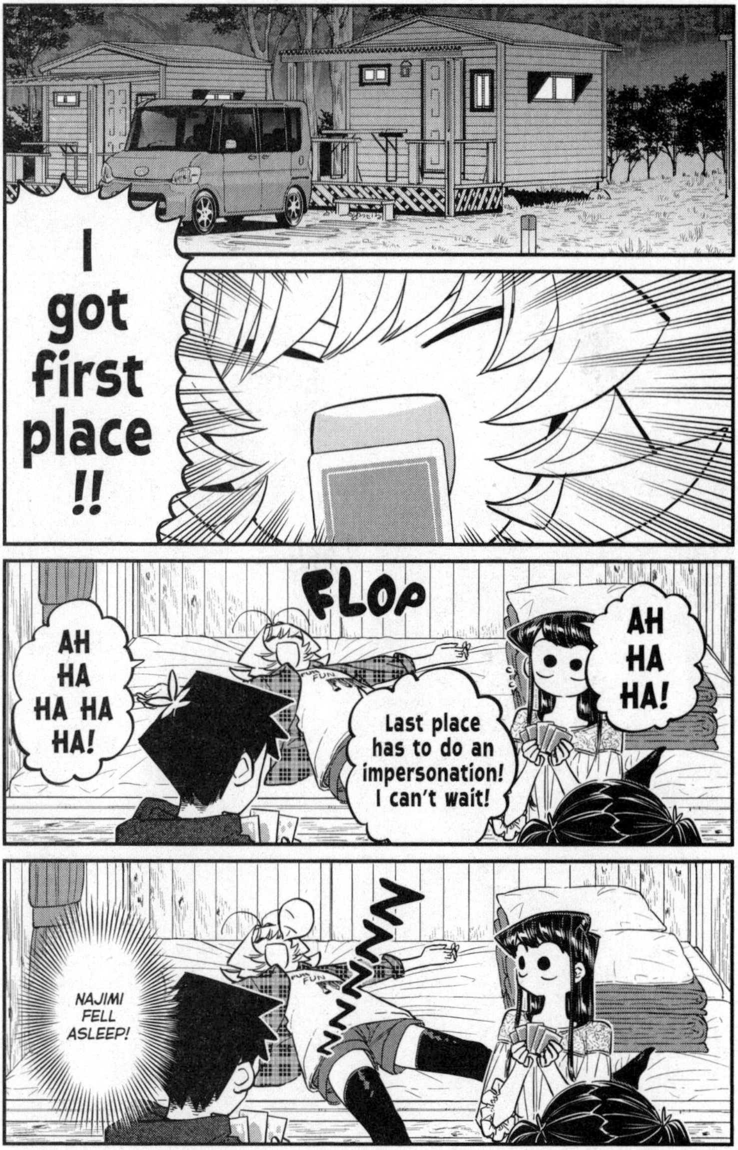

I got first place!!
AH HA HA!
FLOP
Last place has to do an impersonation! I can't wait!
AH HA HA HA HA!
NAJIMI FELL ASLEEP!

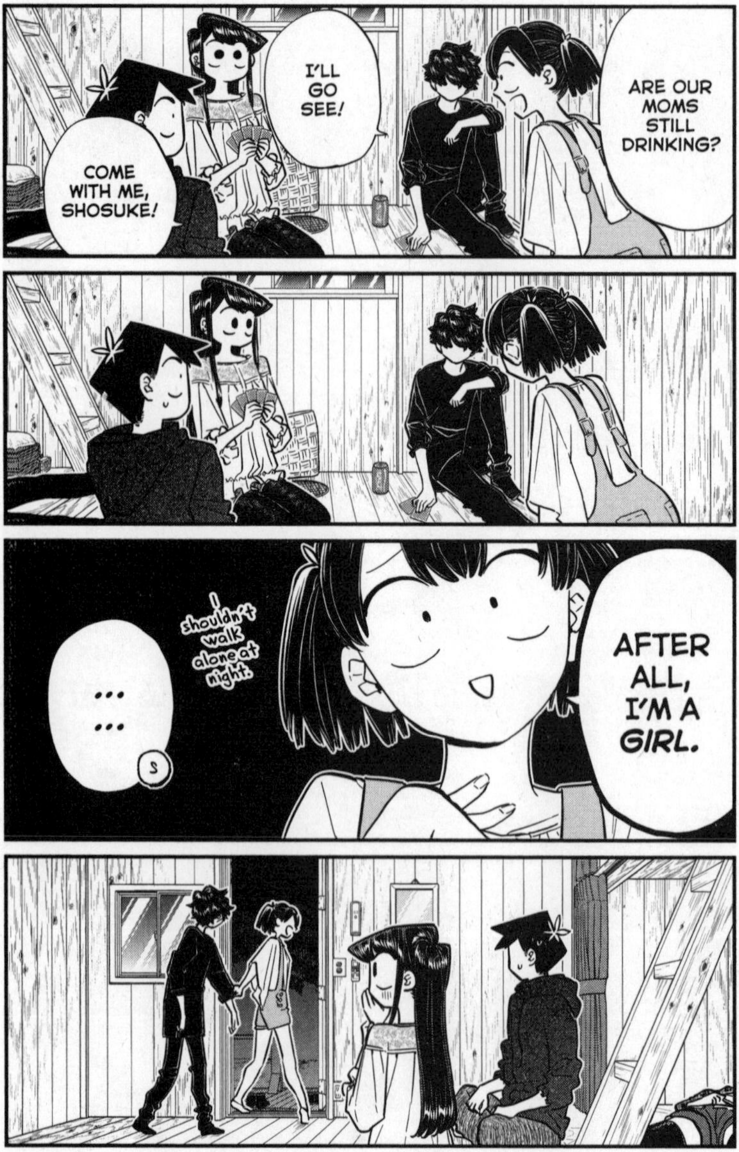
ARE OUR MOMS STILL DRINKING?
I'LL GO SEE!
COME WITH ME, SHOSUKE!
AFTER ALL, I'M A GIRL.
I shouldn't walk alone at night.
... ...
S

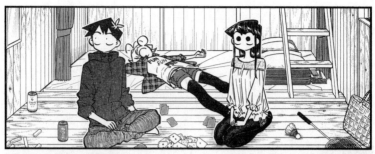

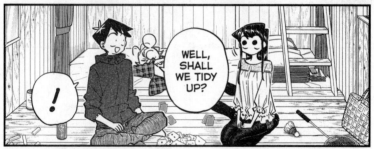

FUN FUN
WELL, SHALL WE TIDY UP?
!
ISN'T IT FUNNY HOW OUR FAMILIES RAN INTO EACH OTHER?
NOD NOD
!
Or, um... IS IT ANNOYING?
!!
SHAKE SHAKE
FUN

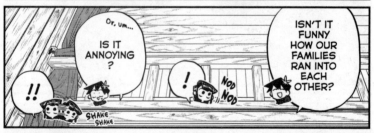

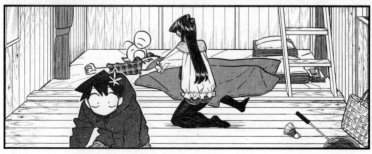

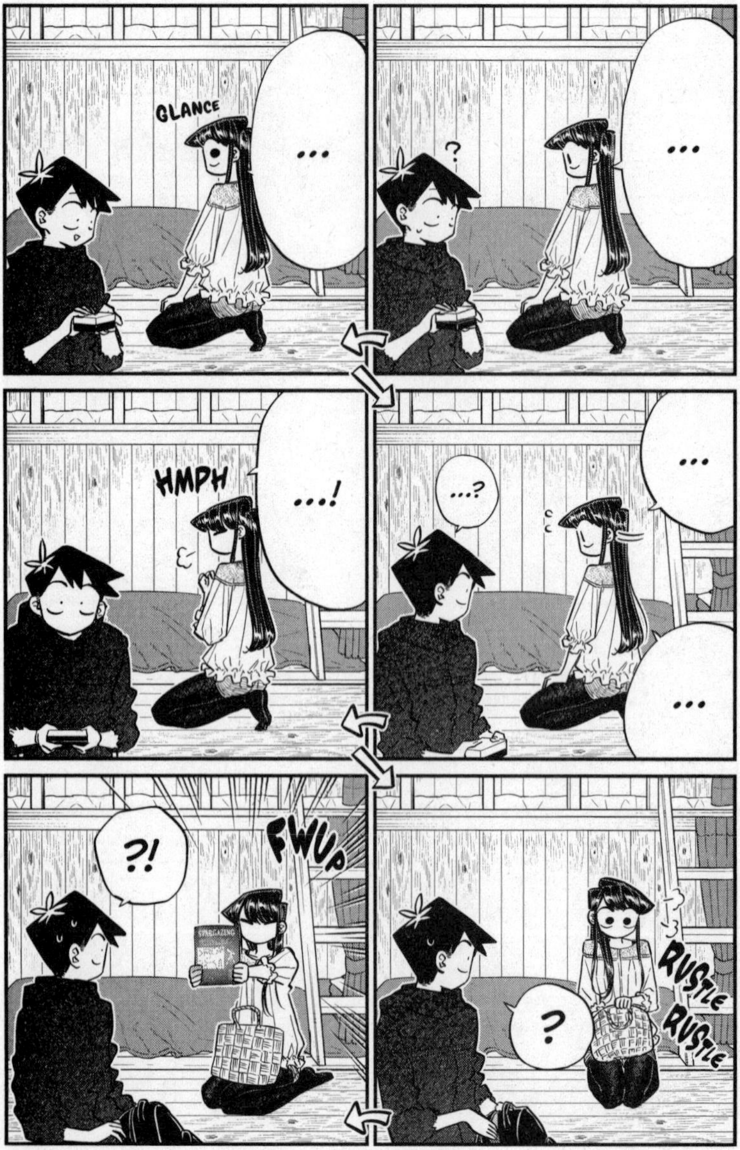
...
?
GLANCE
...
...
...?
...
HMPH
...!
RUSTLE
RUSTLE
?
FWUP
?!
STARGAZING

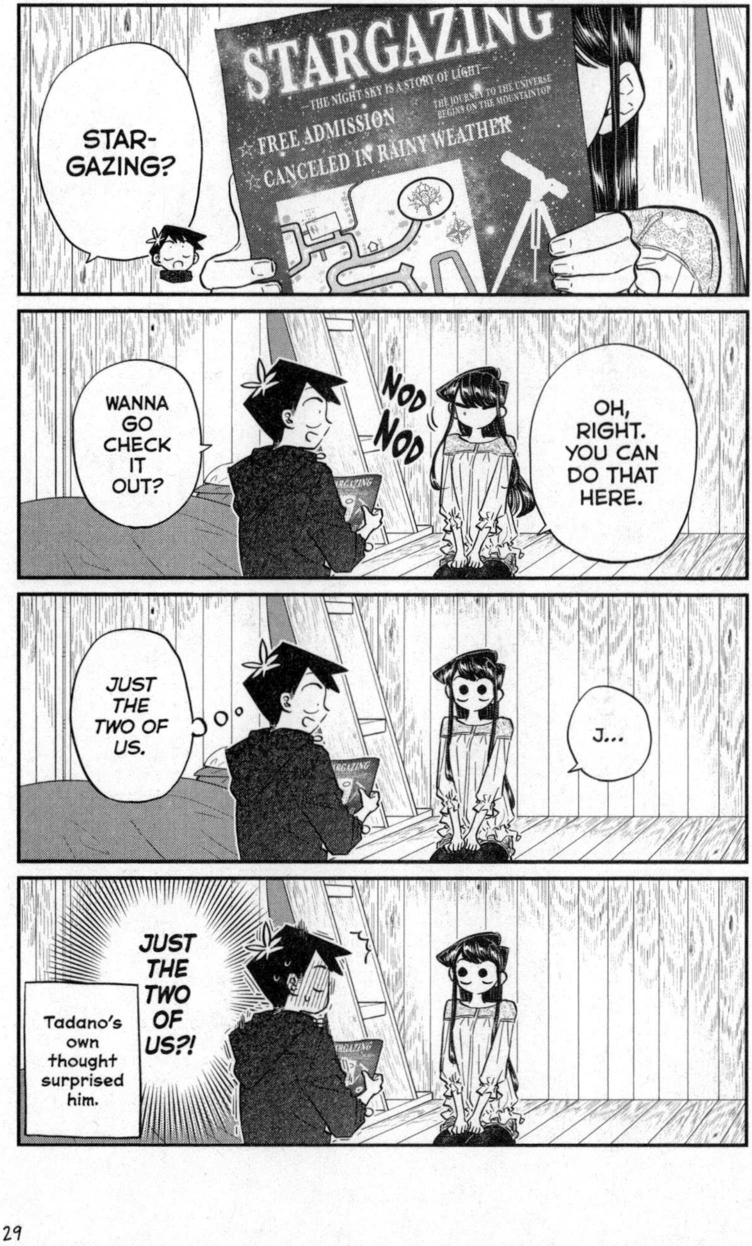
STARGAZING
—THE NIGHT SKY IS A STORY OF LIGHT—
THE JOURNEY TO THE UNIVERSE BEGINS ON THE MOUNTAINTOP
☆FREE ADMISSION
☆CANCELED IN RAINY WEATHER
STAR-GAZING?
OH, RIGHT. YOU CAN DO THAT HERE.
NOD NOD
WANNA GO CHECK IT OUT?
J...
JUST THE TWO OF US.
JUST THE TWO OF US?!
Tadano's own thought surprised him.

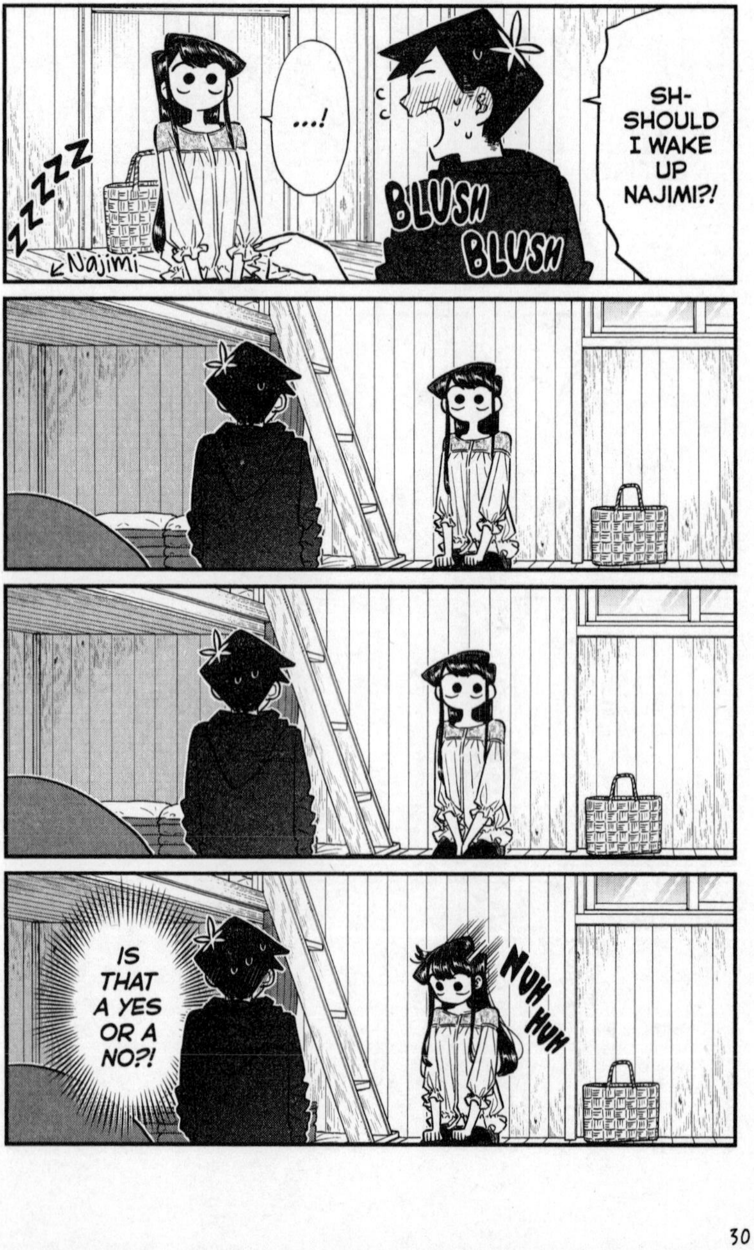
SH- SHOULD I WAKE UP NAJIMI?!
BLUSH BLUSH
...!
ZZZZZ
←Najimi
NUH HUH
IS THAT A YES OR A NO?!

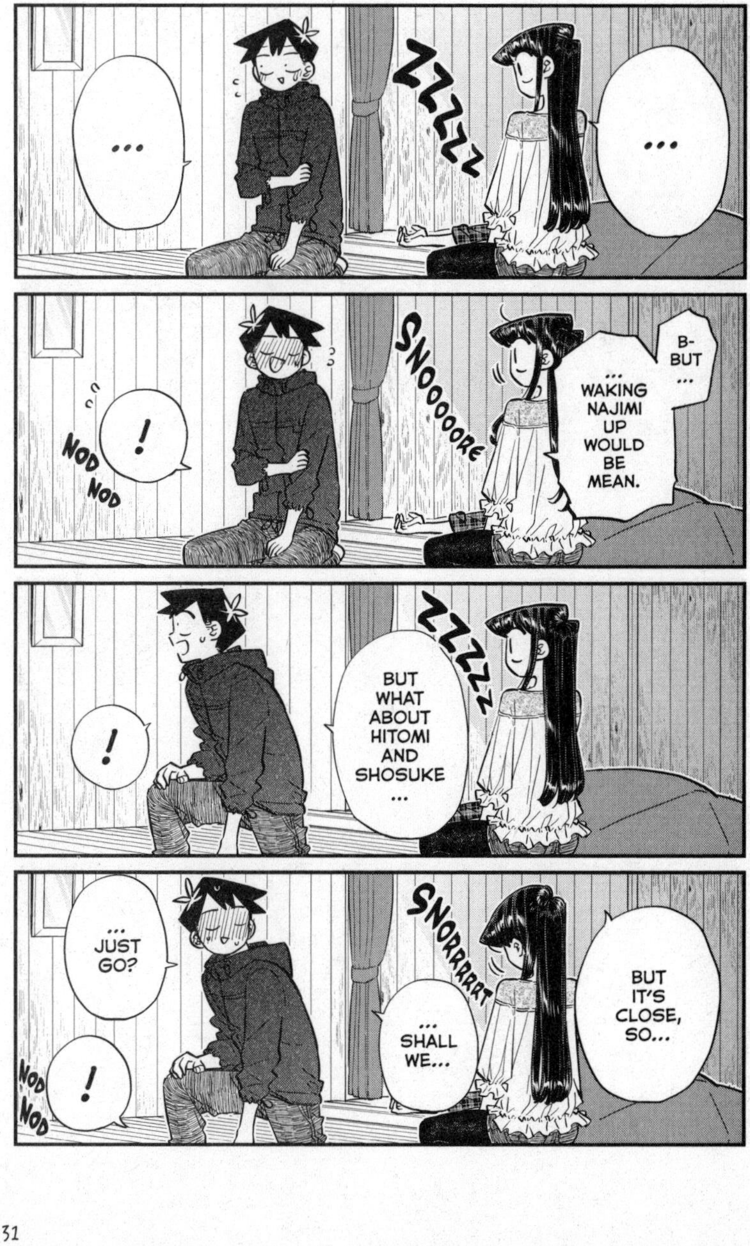
...
ZZZZZZ
...
B-BUT ...
... WAKING NAJIMI UP WOULD BE MEAN.
SNOOOOOORE
!
NOD NOD
ZZZZZZ
BUT WHAT ABOUT HITOMI AND SHOSUKE ...
!
BUT IT'S CLOSE, SO...
SNORRRRRT
... SHALL WE...
... JUST GO?
!
NOD NOD

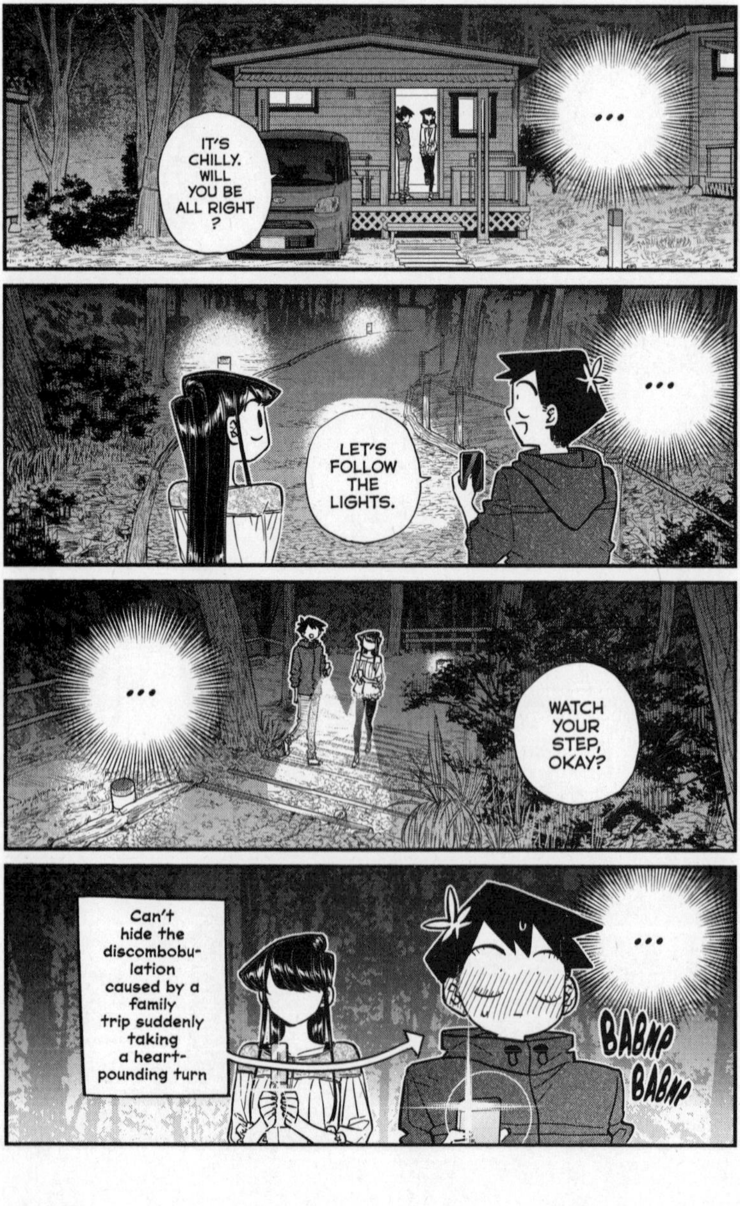
...
IT'S CHILLY. WILL YOU BE ALL RIGHT ?
...
LET'S FOLLOW THE LIGHTS.
WATCH YOUR STEP, OKAY?
...
...
BABMP BABMP
Can't hide the discombobu-lation caused by a family trip suddenly taking a heart-pounding turn

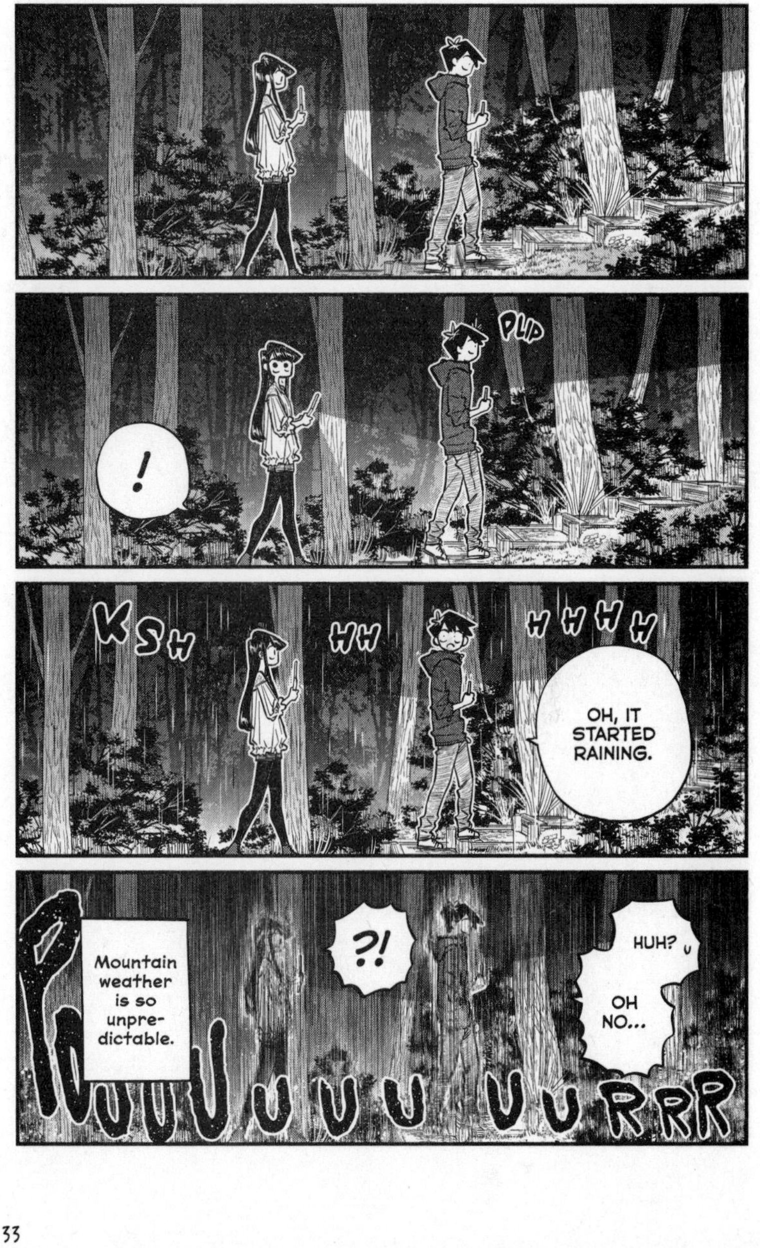
PLIP
!
HHHH
HH
KSH
OH, IT STARTED RAINING.
HUH?
OH NO...
?!
Mountain weather is so unpre-dictable.

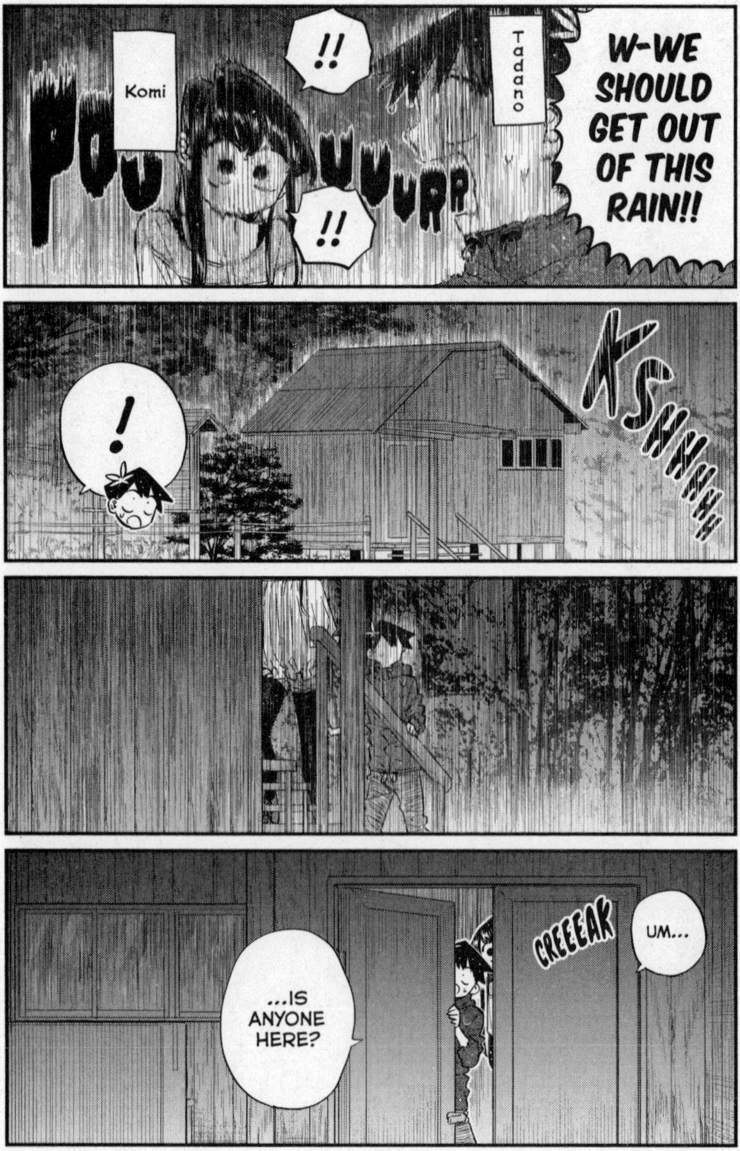
W-WE SHOULD GET OUT OF THIS RAIN!!
Tadano
!!
!!
Komi
POUUUURR
KSHHHHH
!
UM...
CREEEAK
...IS ANYONE HERE?

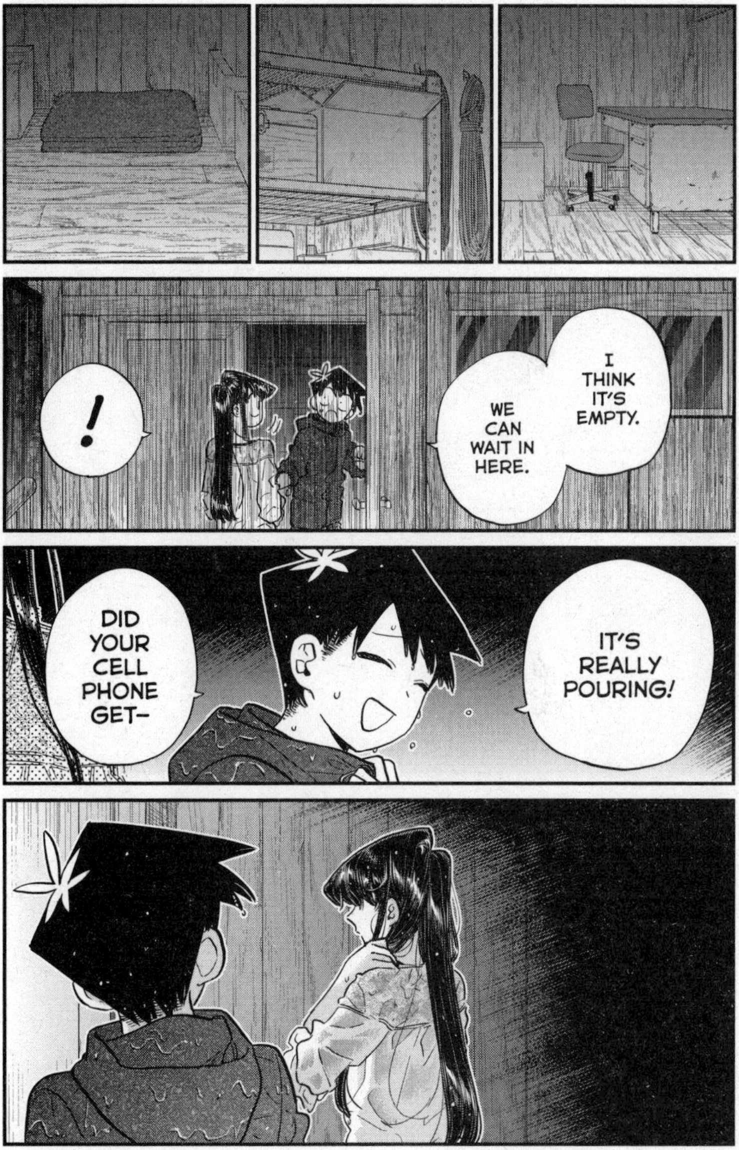
I THINK IT'S EMPTY.
WE CAN WAIT IN HERE.
!
IT'S REALLY POURING!
DID YOUR CELL PHONE GET–

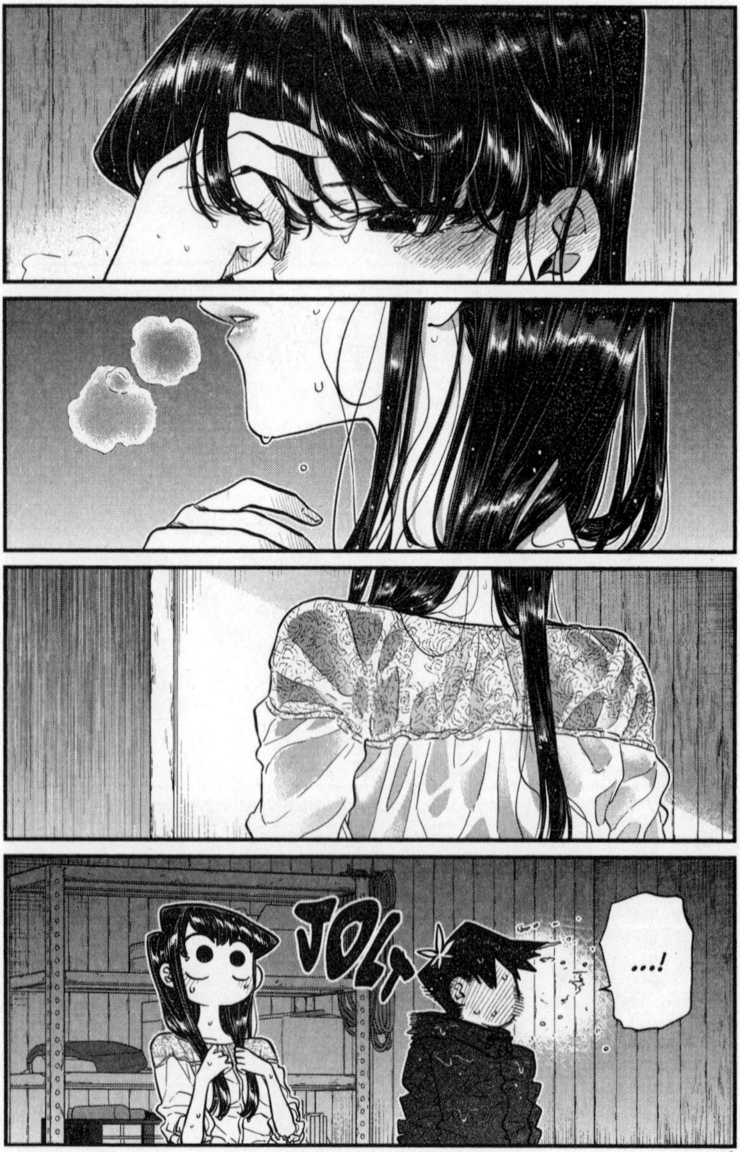
JOLT
...!

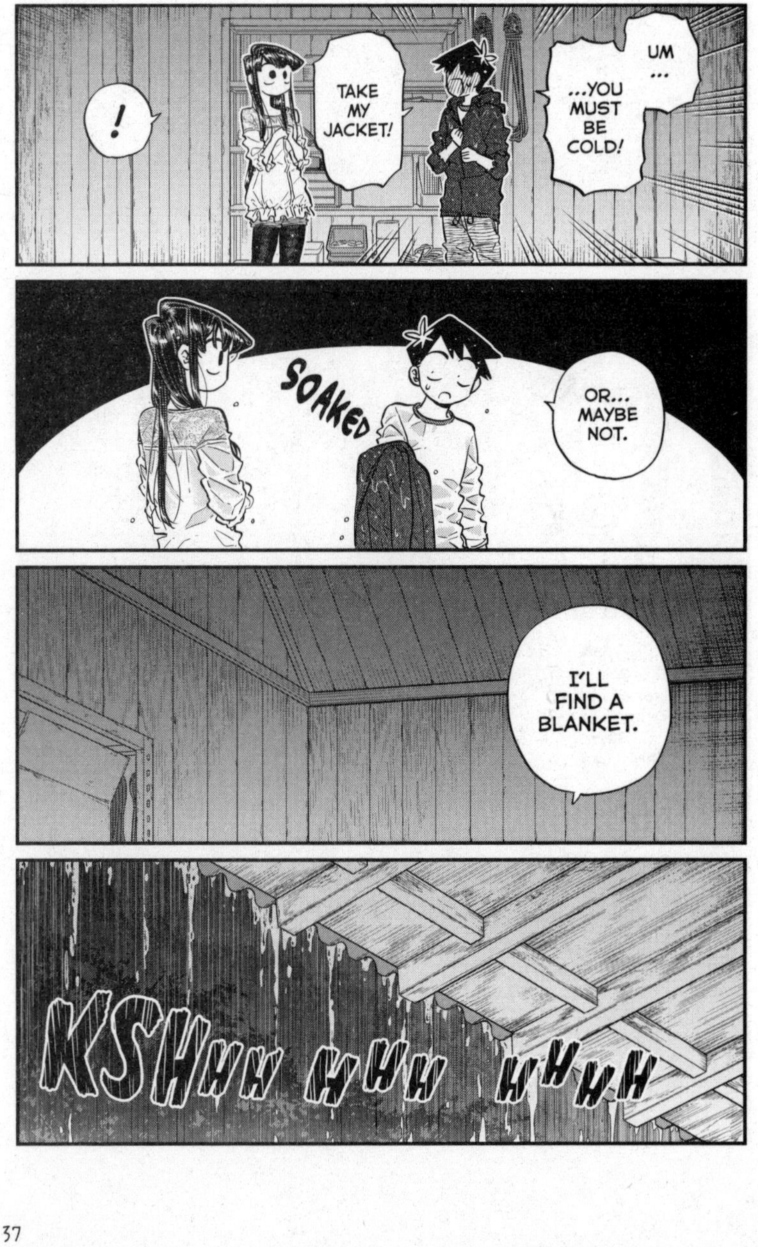
UM ... ...YOU MUST BE COLD!
TAKE MY JACKET!
!
OR... MAYBE NOT.
SOAKED
I'LL FIND A BLANKET.
KSHHH HHH HHHH

...

THE RAIN ISN'T STOPPING.

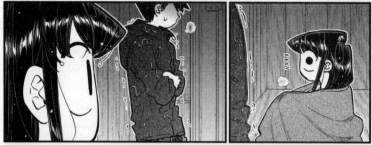

Looking for another blanket (there isn't one)

GLANCE GLANCE

SWUF

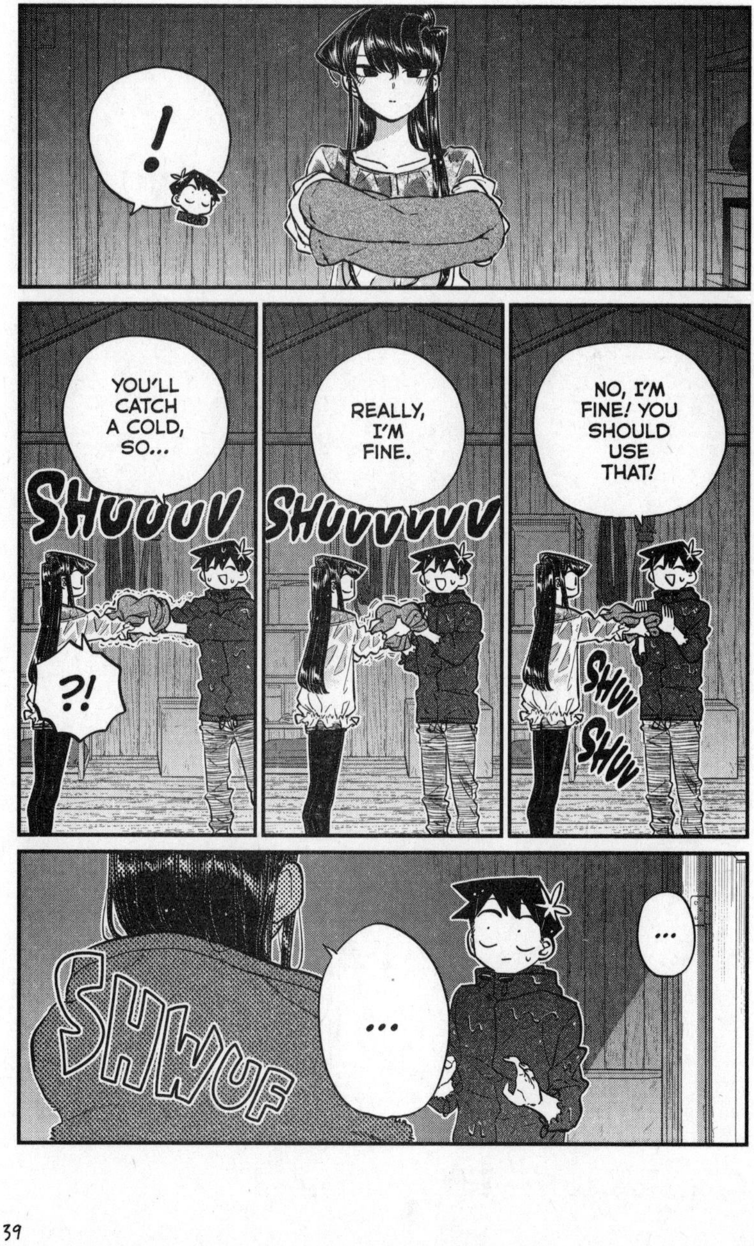
!
NO, I'M FINE! YOU SHOULD USE THAT!
SHUV
SHUV
REALLY, I'M FINE.
SHUVVVVVV
YOU'LL CATCH A COLD, SO...
SHUUUUV
?!
...
...
SHWUF

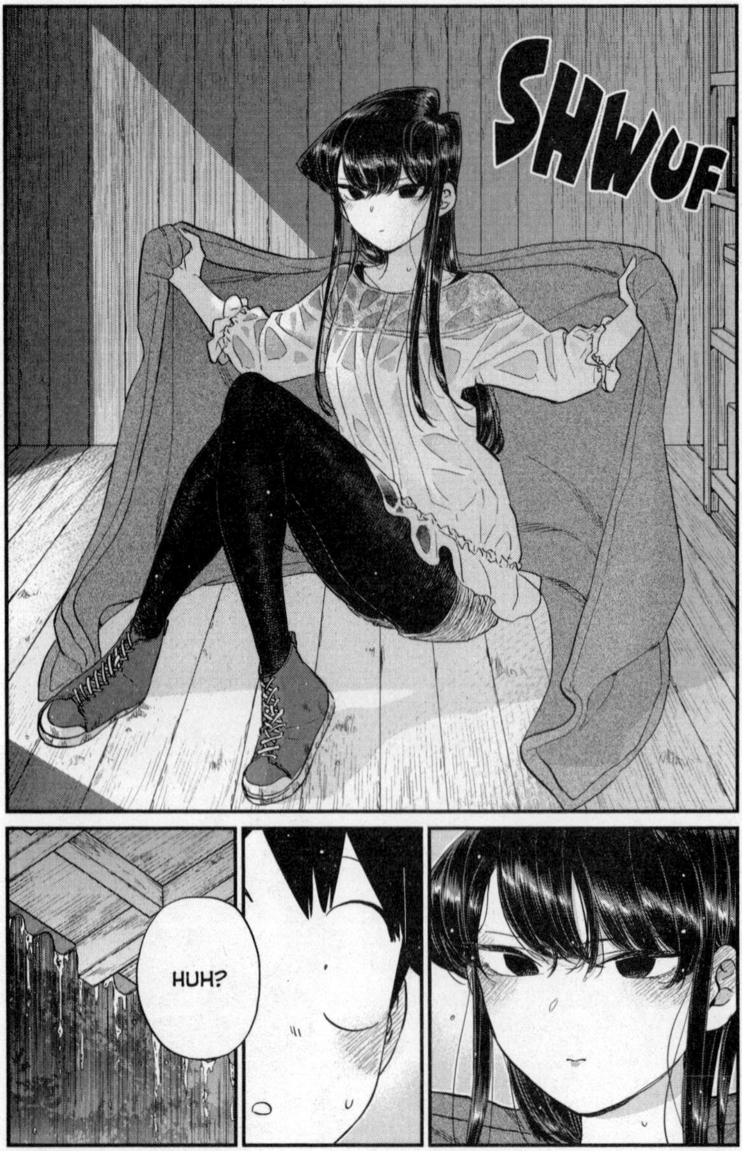
SHWUF
HUH?

Communication 144 — The End

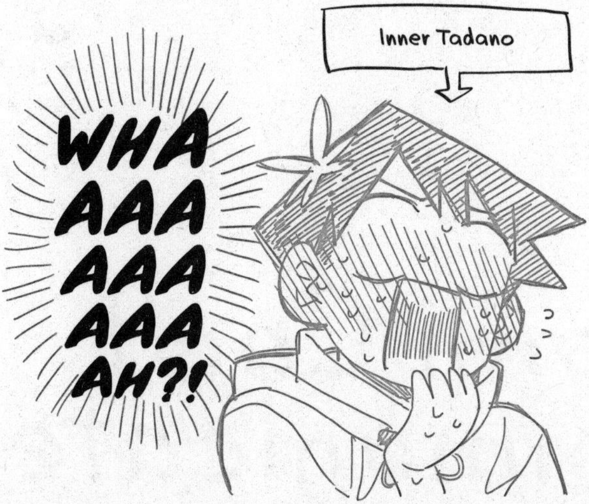
Inner Tadano
WHAAAAAAAAAAAH?!

Komi Can't
Communicate

Komi Can't Communicate

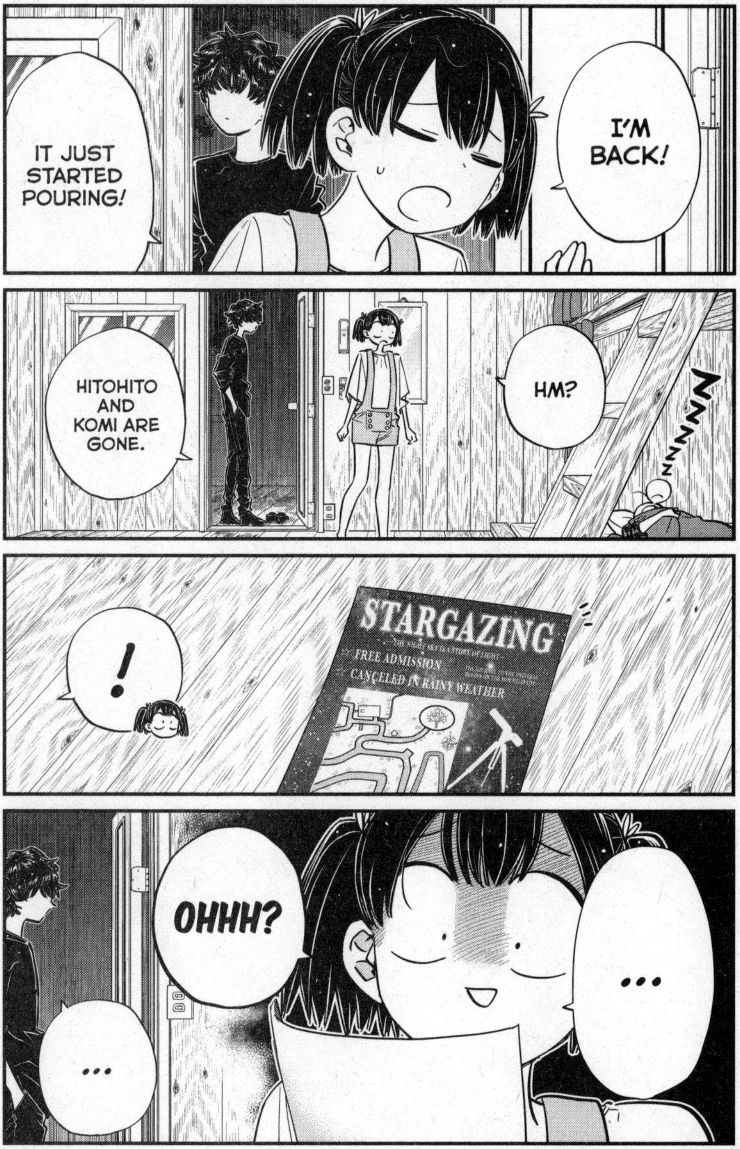
I'M BACK!
IT JUST STARTED POURING!
HM?
HITOHITO AND KOMI ARE GONE.
!
STARGAZING
FREE ADMISSION
CANCELED IN RAINY WEATHER
OHHH?
...
...

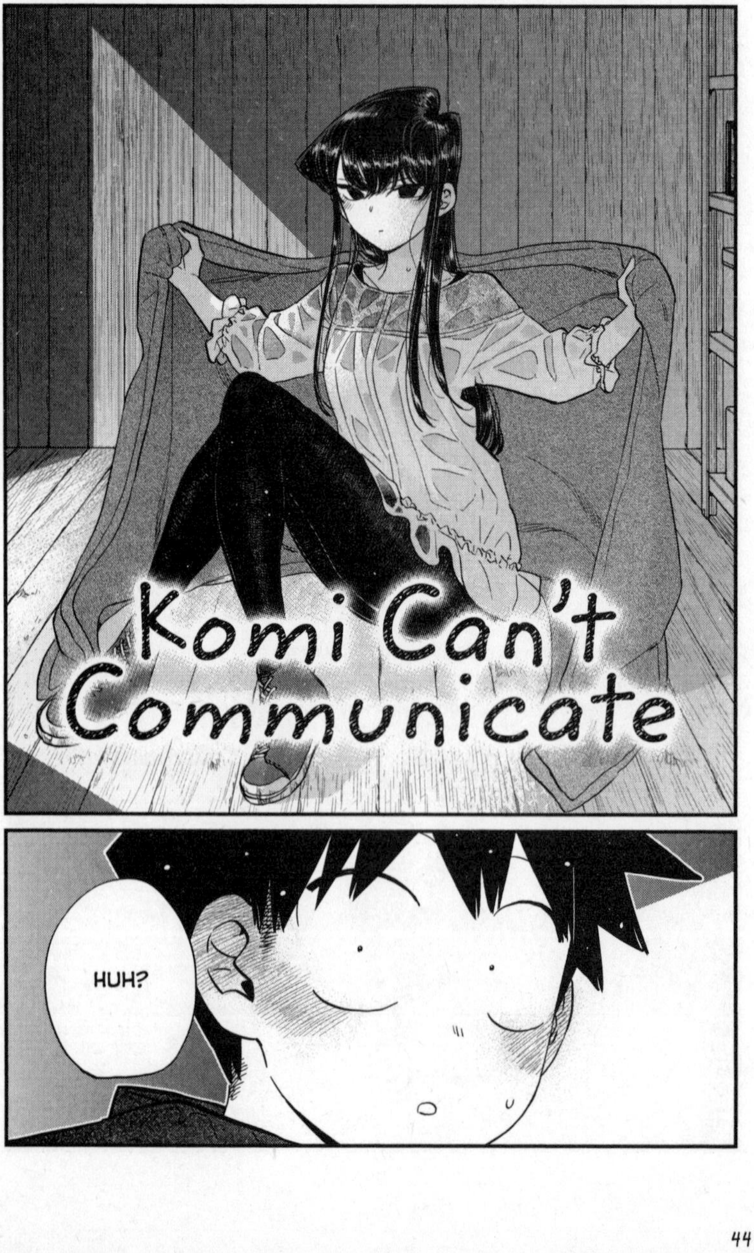
Komi Can't Communicate
HUH?

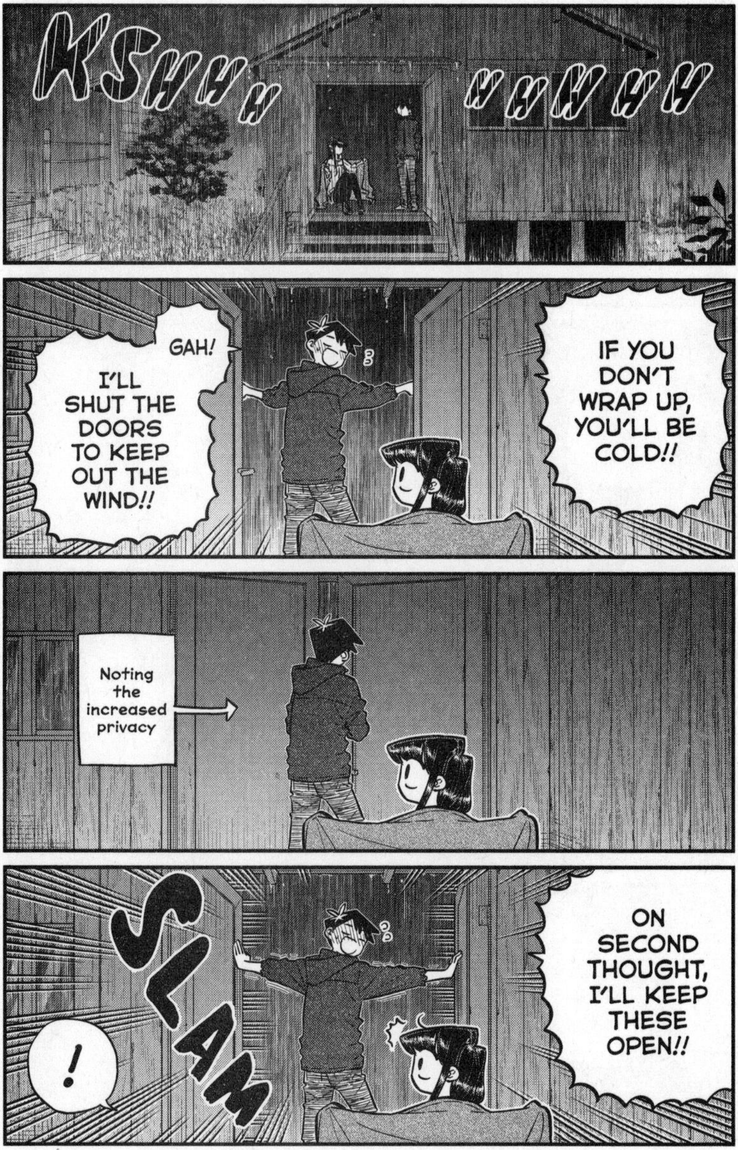
KSHHHH HHHHHH
IF YOU DON'T WRAP UP, YOU'LL BE COLD!!
GAH!
I'LL SHUT THE DOORS TO KEEP OUT THE WIND!!
Noting the increased privacy
ON SECOND THOUGHT, I'LL KEEP THESE OPEN!!
SLAM
!

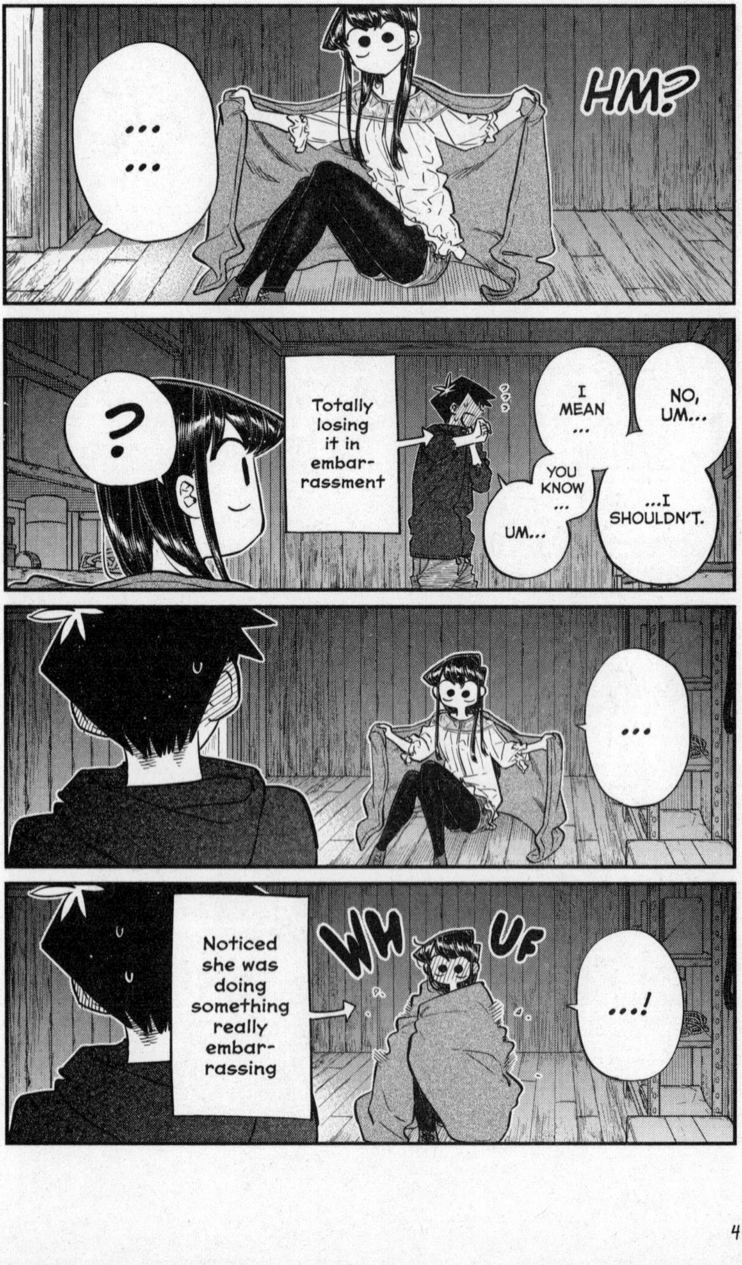
HM?
... ...
NO, UM...
I MEAN ...
YOU KNOW ...
UM...
...I SHOULDN'T.
Totally losing it in embar-rassment
?
...
...!
WH UF
Noticed she was doing something really embar-rassing

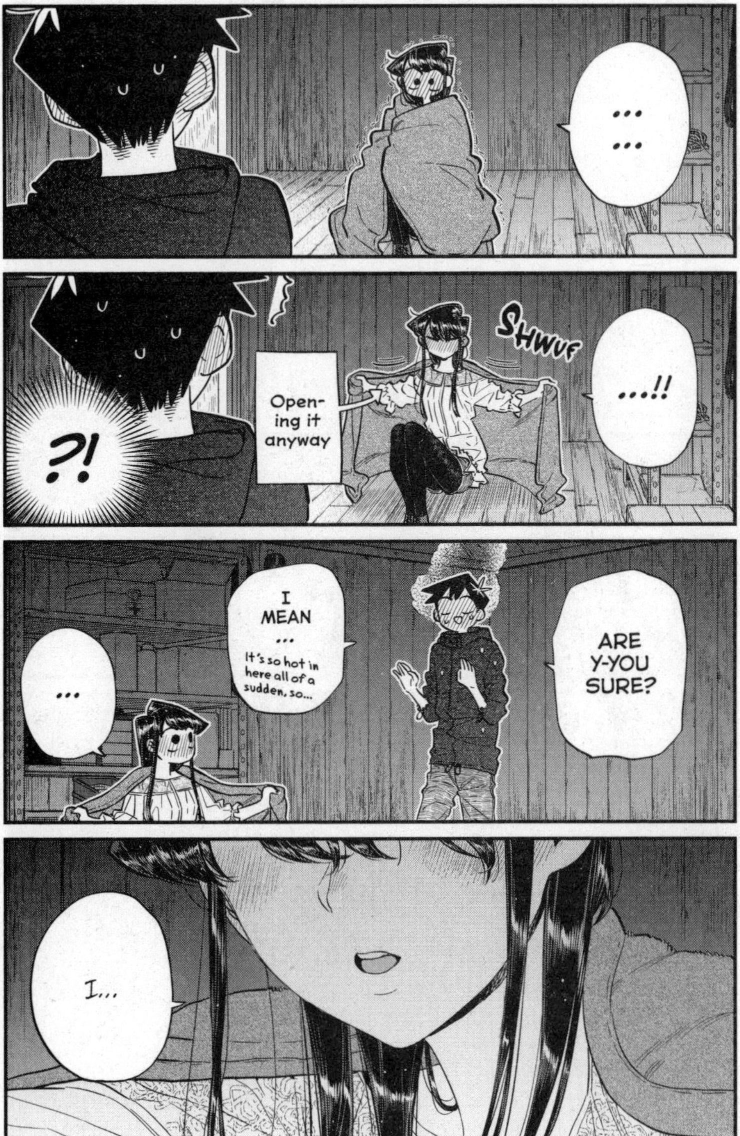

……
SHWUF
…!!
?!
Opening it anyway
ARE Y-YOU SURE?
I MEAN … It's so hot in here all of a sudden, so…
…
I…

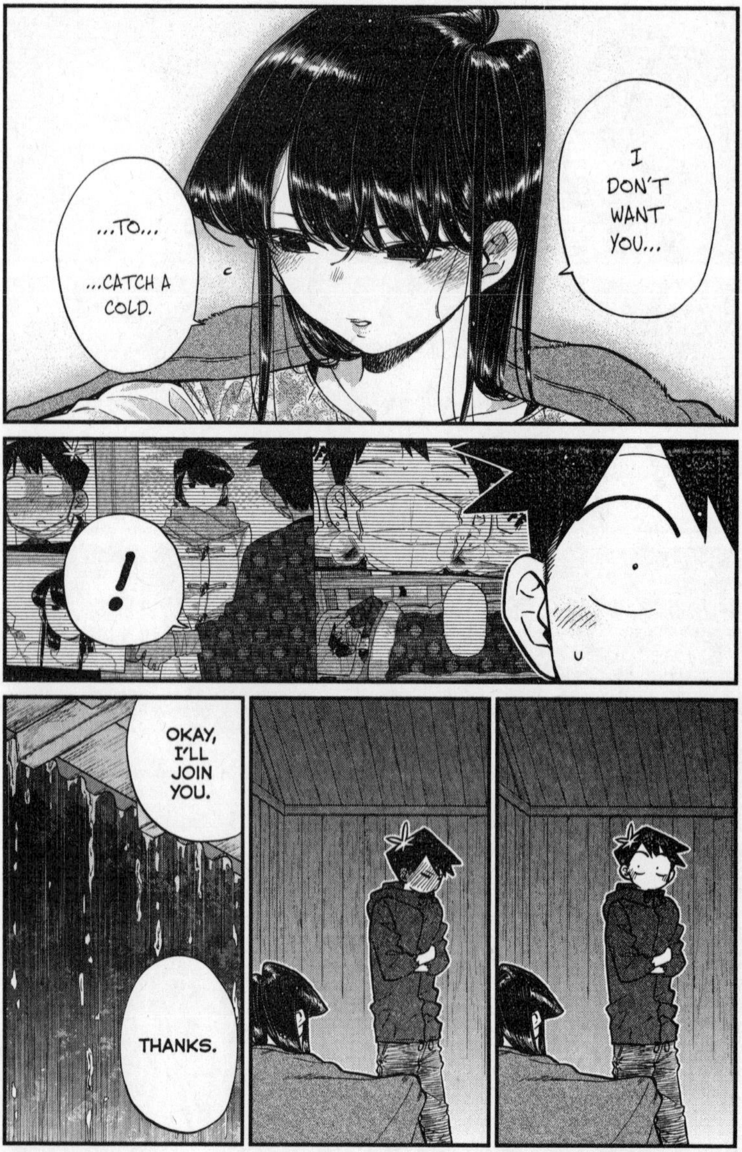

I DON'T WANT YOU...
...TO...
...CATCH A COLD.
!
OKAY, I'LL JOIN YOU.
THANKS.

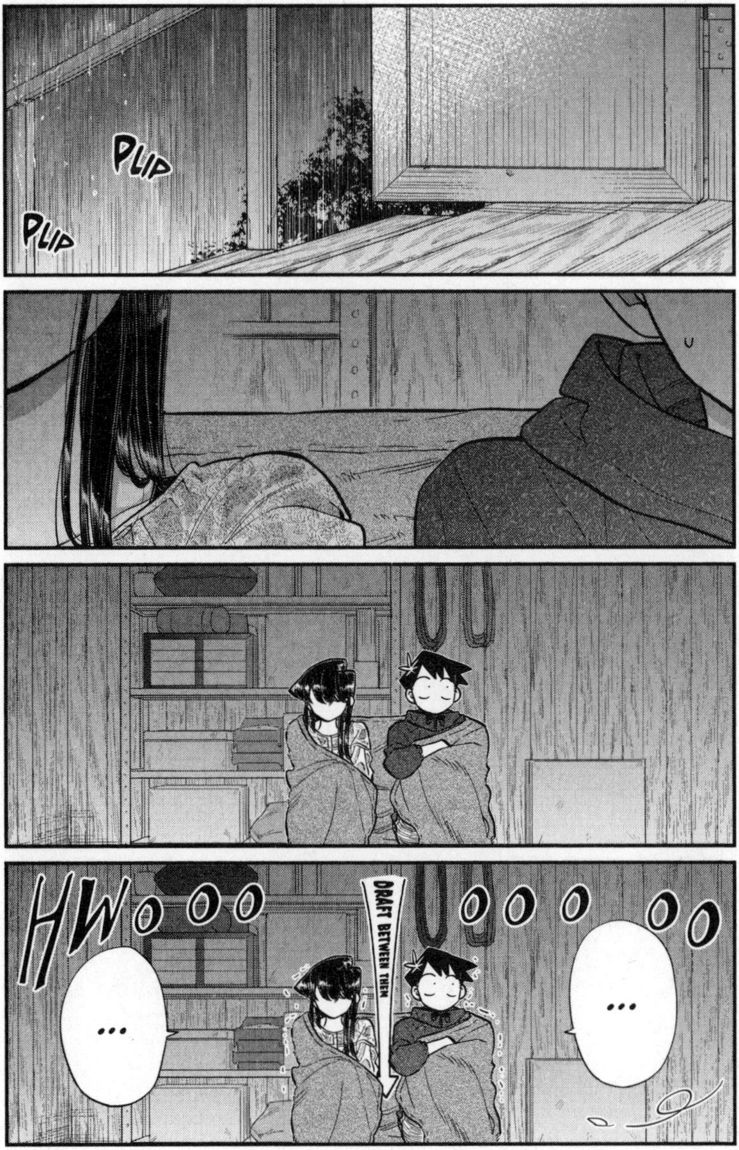
PLIP
PLIP
HWOOOOOOOOO
DRAFT BETWEEN THEM
...
...

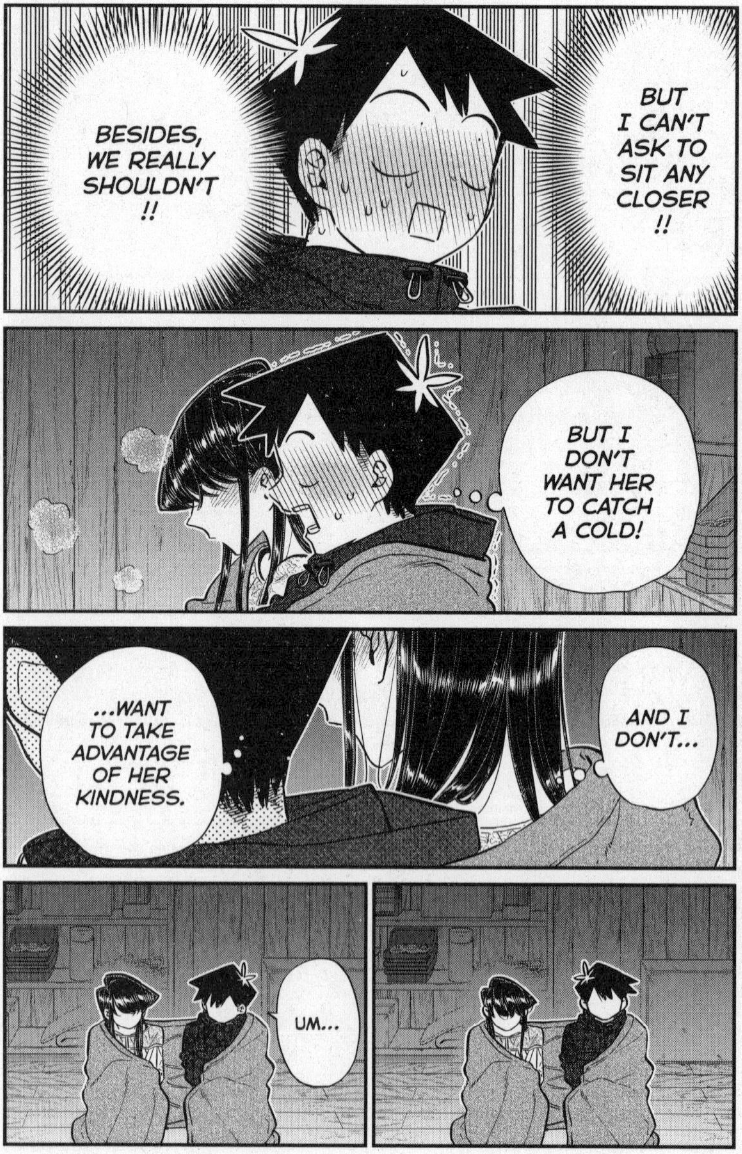
BUT I CAN'T ASK TO SIT ANY CLOSER !!
BESIDES, WE REALLY SHOULDN'T !!
BUT I DON'T WANT HER TO CATCH A COLD!
AND I DON'T...
...WANT TO TAKE ADVANTAGE OF HER KINDNESS.
UM...

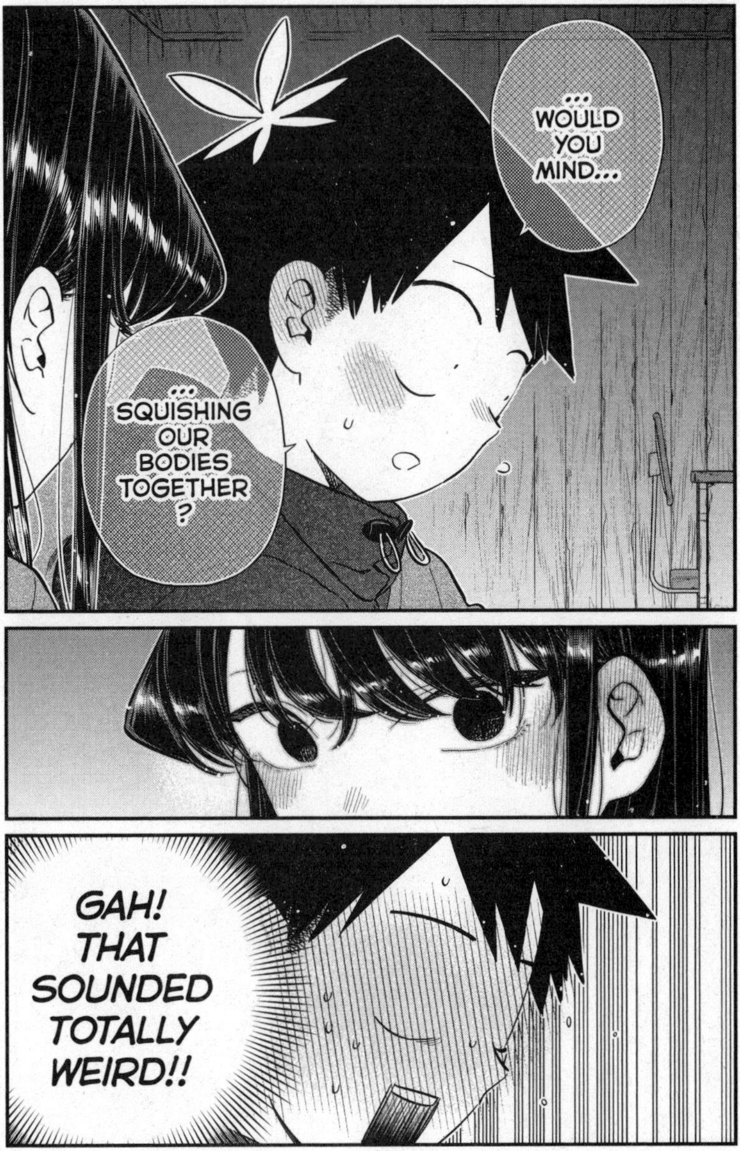
...WOULD YOU MIND...
...SQUISHING OUR BODIES TOGETHER?
GAH! THAT SOUNDED TOTALLY WEIRD!!

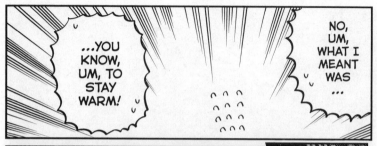

NO, UM, WHAT I MEANT WAS ...
...YOU KNOW, UM, TO STAY WARM!
NO...
...I WOULDN'T MIND.
?!

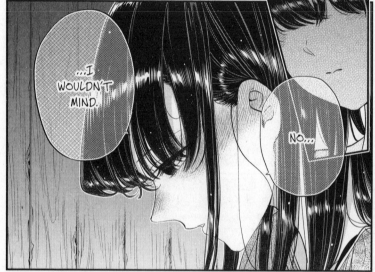

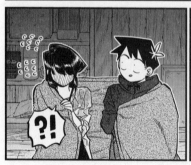

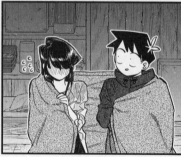

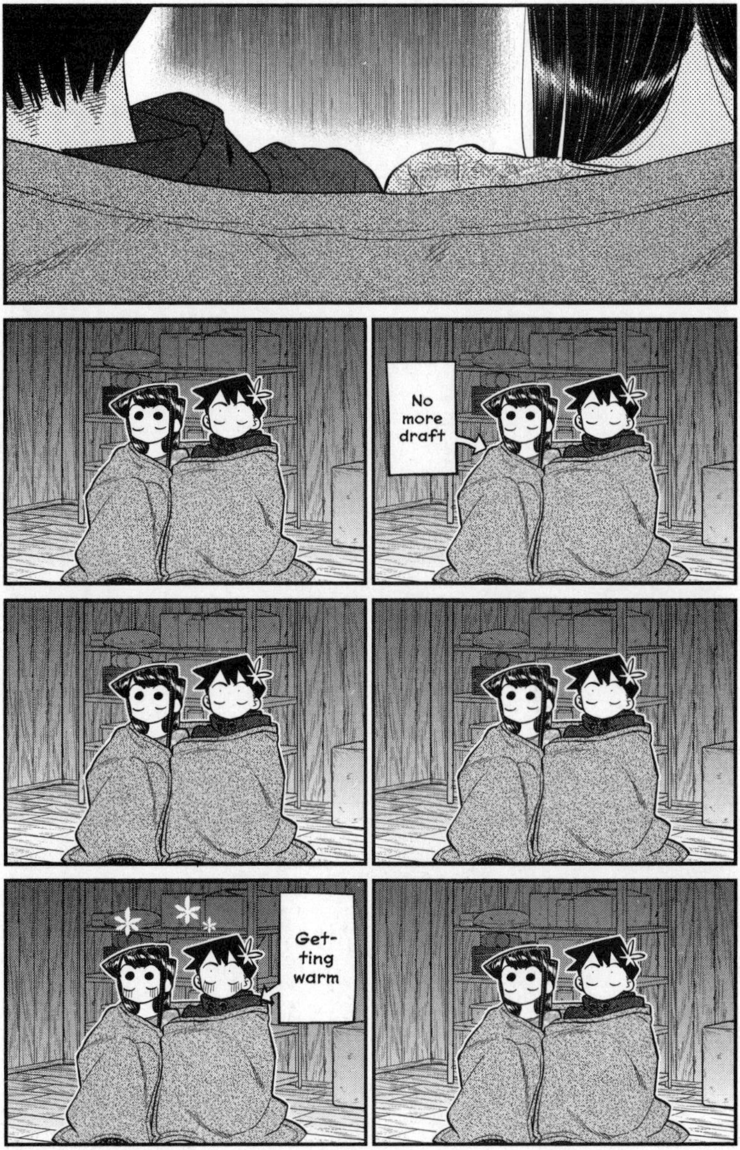
No more draft
Get-ting warm

Any smooching?!

BAM

DID ANY-THING HAP-PEN?!

?!

...

WHOOSH

FLUP

W-WHEN DID YOU GET HERE?!

x

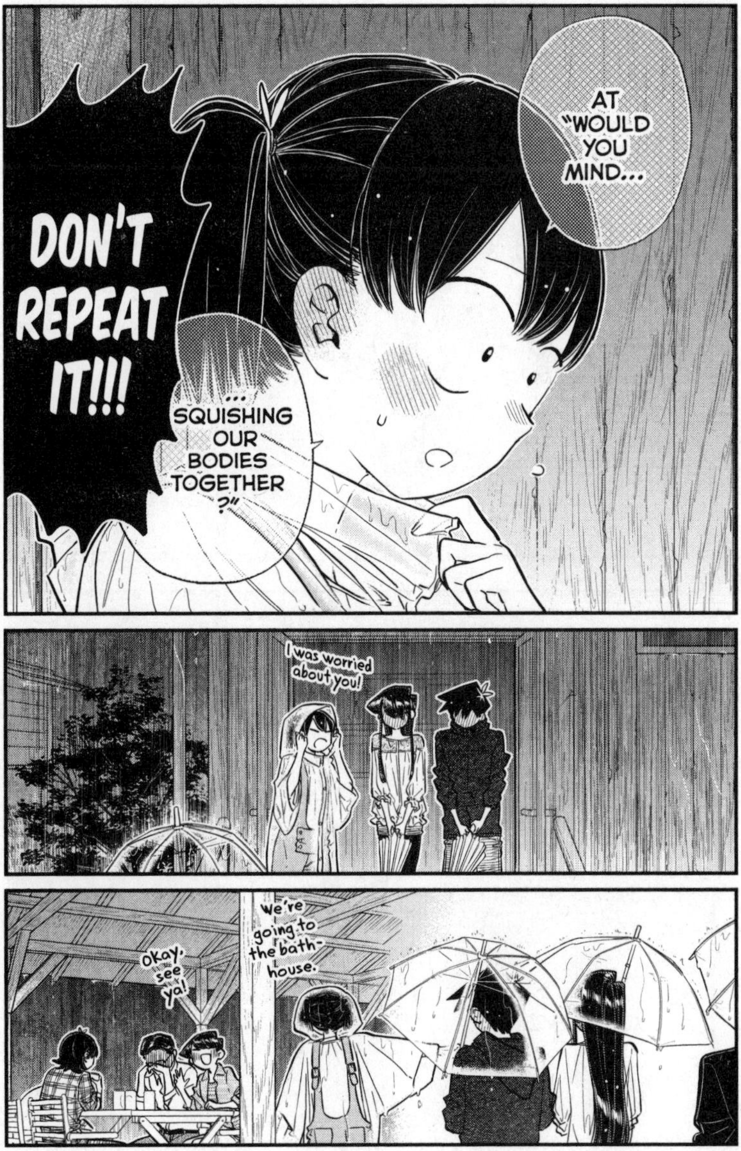
AT "WOULD YOU MIND...
...SQUISHING OUR BODIES TOGETHER?"
DON'T REPEAT IT!!!
I was worried about you!
We're going to the bath-house.
Okay, see ya!

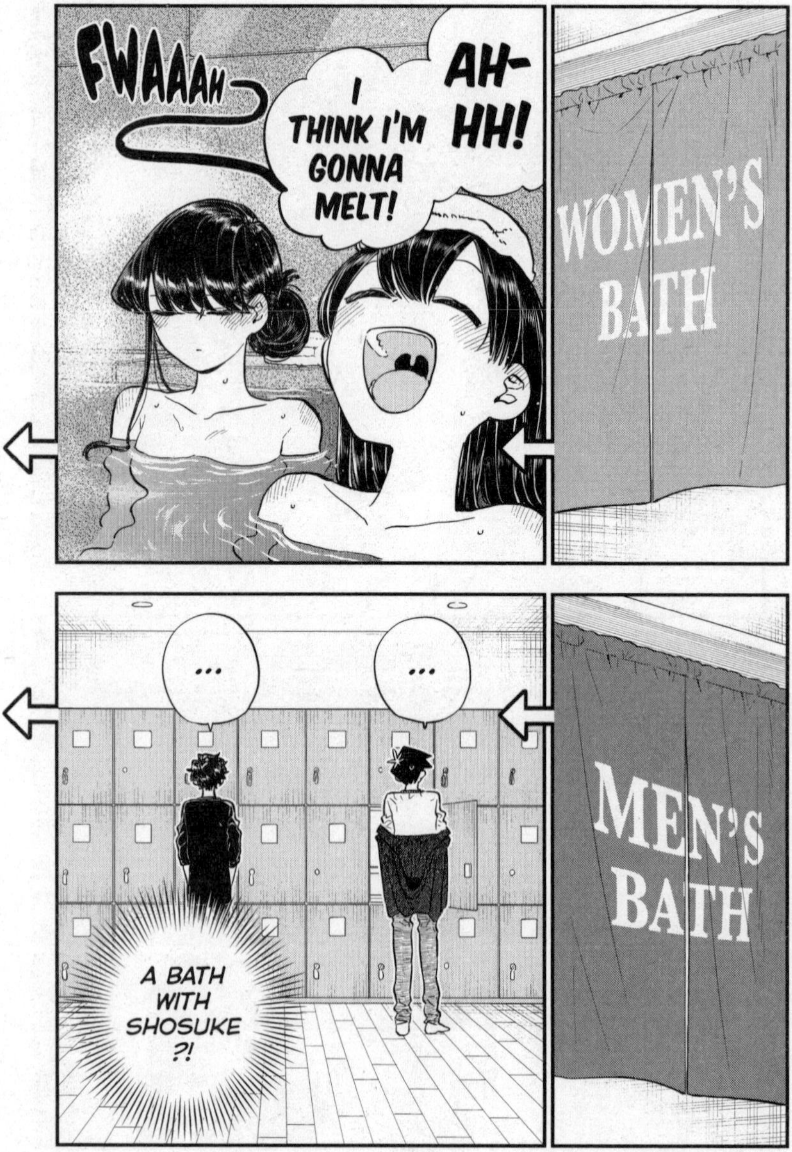
WOMEN'S BATH
AH-HH!
I THINK I'M GONNA MELT!
FWAAAH
MEN'S BATH
...
...
A BATH WITH SHOSUKE ?!

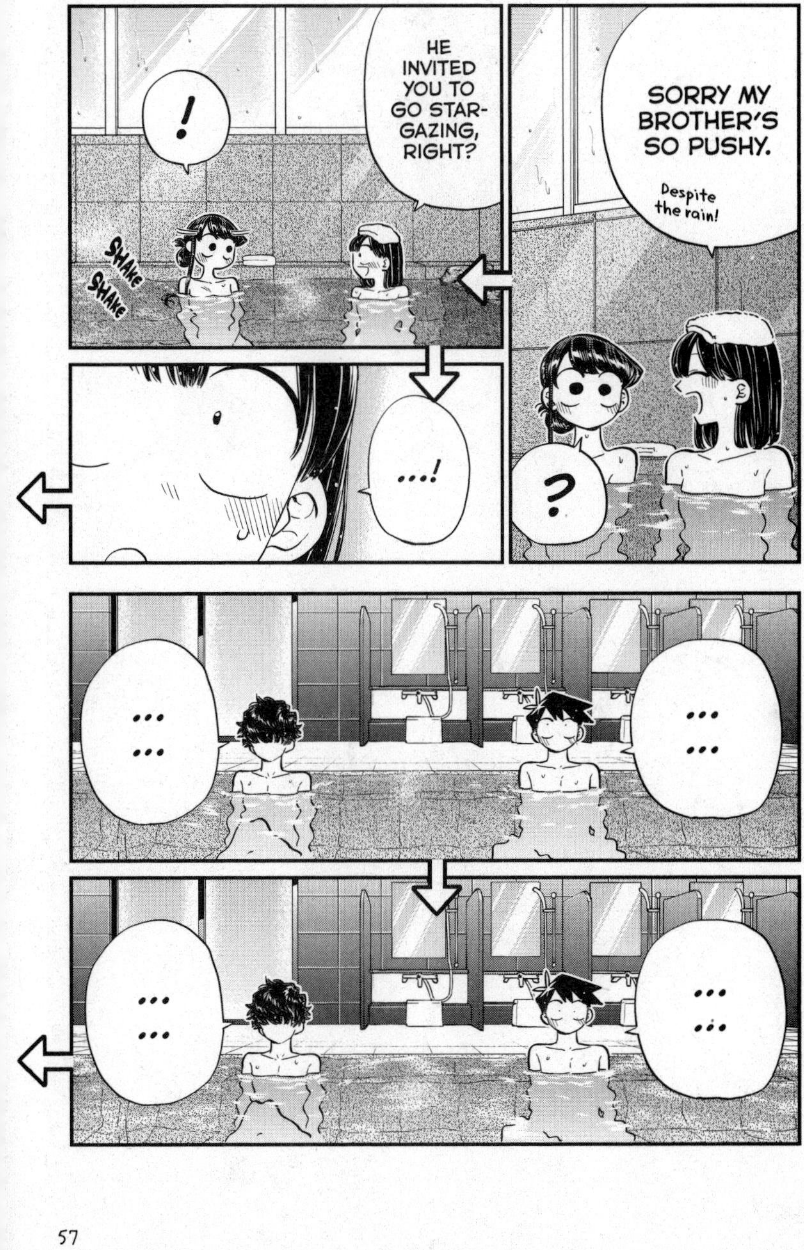
SORRY MY BROTHER'S SO PUSHY.
Despite the rain!
?
HE INVITED YOU TO GO STAR-GAZING, RIGHT?
!
SHAKE SHAKE
...!
... ...
... ...
... ...
... ...

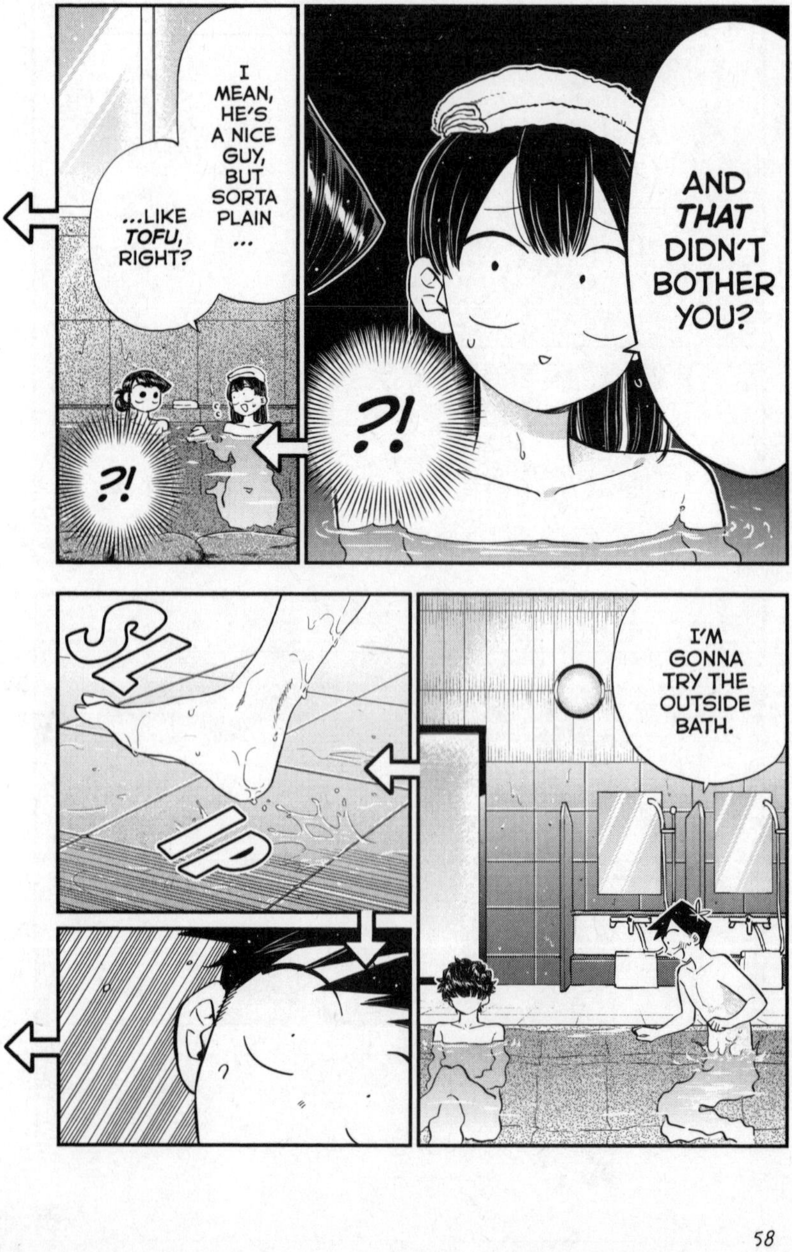
AND THAT DIDN'T BOTHER YOU?
?!
I MEAN, HE'S A NICE GUY, BUT SORTA PLAIN ...
...LIKE TOFU, RIGHT?
?!
I'M GONNA TRY THE OUTSIDE BATH.
SLIP

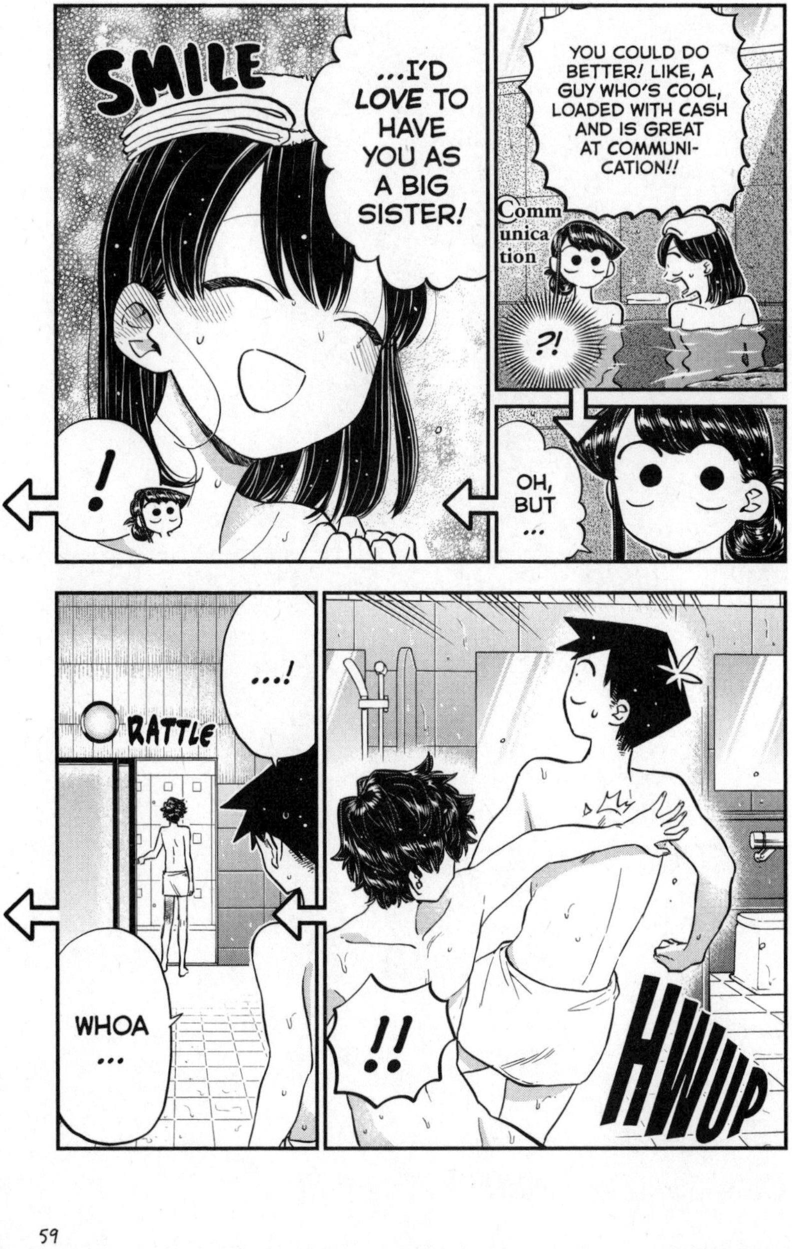
YOU COULD DO BETTER! LIKE, A GUY WHO'S COOL, LOADED WITH CASH AND IS GREAT AT COMMUNI-CATION!!
Communication
?!
OH, BUT ...
SMILE
...I'D LOVE TO HAVE YOU AS A BIG SISTER!
!
HWUP
!!
...!
RATTLE
WHOA ...

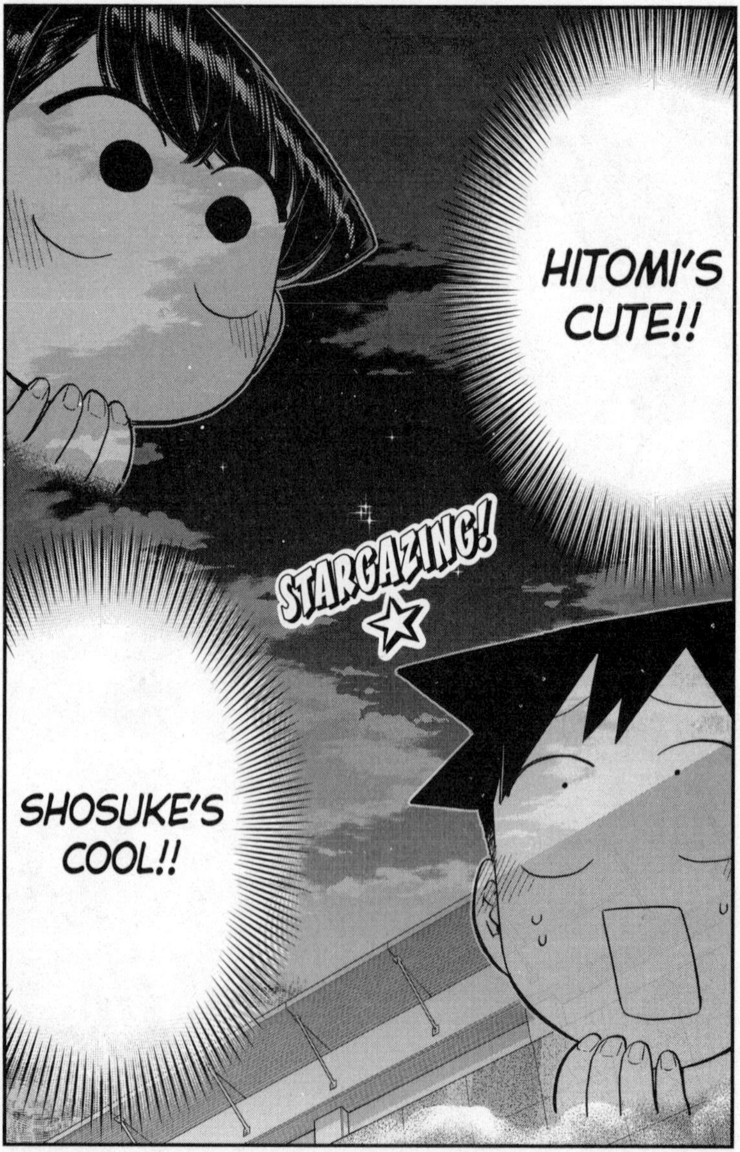
HITOMI'S CUTE!!
STARGAZING! ☆
SHOSUKE'S COOL!!

Communication 144 — The End

Komi Can't Communicate

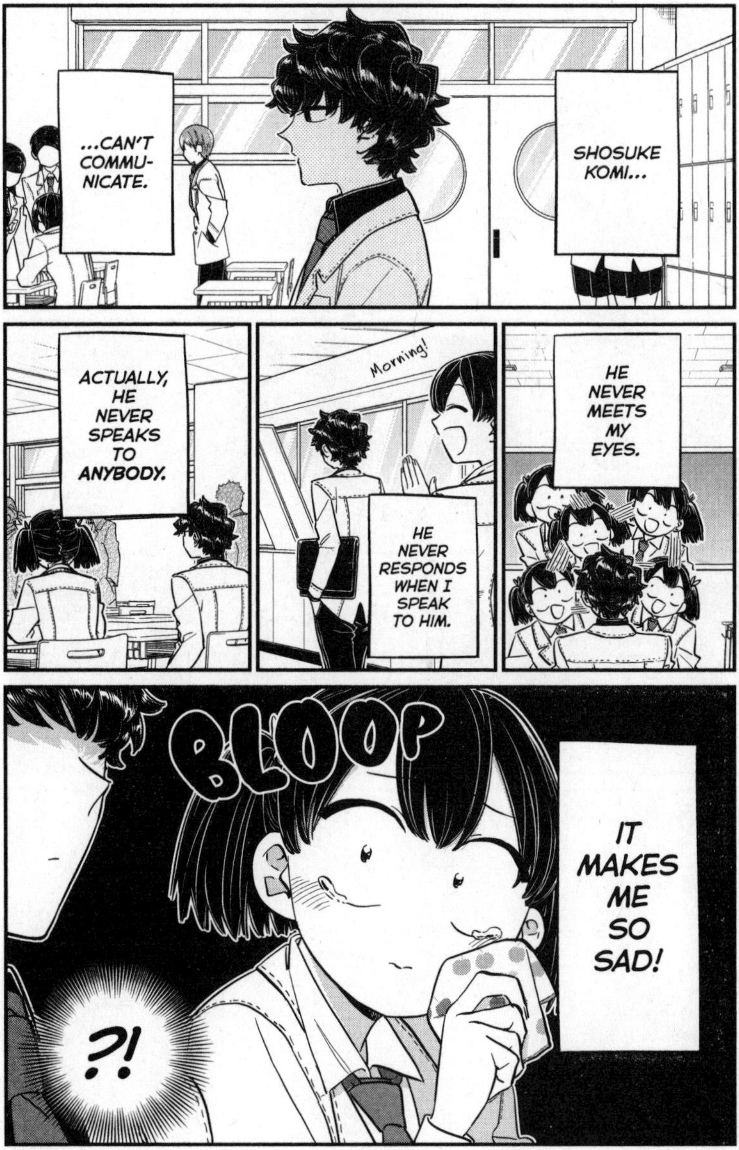
SHOSUKE KOMI...
...CAN'T COMMUNICATE.
HE NEVER MEETS MY EYES.
Morning!
HE NEVER RESPONDS WHEN I SPEAK TO HIM.
ACTUALLY, HE NEVER SPEAKS TO ANYBODY.
BLOOP
IT MAKES ME SO SAD!
?!

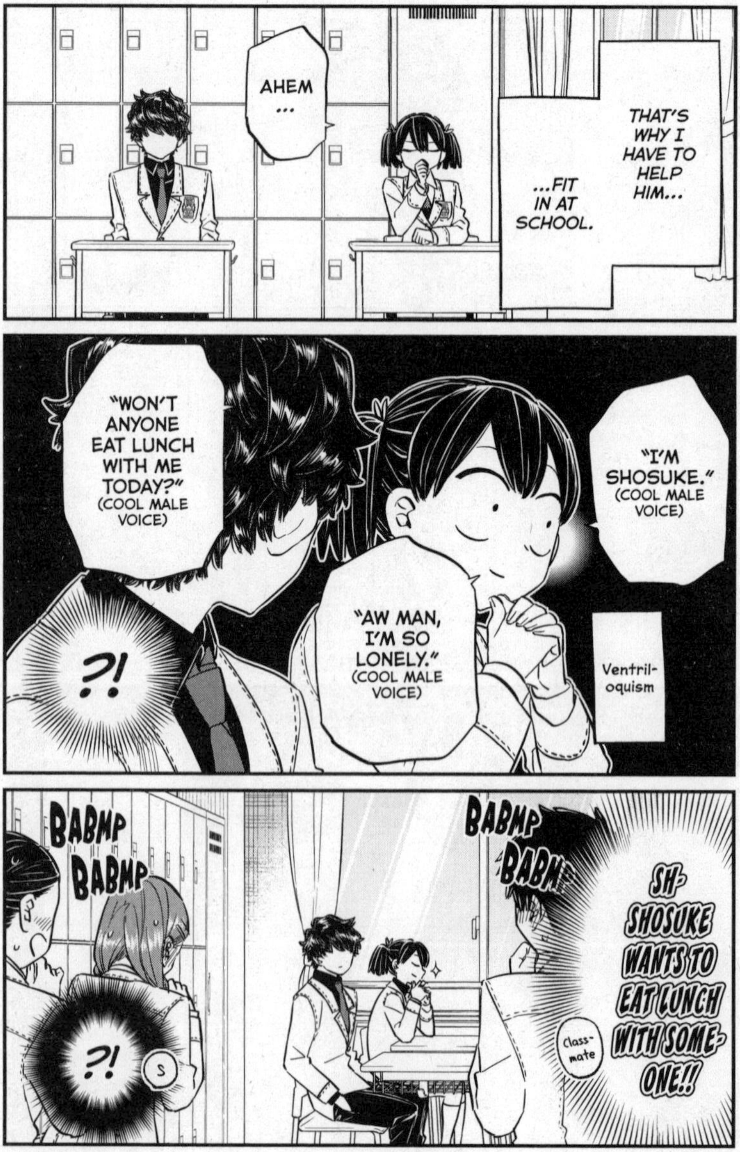
THAT'S WHY I HAVE TO HELP HIM...
...FIT IN AT SCHOOL.
AHEM ...
"I'M SHOSUKE." (COOL MALE VOICE)
"WON'T ANYONE EAT LUNCH WITH ME TODAY?" (COOL MALE VOICE)
Ventril-oquism
"AW MAN, I'M SO LONELY." (COOL MALE VOICE)
?!
BABMP BABM
SH-SHOSUKE WANTS TO EAT LUNCH WITH SOME-ONE!!
Class-mate
BABMP BABMP
?!
S

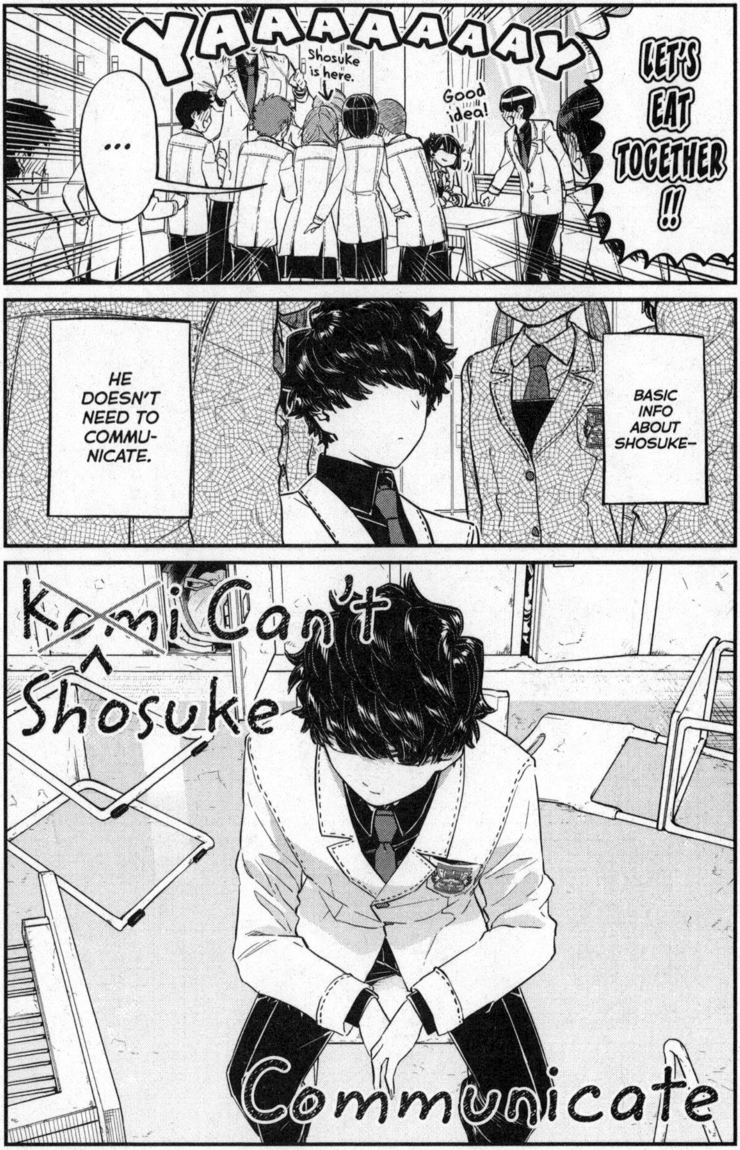
LET'S EAT TOGETHER!!
Good idea!
Shosuke is here.
YAAAAAAAY
...
BASIC INFO ABOUT SHOSUKE—
HE DOESN'T NEED TO COMMUNICATE.
Komi Can't
Shosuke
Communicate

Communication 145: Soccer

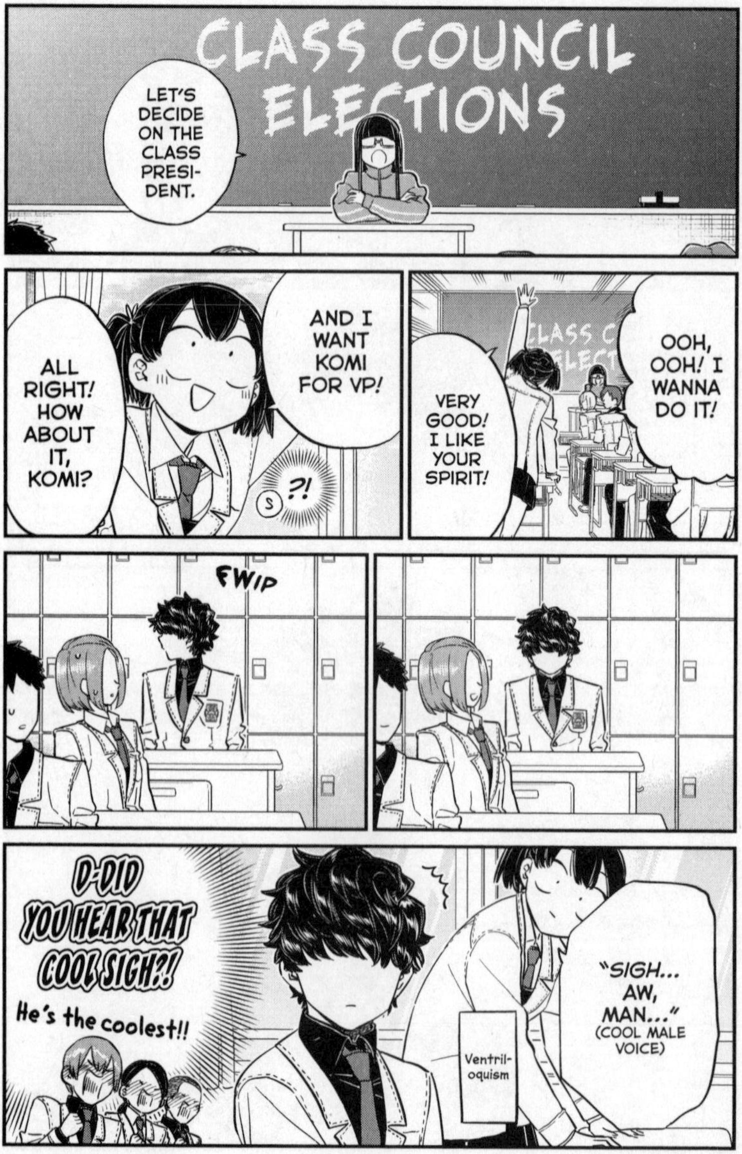
CLASS COUNCIL ELECTIONS
LET'S DECIDE ON THE CLASS PRESIDENT.
OOH, OOH! I WANNA DO IT!
VERY GOOD! I LIKE YOUR SPIRIT!
AND I WANT KOMI FOR VP!
ALL RIGHT! HOW ABOUT IT, KOMI?
?!
S
FWIP
"SIGH... AW, MAN..." (COOL MALE VOICE)
Ventril-oquism
D-DID YOU HEAR THAT COOL SIGH?!
He's the coolest!!

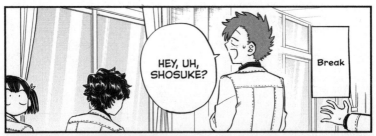

Break
HEY, UH, SHOSUKE?
...
!
S-S-SORRY! I W-WAS JUST G-GONNA CHAT, BUT...
NEVER MIND! MY DEEPEST APOLOGIES!
"DID YOU SEE CHIBI MARUKO-CHAN YESTERDAY? YAMANA WAS GREAT!"
HE'S GOT GOOD LOOKS AND HE'S CONGENIAL!!

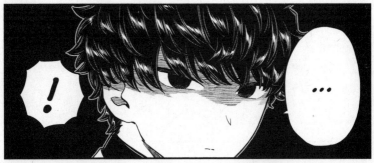

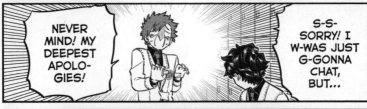

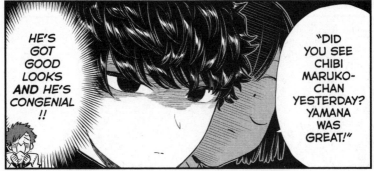

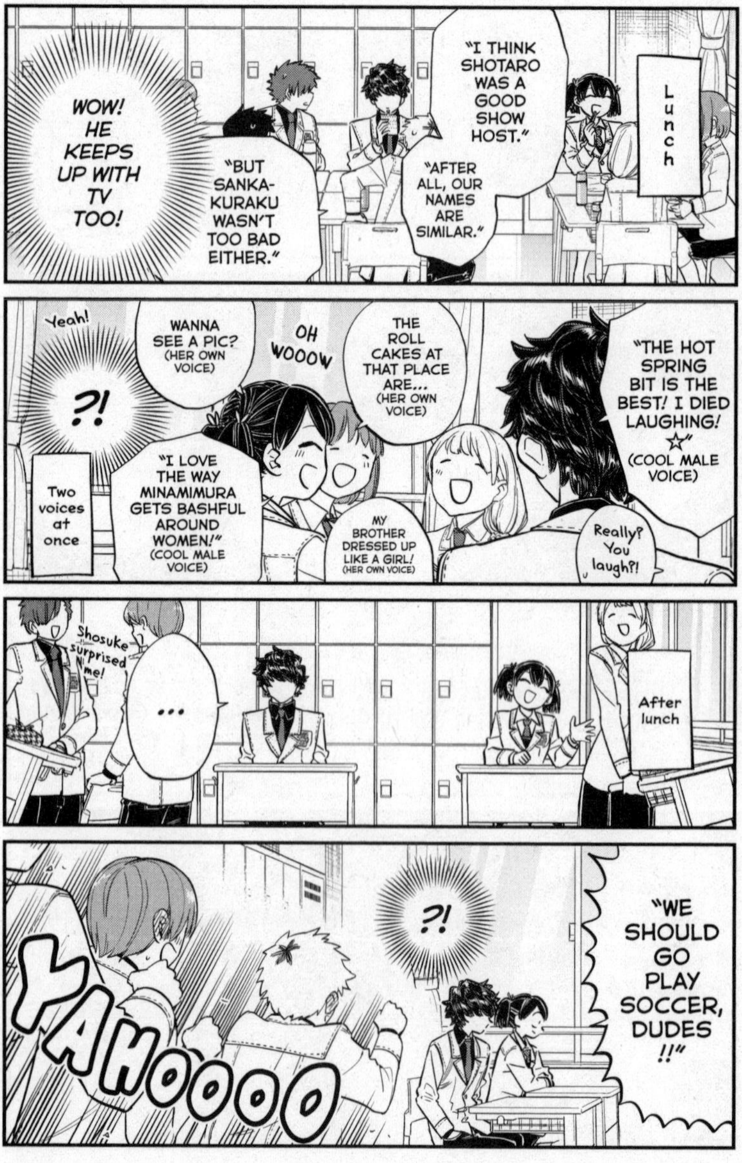
Lunch
"I THINK SHOTARO WAS A GOOD SHOW HOST."
"AFTER ALL, OUR NAMES ARE SIMILAR."
"BUT SANKA-KURAKU WASN'T TOO BAD EITHER."
WOW! HE KEEPS UP WITH TV TOO!
"THE HOT SPRING BIT IS THE BEST! I DIED LAUGHING! ☆" (COOL MALE VOICE)
THE ROLL CAKES AT THAT PLACE ARE... (HER OWN VOICE)
OH WOOOW
WANNA SEE A PIC? (HER OWN VOICE)
Yeah!
Really? You laugh?!
MY BROTHER DRESSED UP LIKE A GIRL! (HER OWN VOICE)
"I LOVE THE WAY MINAMIMURA GETS BASHFUL AROUND WOMEN!" (COOL MALE VOICE)
?!
Two voices at once
After lunch
...
Shosuke surprised me!
"WE SHOULD GO PLAY SOCCER, DUDES!!"
?!
YAHOOOO

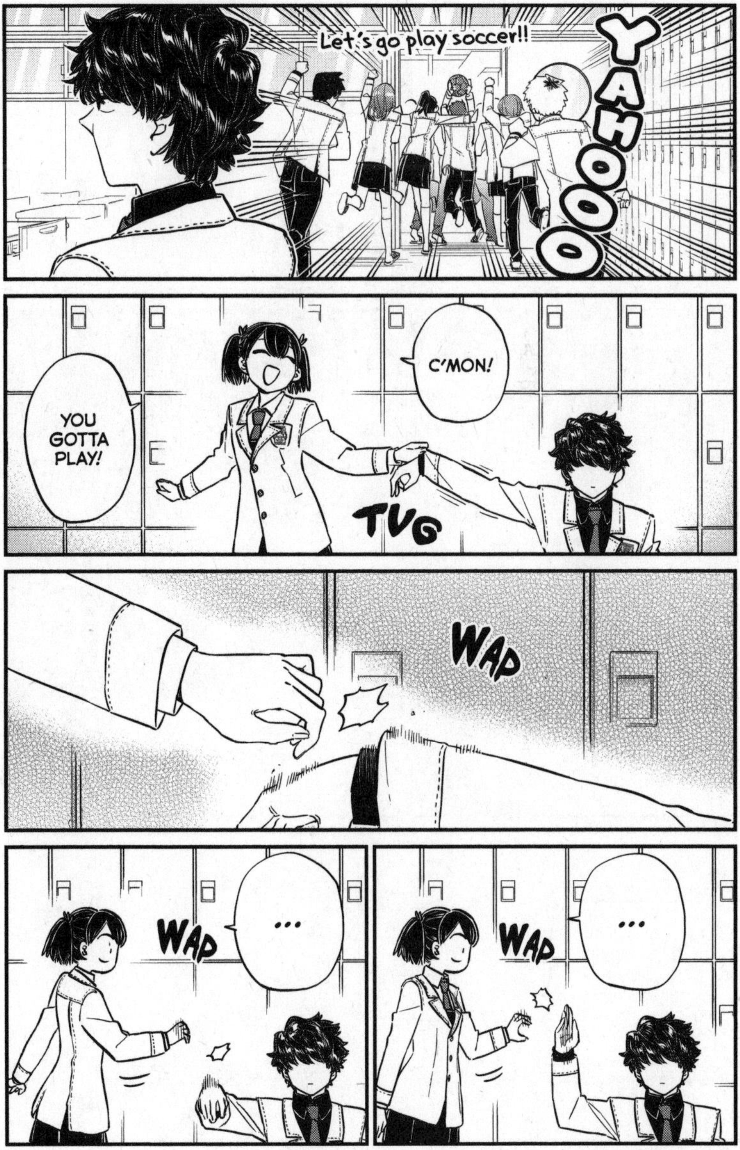
YAHOOO
Let's go play soccer!!
C'MON!
YOU GOTTA PLAY!
TUG
WAP
...
WAP
...
WAP

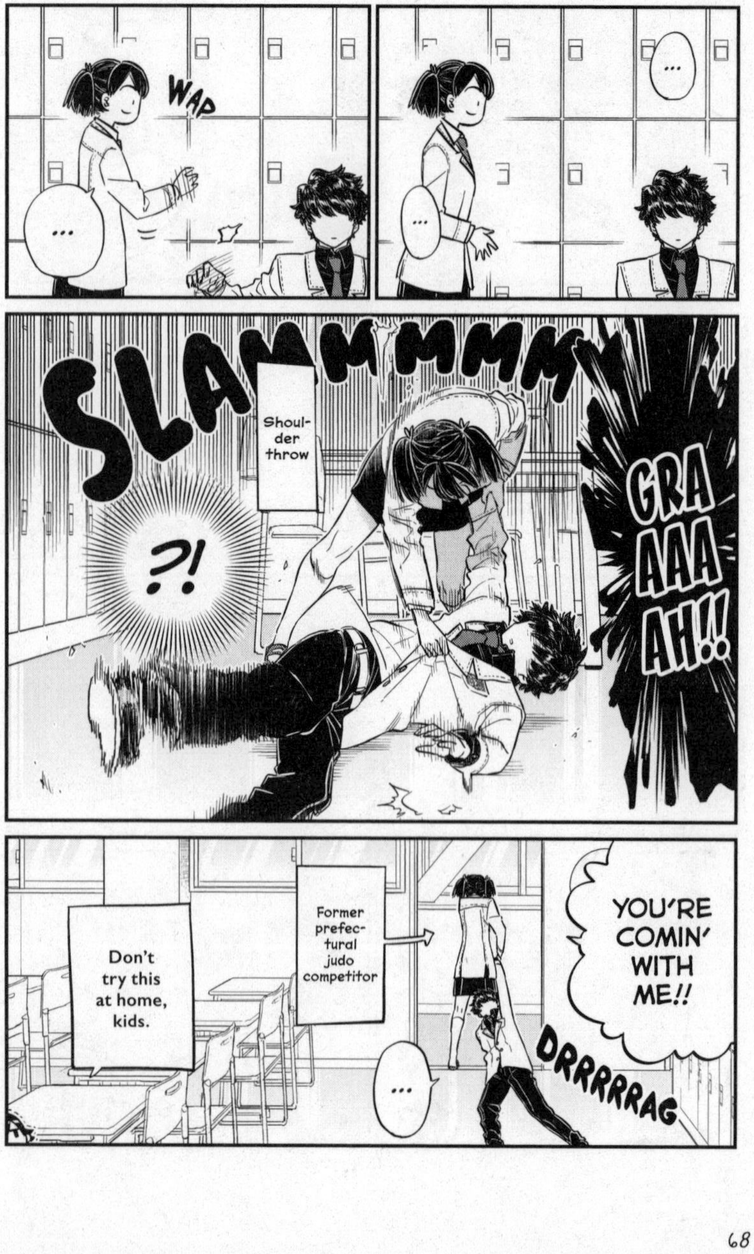
...
...
WAP
...
GRAAAAAH!!
SLAMMMMMM
Shoulder-throw
?!
YOU'RE COMIN' WITH ME!!
DRRRRRRAG
...
Former prefectural judo competitor
Don't try this at home, kids.

WAAAH

YAAAH

RAAAH

UWAAH

FWEEET

SHOSUKE!!

SWIP

SH-SHO-SUKE! GET THE BALL!

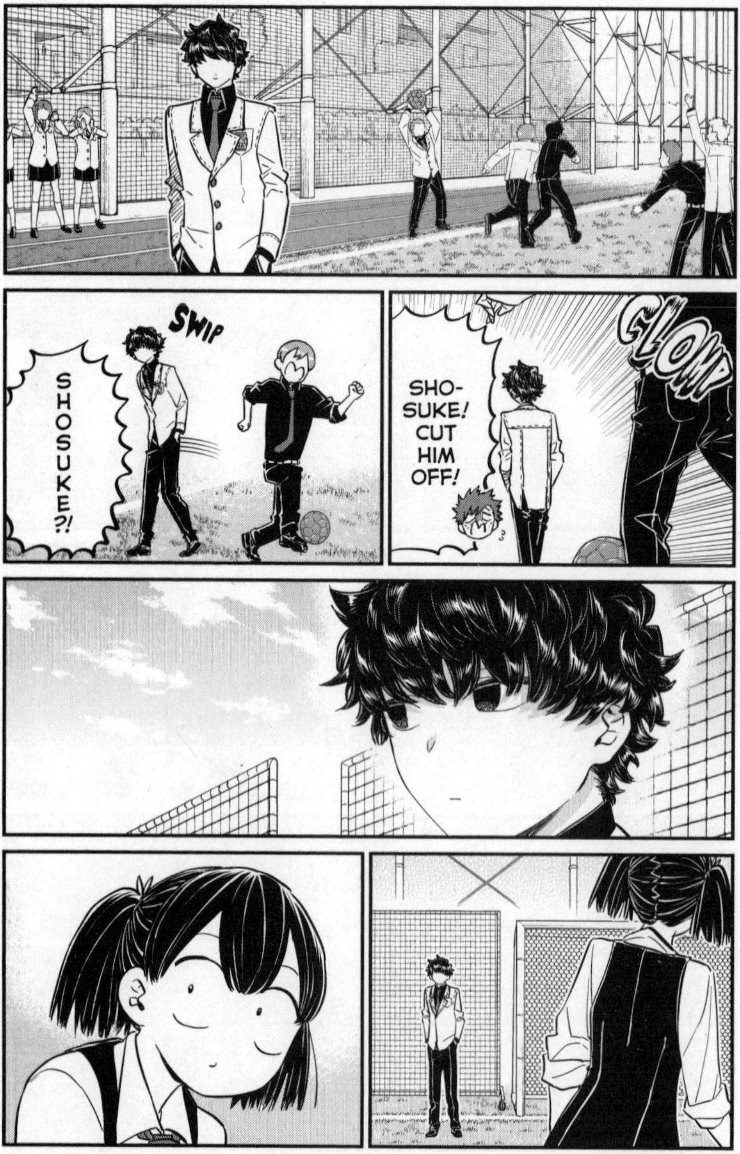
GLOMP
SHO-SUKE! CUT HIM OFF!
SWIP
SHOSUKE?!

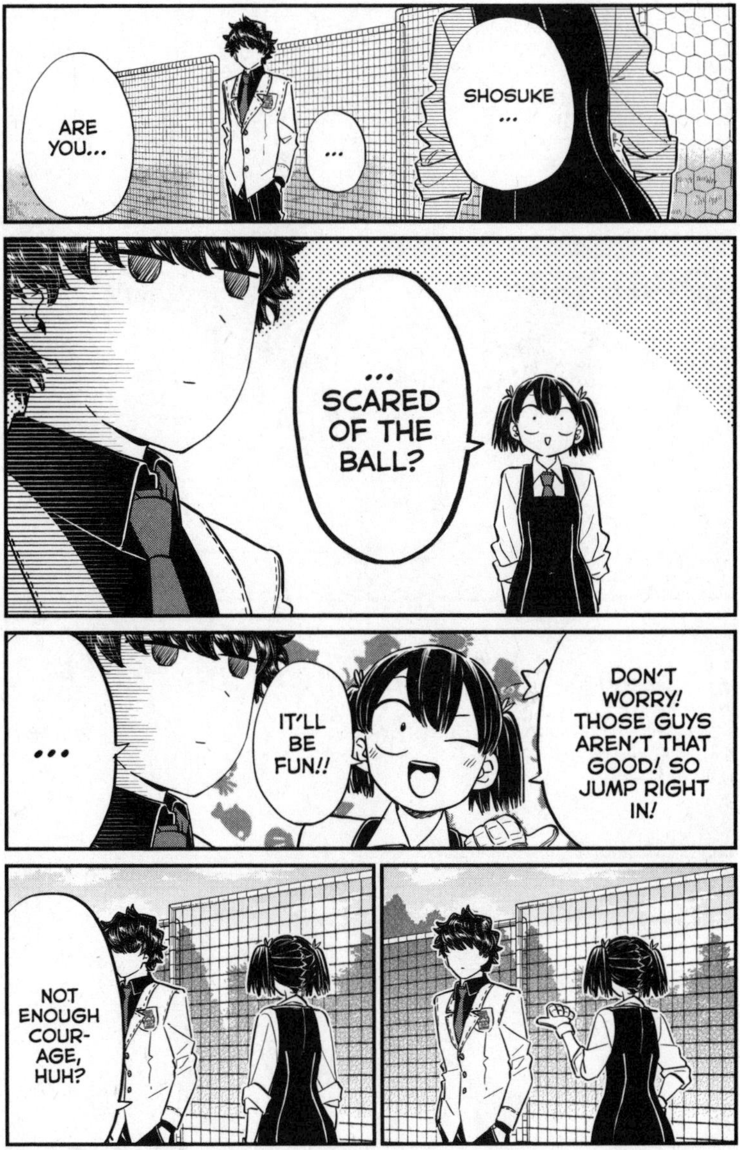
SHOSUKE ...
...
ARE YOU...
... SCARED OF THE BALL?
DON'T WORRY! THOSE GUYS AREN'T THAT GOOD! SO JUMP RIGHT IN!
IT'LL BE FUN!!
...
NOT ENOUGH COURAGE, HUH?

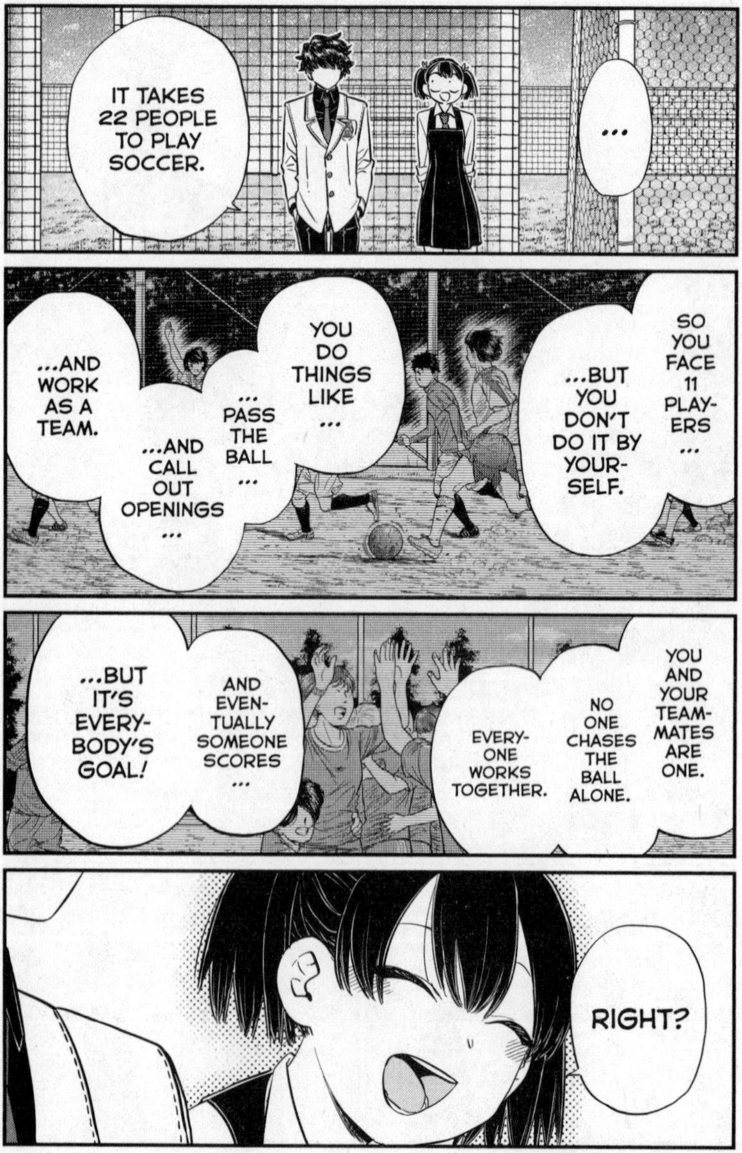
...
IT TAKES 22 PEOPLE TO PLAY SOCCER.
SO YOU FACE 11 PLAYERS...
...BUT YOU DON'T DO IT BY YOURSELF.
YOU DO THINGS LIKE...
...PASS THE BALL...
...AND CALL OUT OPENINGS...
...AND WORK AS A TEAM.
YOU AND YOUR TEAMMATES ARE ONE.
NO ONE CHASES THE BALL ALONE.
EVERYONE WORKS TOGETHER.
AND EVENTUALLY SOMEONE SCORES...
...BUT IT'S EVERYBODY'S GOAL!
RIGHT?

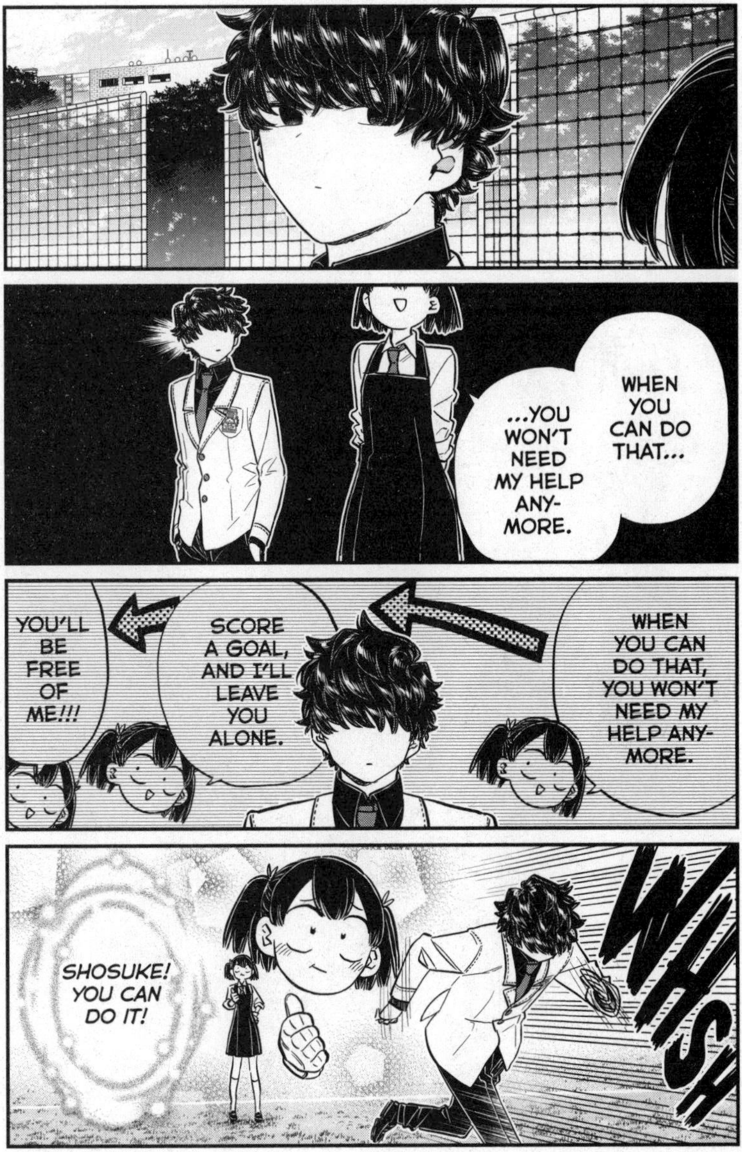
WHEN YOU CAN DO THAT...
...YOU WON'T NEED MY HELP ANY-MORE.
WHEN YOU CAN DO THAT, YOU WON'T NEED MY HELP ANY-MORE.
SCORE A GOAL, AND I'LL LEAVE YOU ALONE.
YOU'LL BE FREE OF ME!!!
WHSH
SHOSUKE! YOU CAN DO IT!

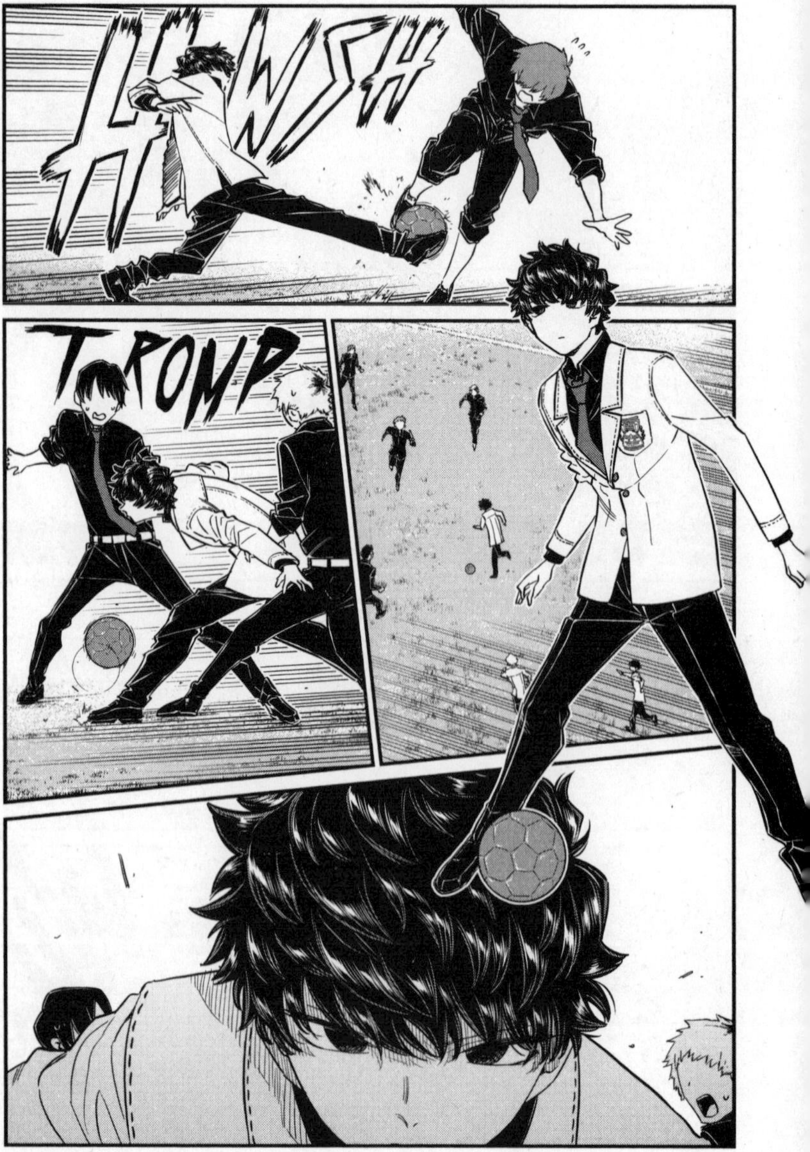
FWISH
TROMP

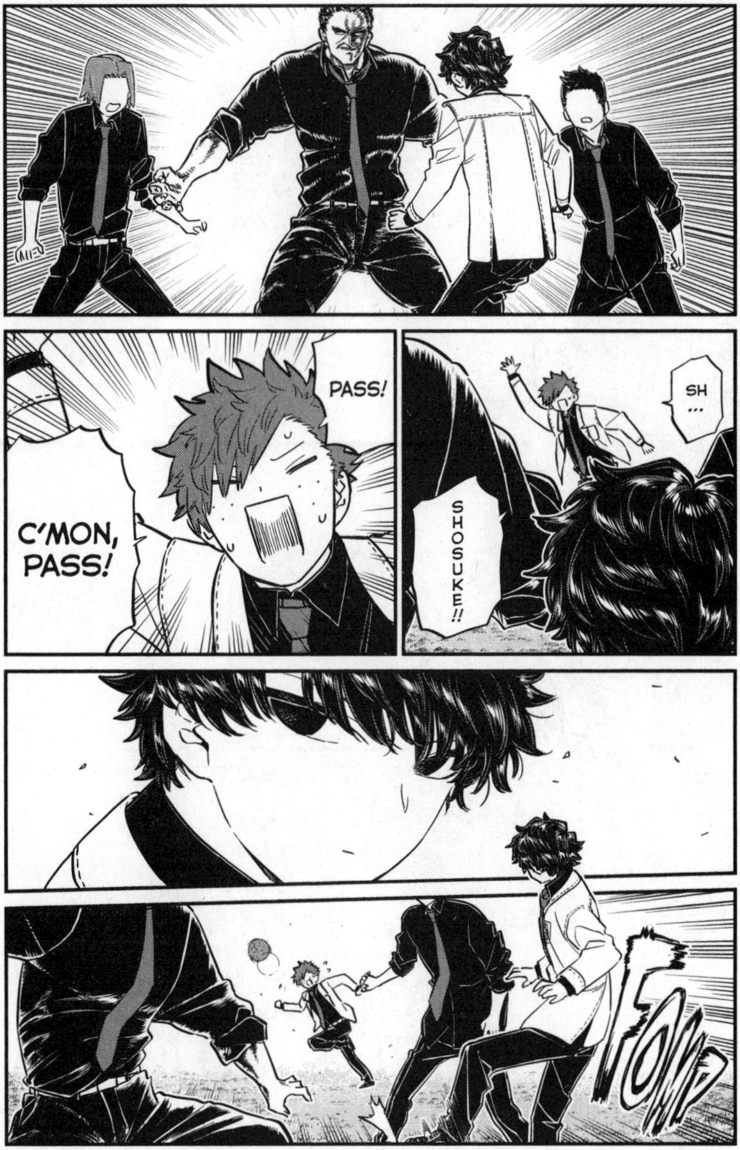
SH ...
SHOSUKE!!
PASS!
C'MON, PASS!

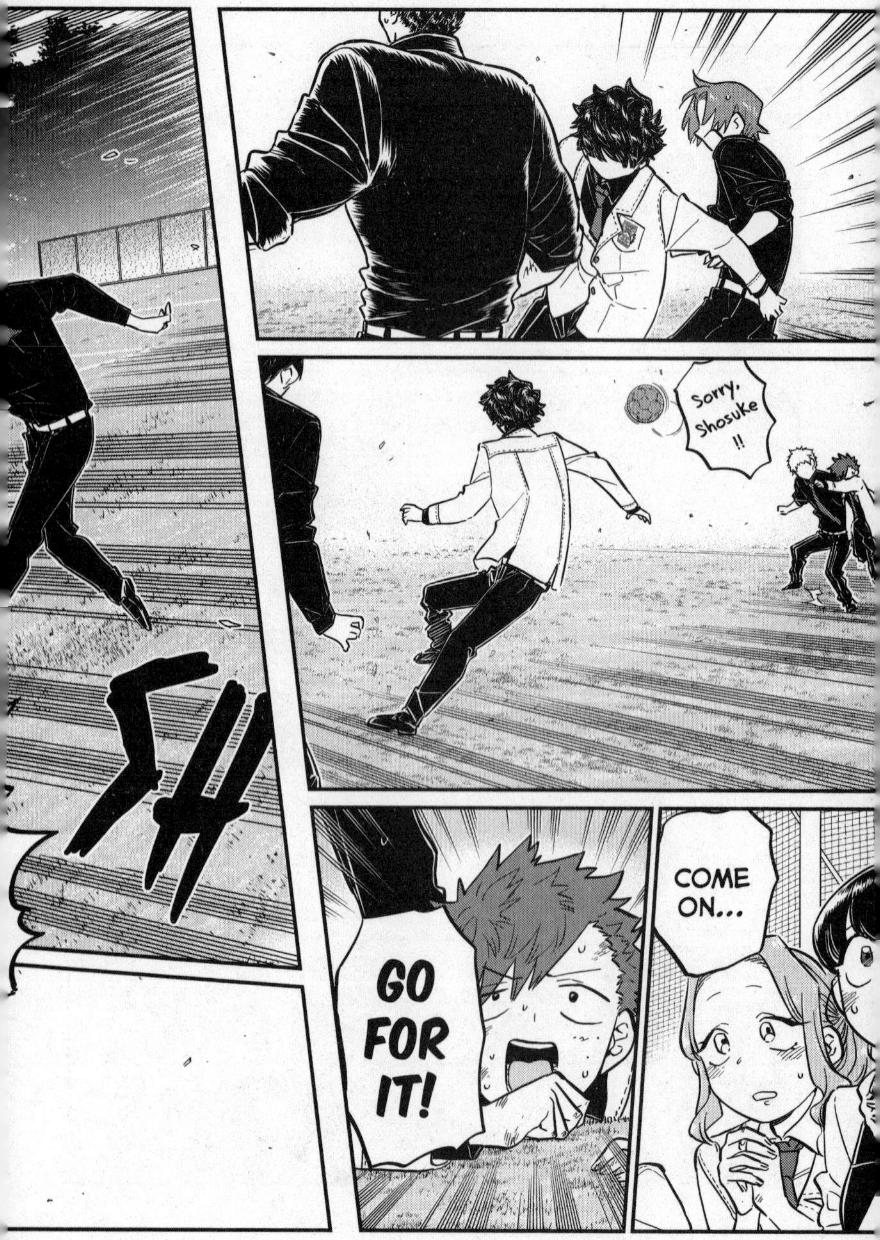
Sorry, Shosuke !!
COME ON...
GO FOR IT!

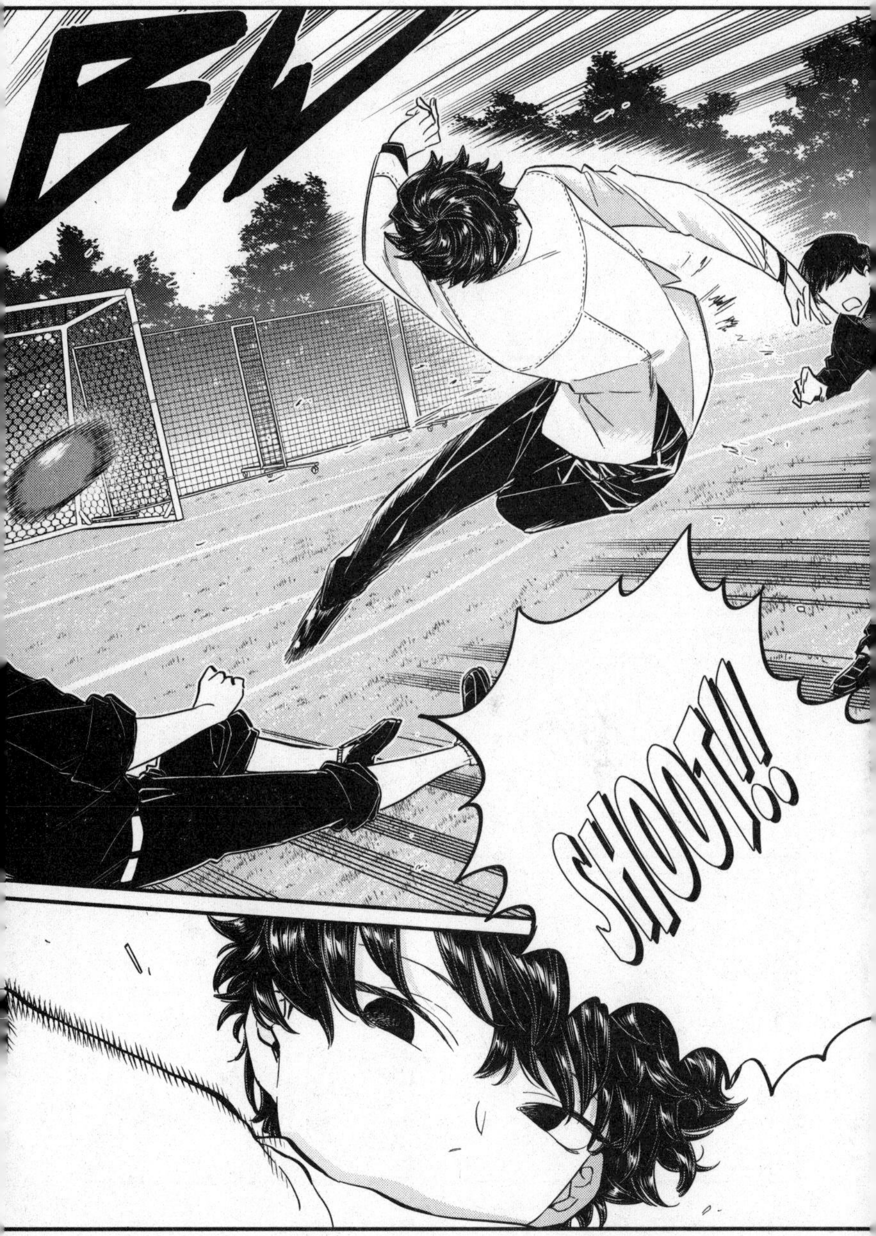
BW
SHOOT!!

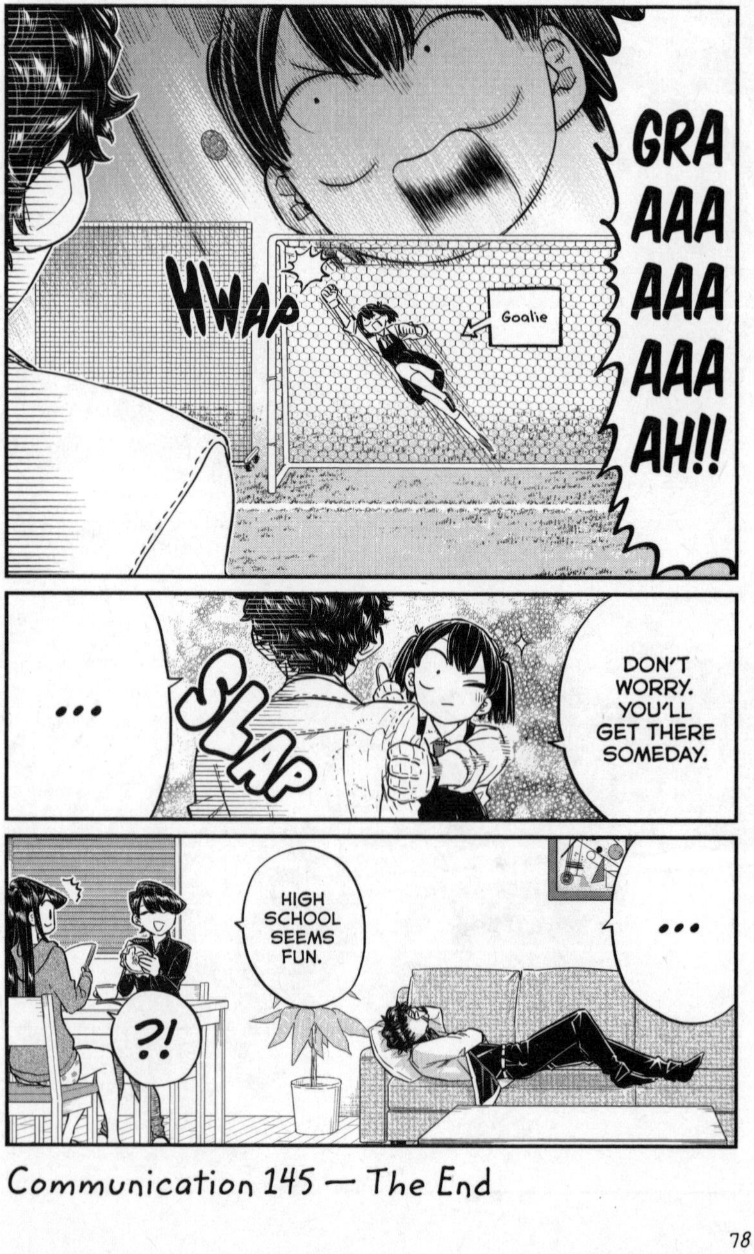
GRAAAAAAAAAAAAAH!!
HWAP
Goalie
DON'T WORRY. YOU'LL GET THERE SOMEDAY.
SLAP
...
...
HIGH SCHOOL SEEMS FUN.
?!

Communication 145 — The End

Komi Can't Communicate

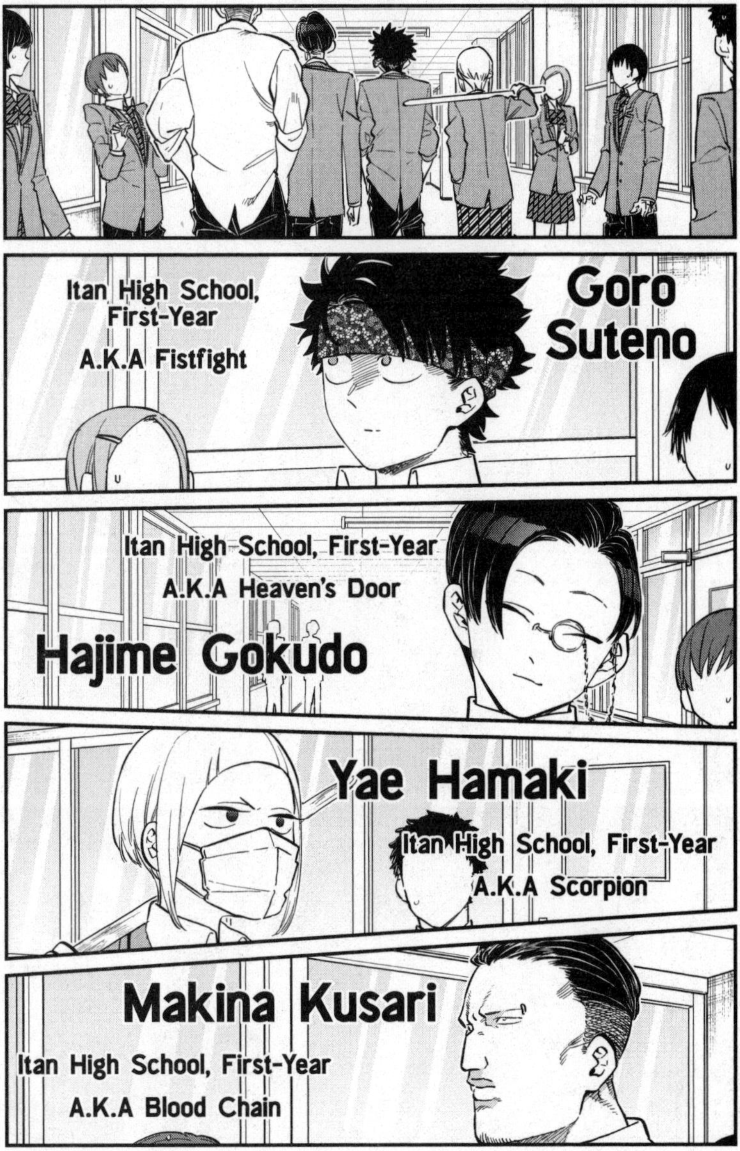
Goro Suteno
Itan High School, First-Year
A.K.A Fistfight
Itan High School, First-Year
A.K.A Heaven's Door
Hajime Gokudo
Yae Hamaki
Itan High School, First-Year
A.K.A Scorpion
Makina Kusari
Itan High School, First-Year
A.K.A Blood Chain

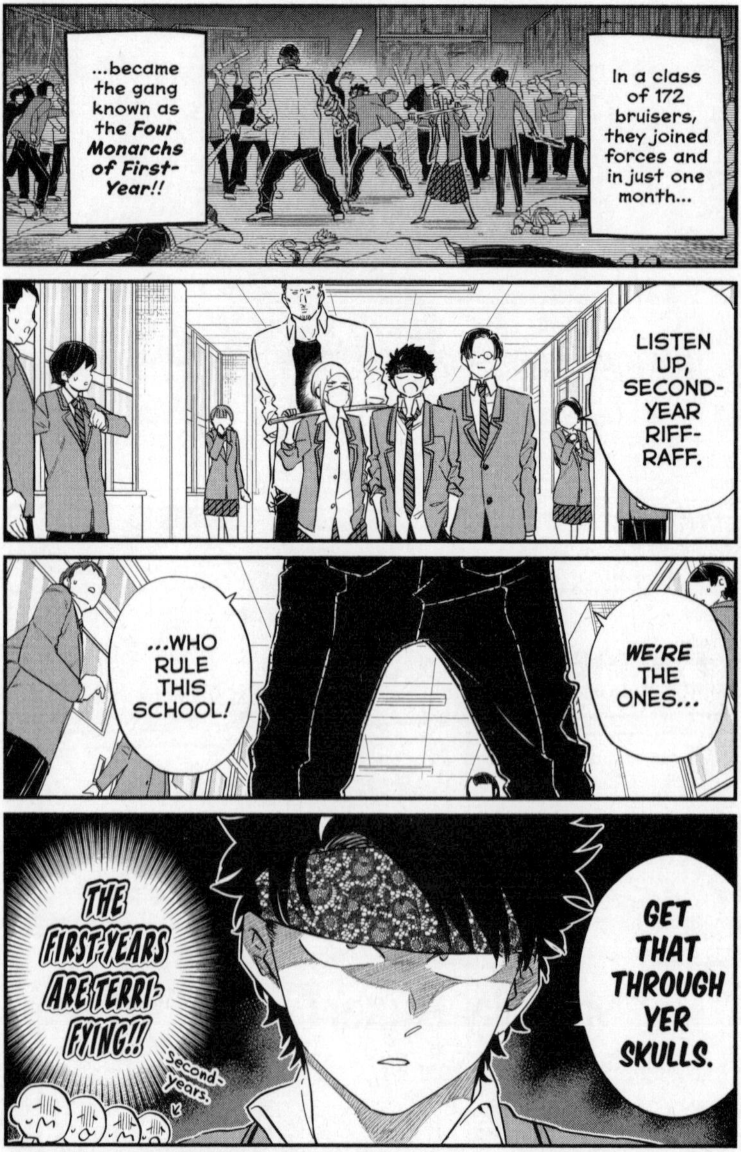
In a class of 172 bruisers, they joined forces and in just one month...
...became the gang known as the *Four Monarchs of First-Year!!*
LISTEN UP, SECOND-YEAR RIFF-RAFF.
WE'RE THE ONES...
...WHO RULE THIS SCHOOL!
GET THAT THROUGH YER SKULLS.
THE FIRST-YEARS ARE TERRI-FYING!!
Second-years.

Communication 146: Delinquent, Part 2

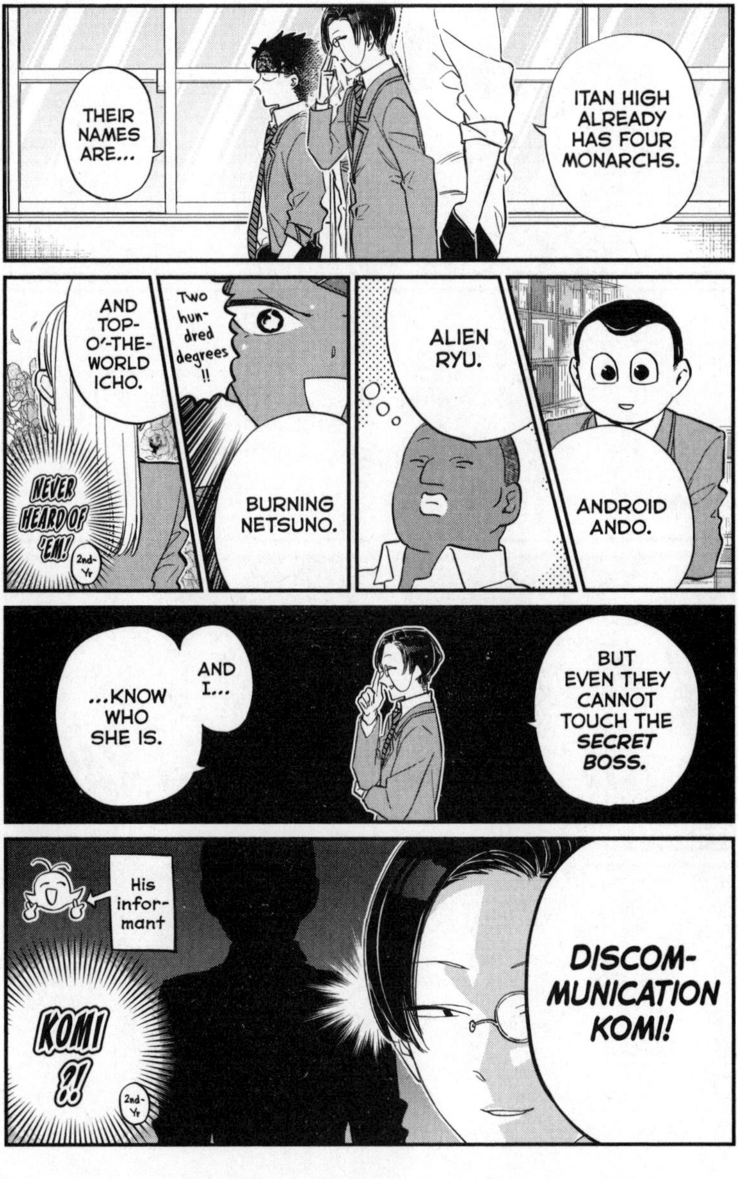
ITAN HIGH ALREADY HAS FOUR MONARCHS.
THEIR NAMES ARE...
ANDROID ANDO.
ALIEN RYU.
Two hundred degrees!!
BURNING NETSUNO.
AND TOP-O'-THE-WORLD ICHO.
NEVER HEARD OF 'EM!
2nd-Yr
BUT EVEN THEY CANNOT TOUCH THE *SECRET BOSS.*
AND I...
...KNOW WHO SHE IS.
DISCOM-MUNICATION KOMI!
His informant
KOMI?!
2nd-Yr

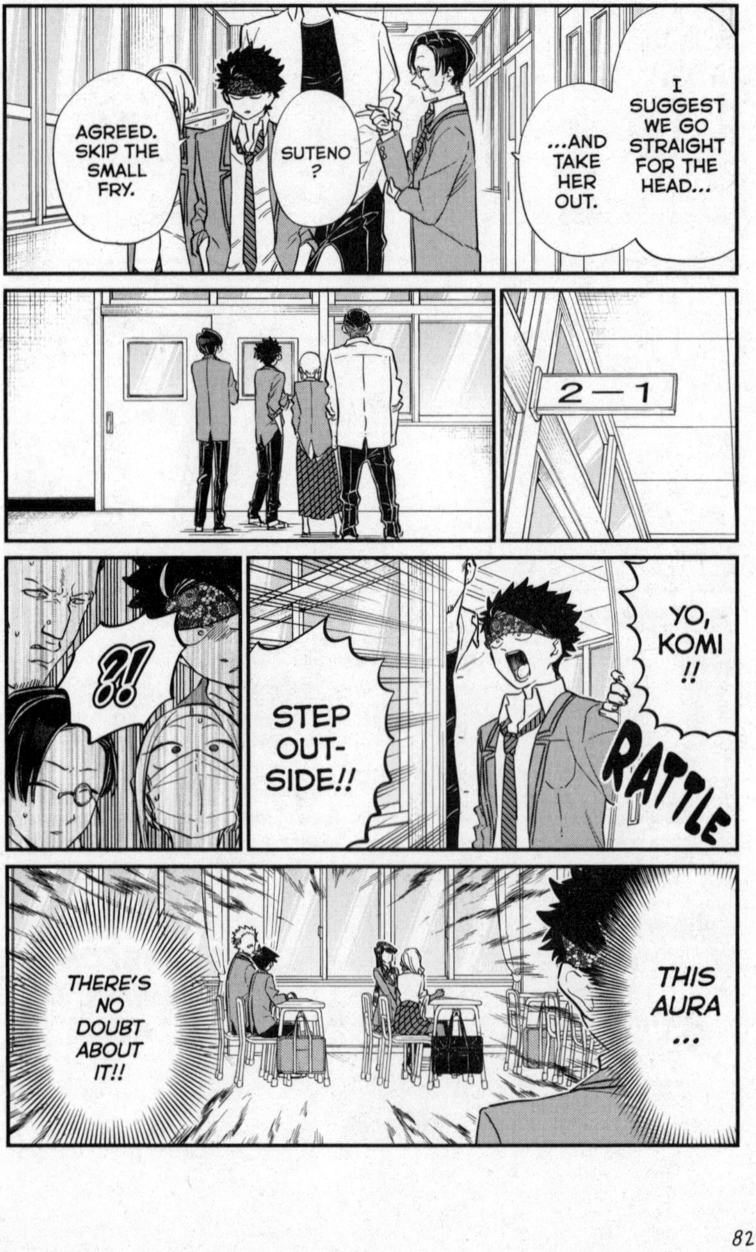
I SUGGEST WE GO STRAIGHT FOR THE HEAD...
...AND TAKE HER OUT.
SUTENO?
AGREED. SKIP THE SMALL FRY.
2—1
YO, KOMI!!
RATTLE
STEP OUT-SIDE!!
?!
THIS AURA...
THERE'S NO DOUBT ABOUT IT!!

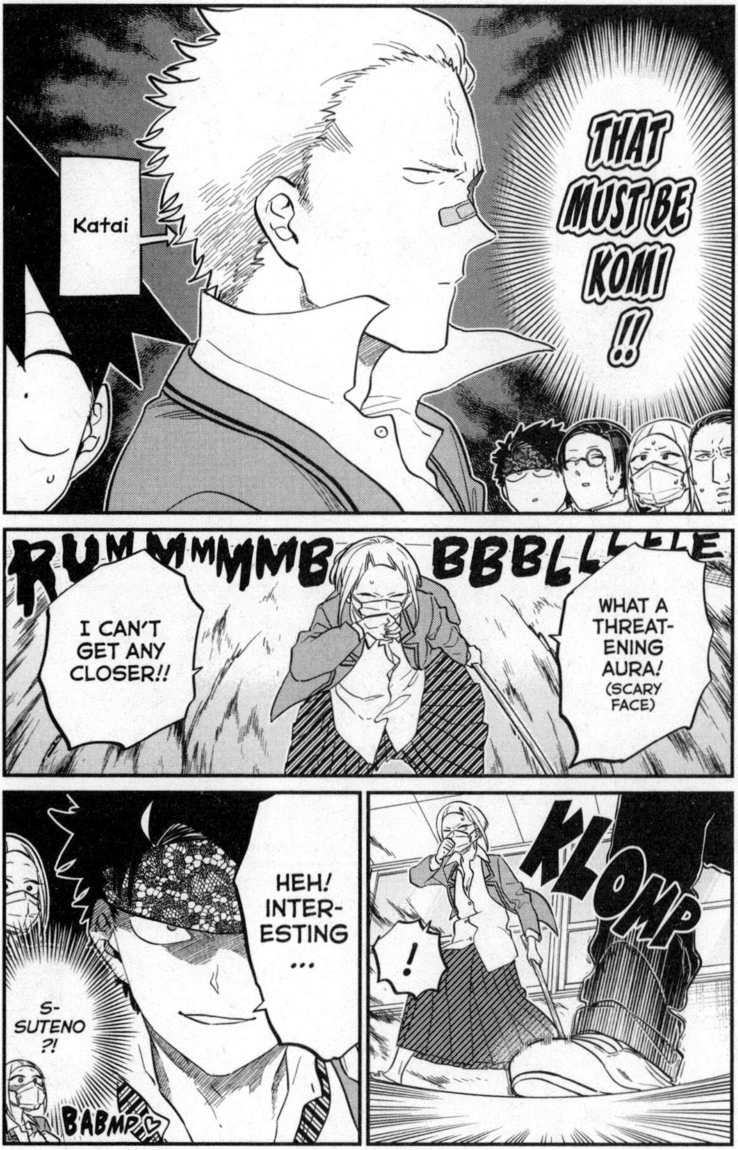
THAT MUST BE KOMI!!
Katai
RUMMMMMB BBBLLLLE
WHAT A THREATENING AURA! (SCARY FACE)
I CAN'T GET ANY CLOSER!!
KLOMP
!
HEH! INTERESTING...
S-SUTENO?!
BABMP♡

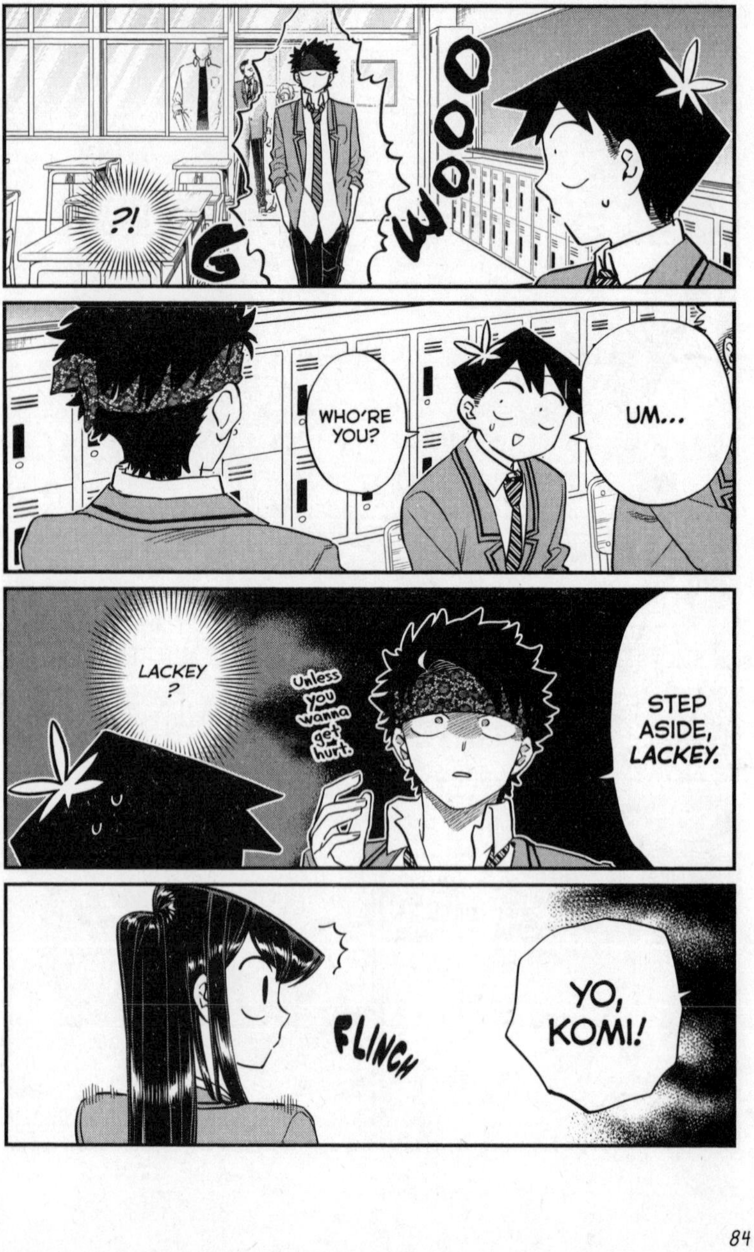
GWOOOO
?!
UM...
WHO'RE YOU?
STEP ASIDE, LACKEY.
Unless you wanna get hurt.
LACKEY?
YO, KOMI!
FLINCH

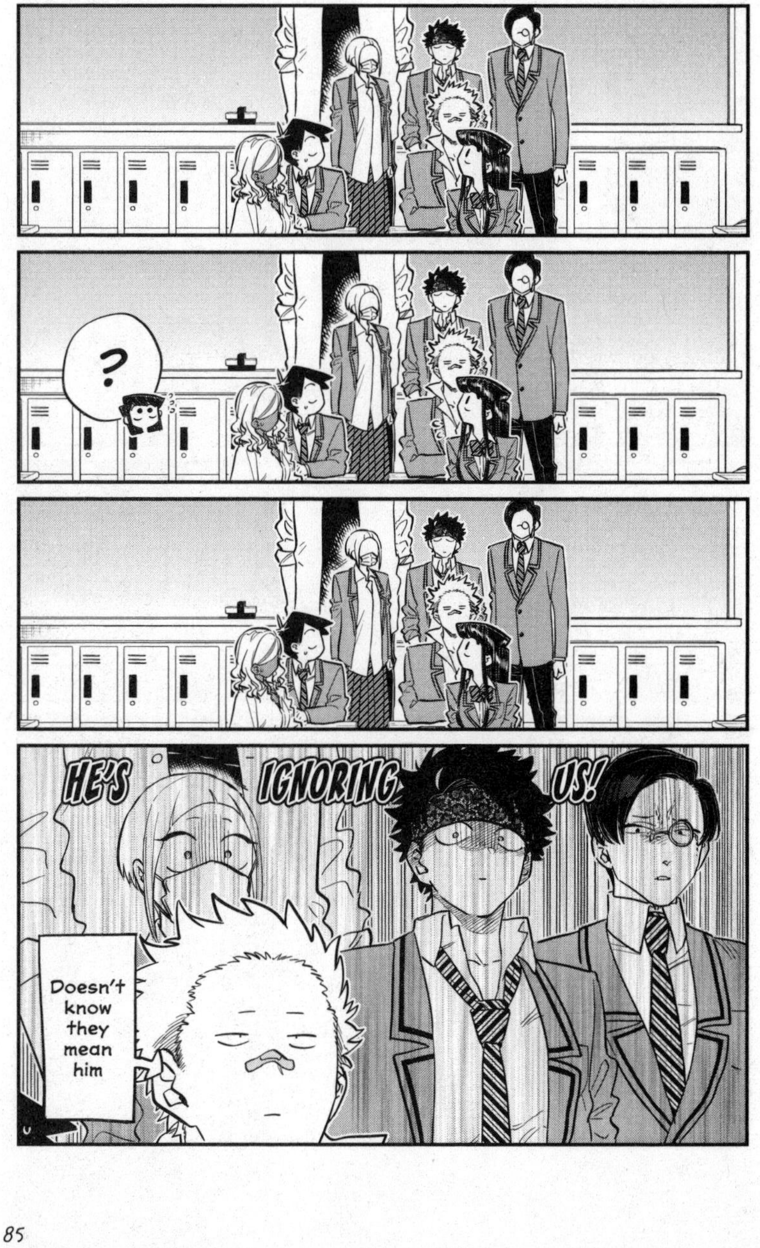
?
HE'S IGNORING US!
Doesn't know they mean him

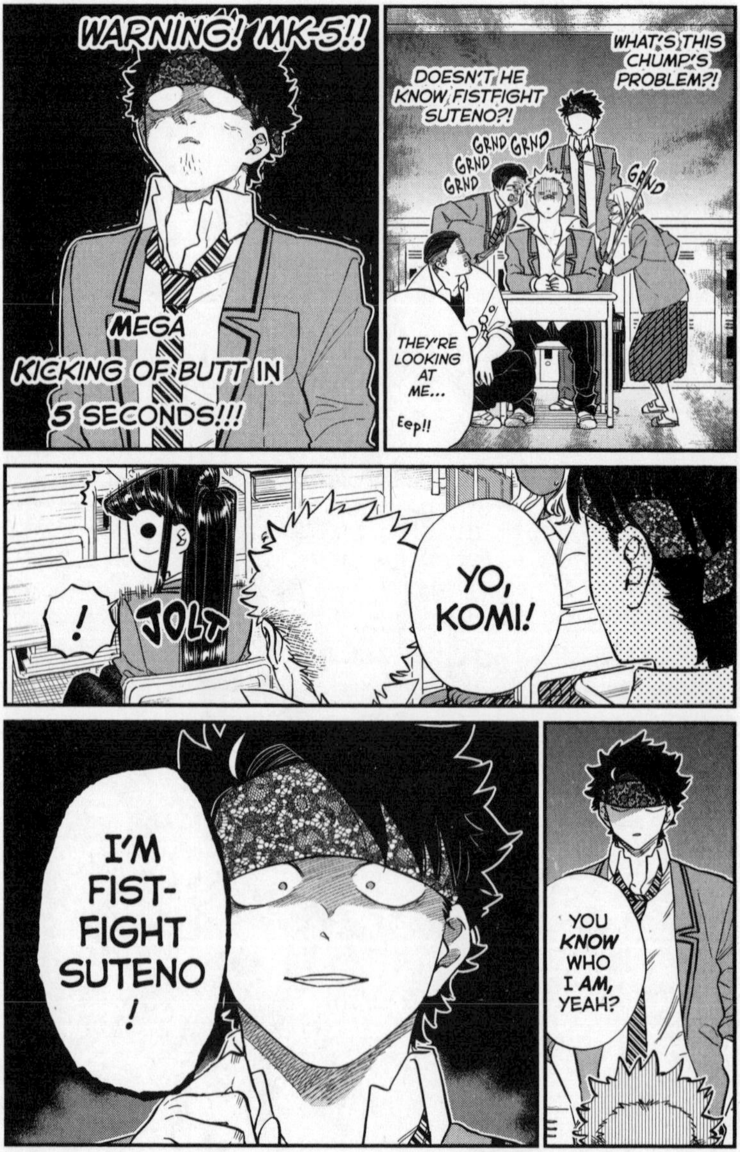
WHAT'S THIS CHUMP'S PROBLEM?!
DOESN'T HE KNOW FISTFIGHT SUTENO?!
GRND GRND
GRND GRND
GRND
THEY'RE LOOKING AT ME...
Eep!!
WARNING! MK-5!!
MEGA KICKING OF BUTT IN 5 SECONDS!!!
YO, KOMI!
JOLT
!
YOU KNOW WHO I AM, YEAH?
I'M FIST-FIGHT SUTENO!

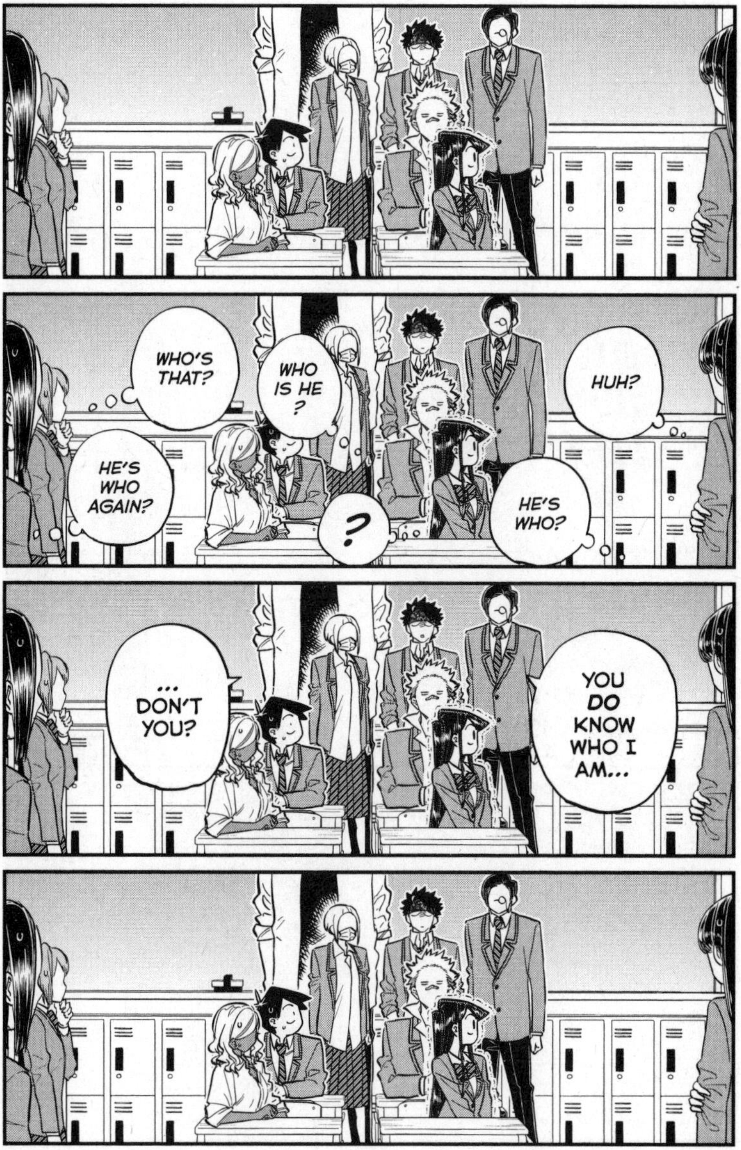
HUH?
HE'S WHO?
WHO IS HE ?
?
WHO'S THAT?
HE'S WHO AGAIN?
YOU *DO* KNOW WHO I AM...
... DON'T YOU?

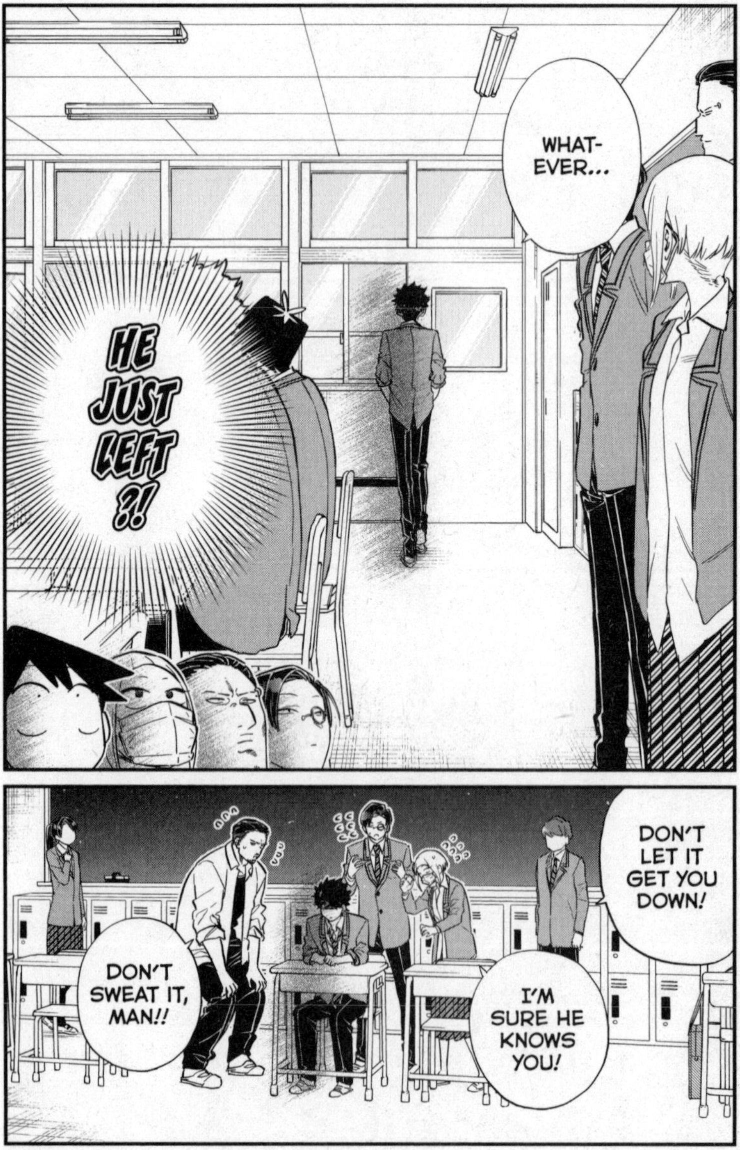
WHAT-EVER...
HE JUST LEFT?!
DON'T LET IT GET YOU DOWN!
I'M SURE HE KNOWS YOU!
DON'T SWEAT IT, MAN!!

Communication 146 — The End

Komi Can't Communicate

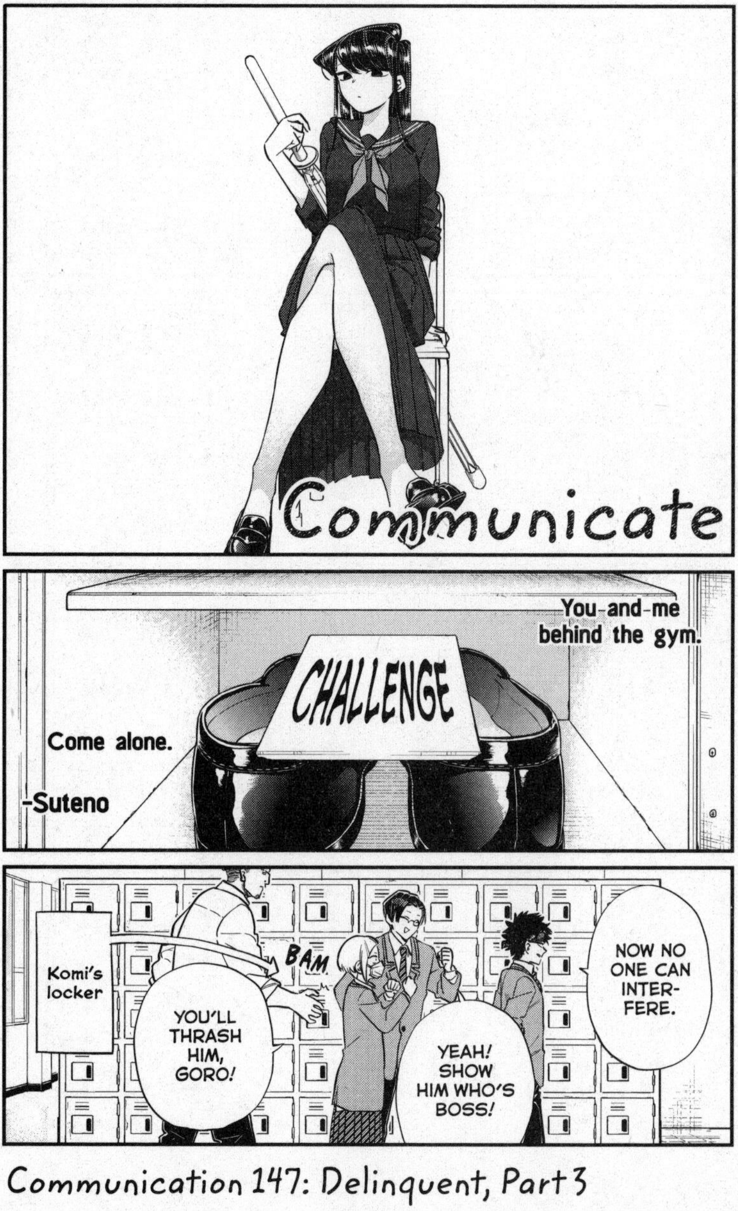

CHALLENGE
You-and-me behind the gym.
Come alone.
-Suteno
NOW NO ONE CAN INTER-FERE.
YEAH! SHOW HIM WHO'S BOSS!
YOU'LL THRASH HIM, GORO!
BAM
Komi's locker

Communication 147: Delinquent, Part 3

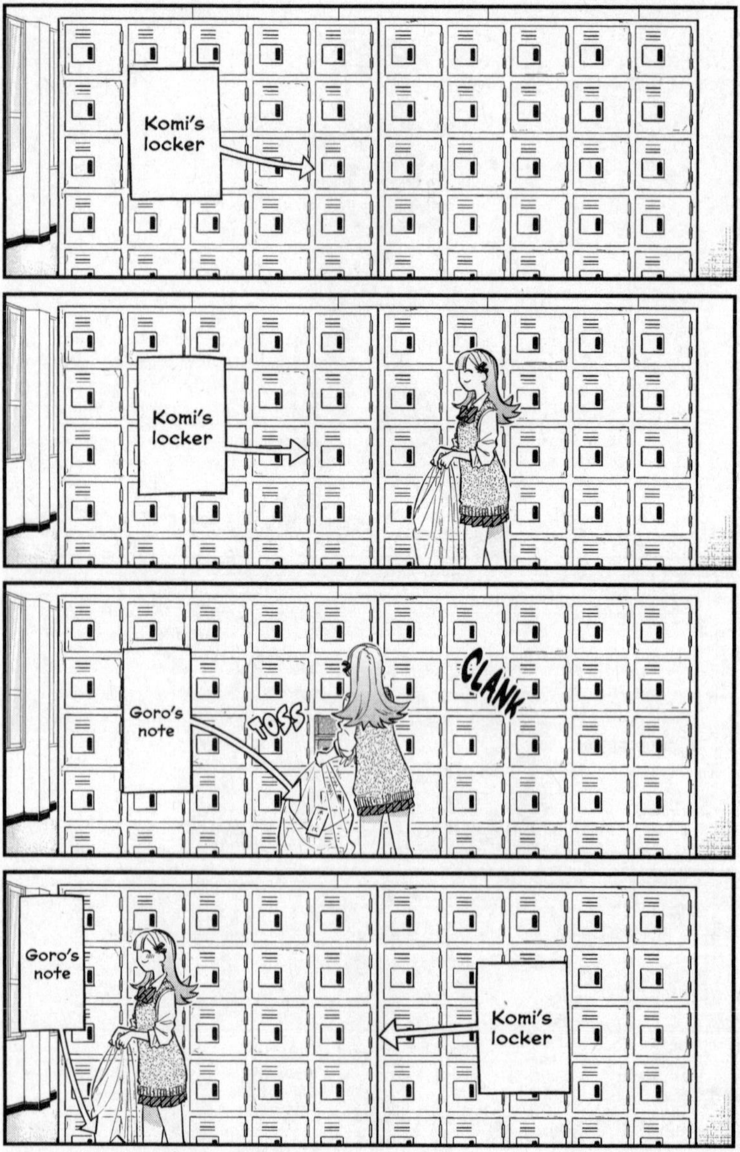
Komi's locker
Komi's locker
Goro's note
TOSS
CLANK
Goro's note
Komi's locker

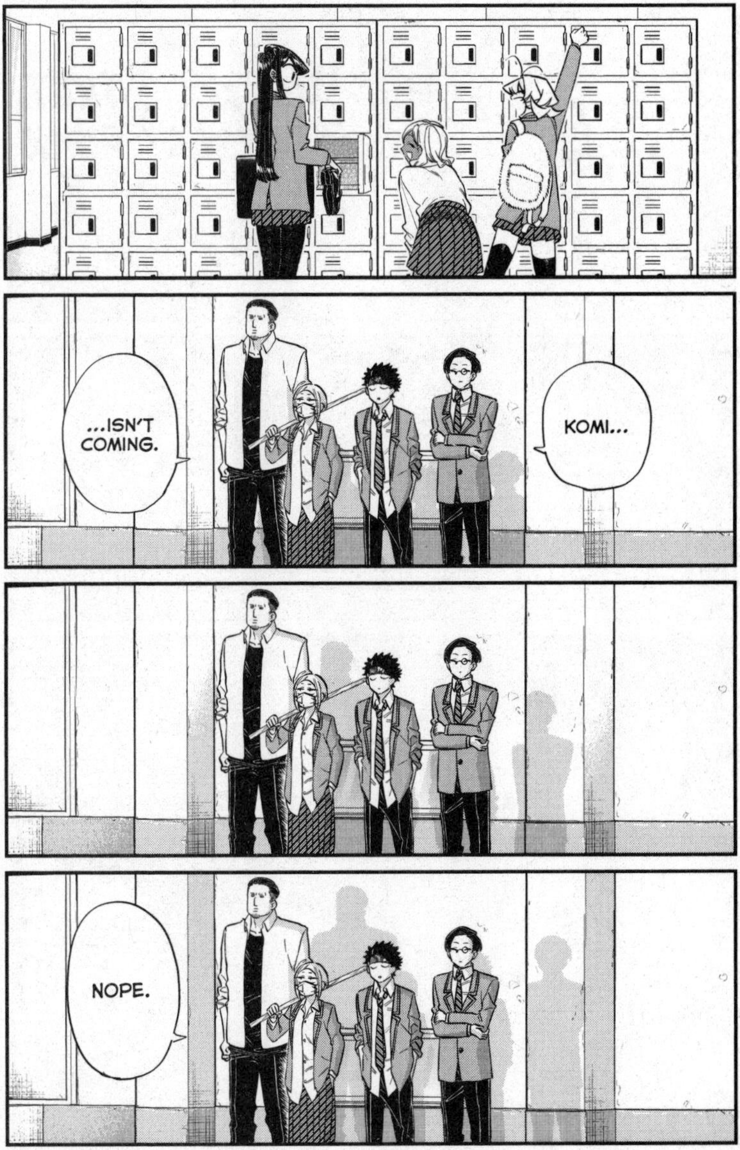
KOMI...
...ISN'T COMING.
NOPE.

Communication 147 — The End

Komi Can't Communicate

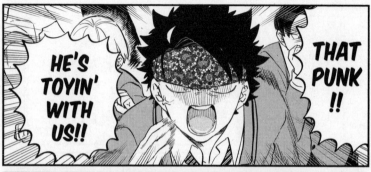

THAT PUNK!!
HE'S TOYIN' WITH US!!
WHETHER HE'S STALLIN' OR JUST A COWARD ...
...I'LL PUNCH HIM! THAT'LL LEARN HIM!!
THERE HE IS!!
So many beverages to choose from...

Communication 148: Delinquent, Part 4

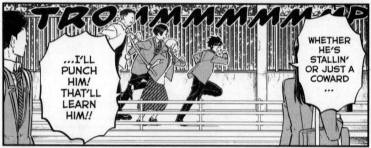

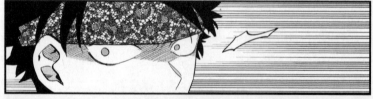

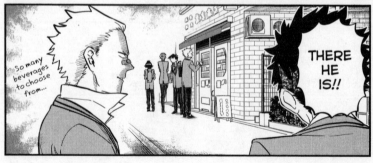

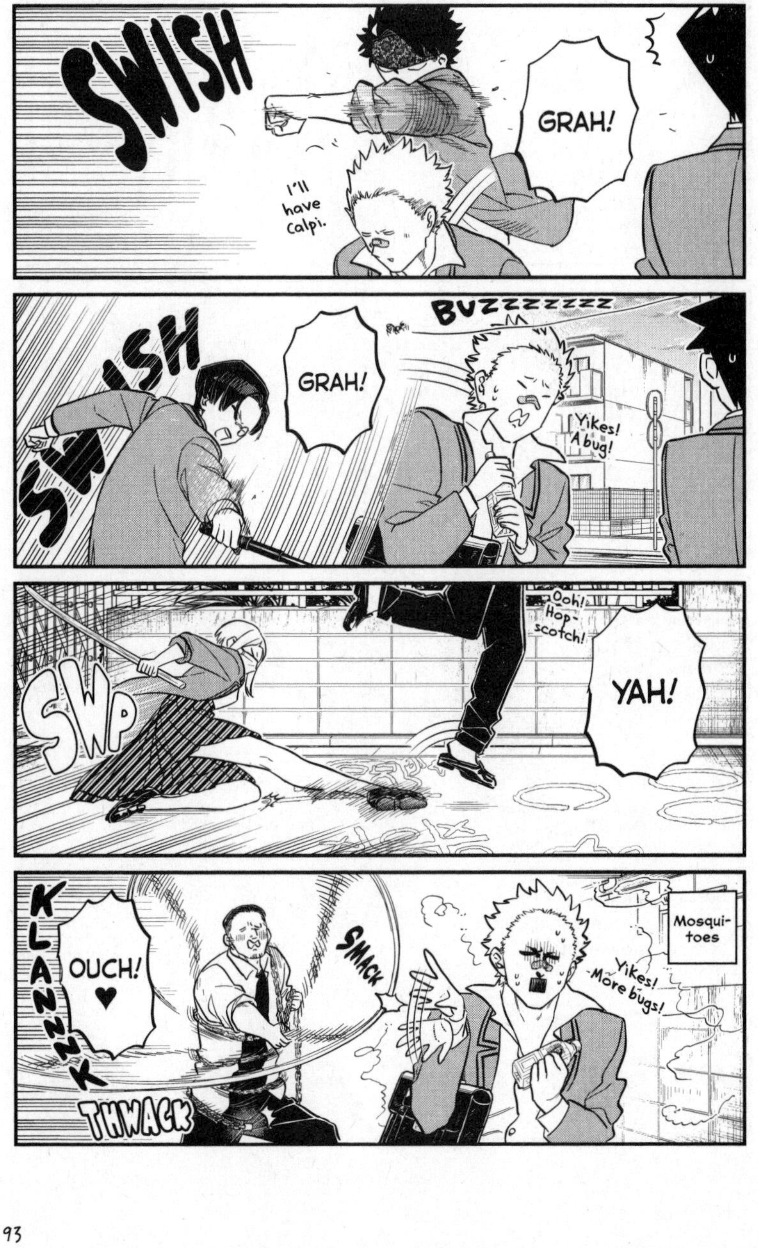
GRAH!
SWISH
I'll have calpi.
BUZZZZZZZZ
Yikes! A bug!
GRAH!
SWISH
YAH!
Ooh! Hop-scotch!
SWP
Mosqui-toes
Yikes! More bugs!
SMACK
OUCH! ♥
KLANNNK
THWACK

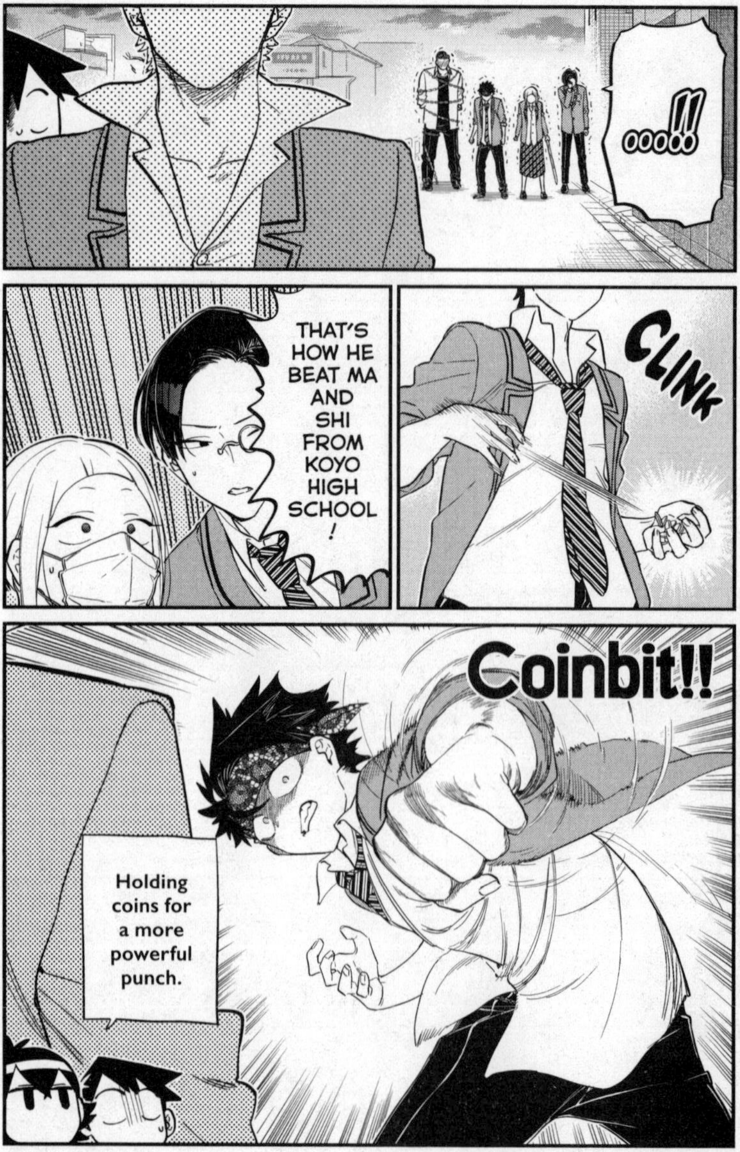
OOOO!!
CLINK
THAT'S HOW HE BEAT MA AND SHI FROM KOYO HIGH SCHOOL!
Coinbit!!
Holding coins for a more powerful punch.

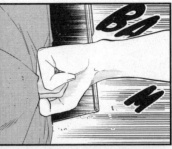

BA
M

LIKE PUNCHING A PLANET!

CLATTER

!

OW...

WHAT ...?

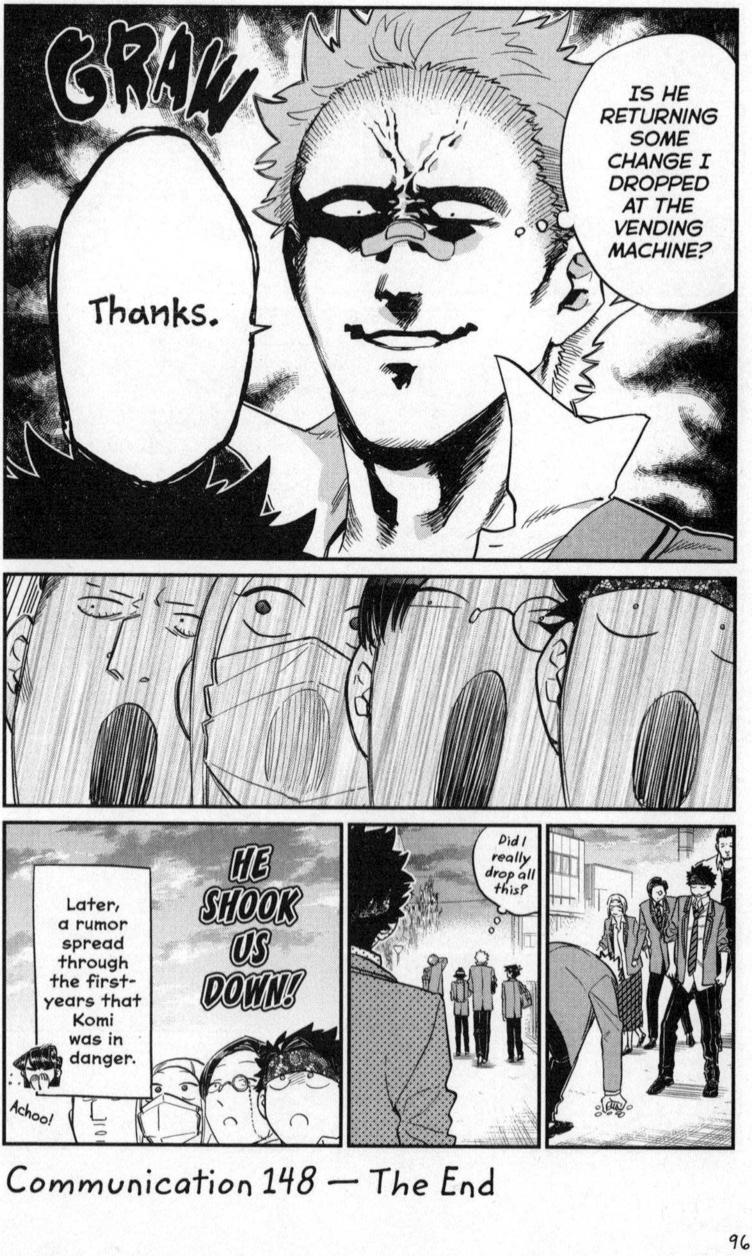
IS HE RETURNING SOME CHANGE I DROPPED AT THE VENDING MACHINE?
GRAW
Thanks.
Did I really drop all this?
HE SHOOK US DOWN!
Later, a rumor spread through the first-years that Komi was in danger.
Achoo!

Communication 148 — The End

Komi Can't Communicate

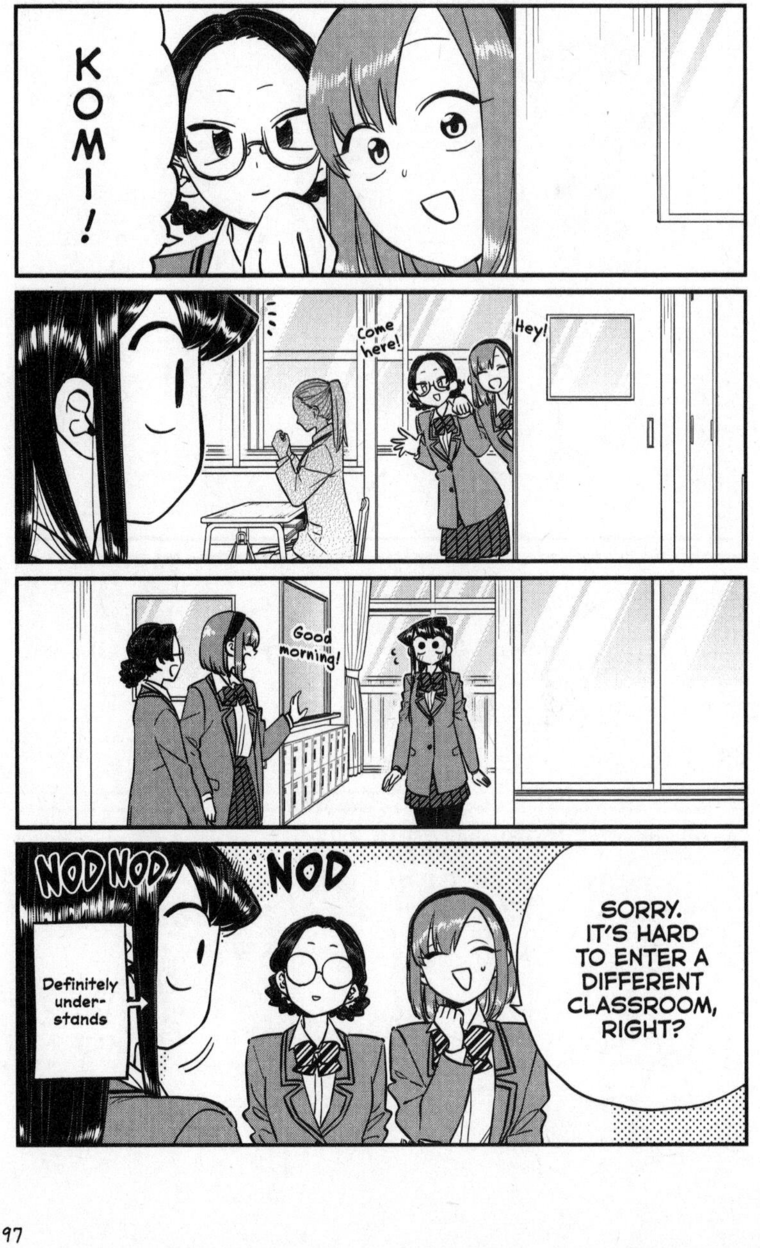
KOMI!
Hey!
Come here!
Good morning!
SORRY. IT'S HARD TO ENTER A DIFFERENT CLASSROOM, RIGHT?
NOD
NOD NOD
Definitely under-stands

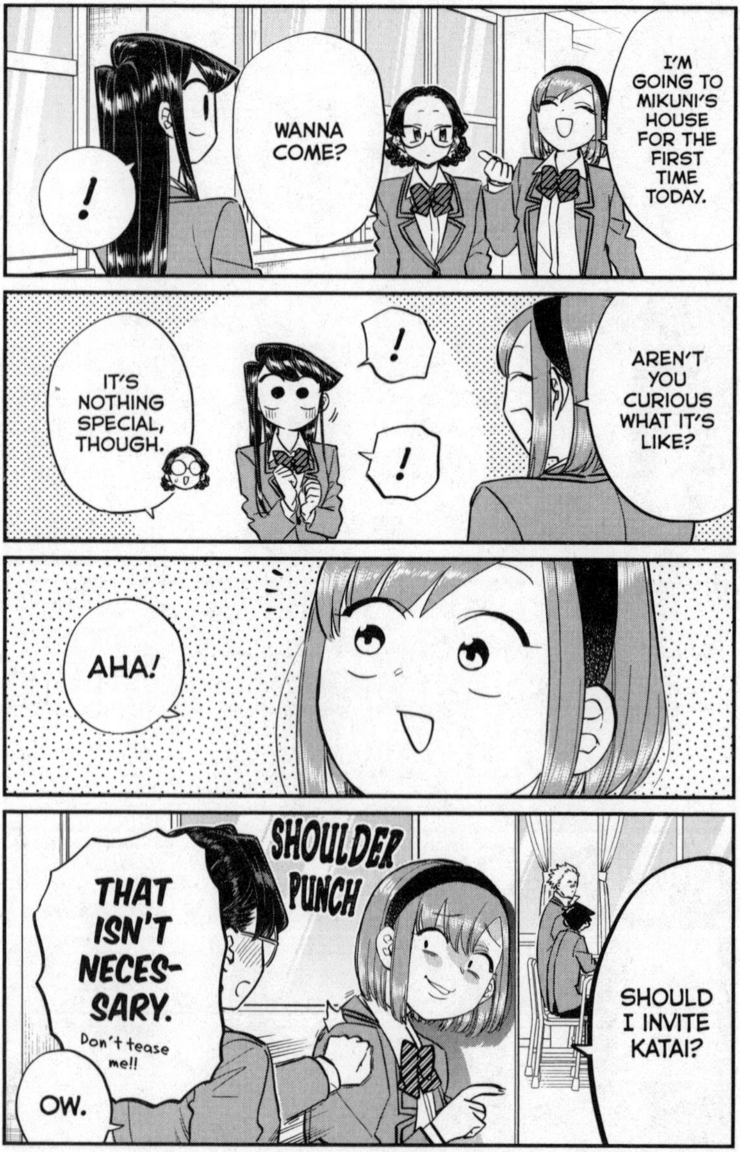
I'M GOING TO MIKUNI'S HOUSE FOR THE FIRST TIME TODAY.
WANNA COME?
!
AREN'T YOU CURIOUS WHAT IT'S LIKE?
!
!
IT'S NOTHING SPECIAL, THOUGH.
AHA!
SHOULD I INVITE KATAI?
SHOULDER PUNCH
THAT ISN'T NECES-SARY.
Don't tease me!!
OW.

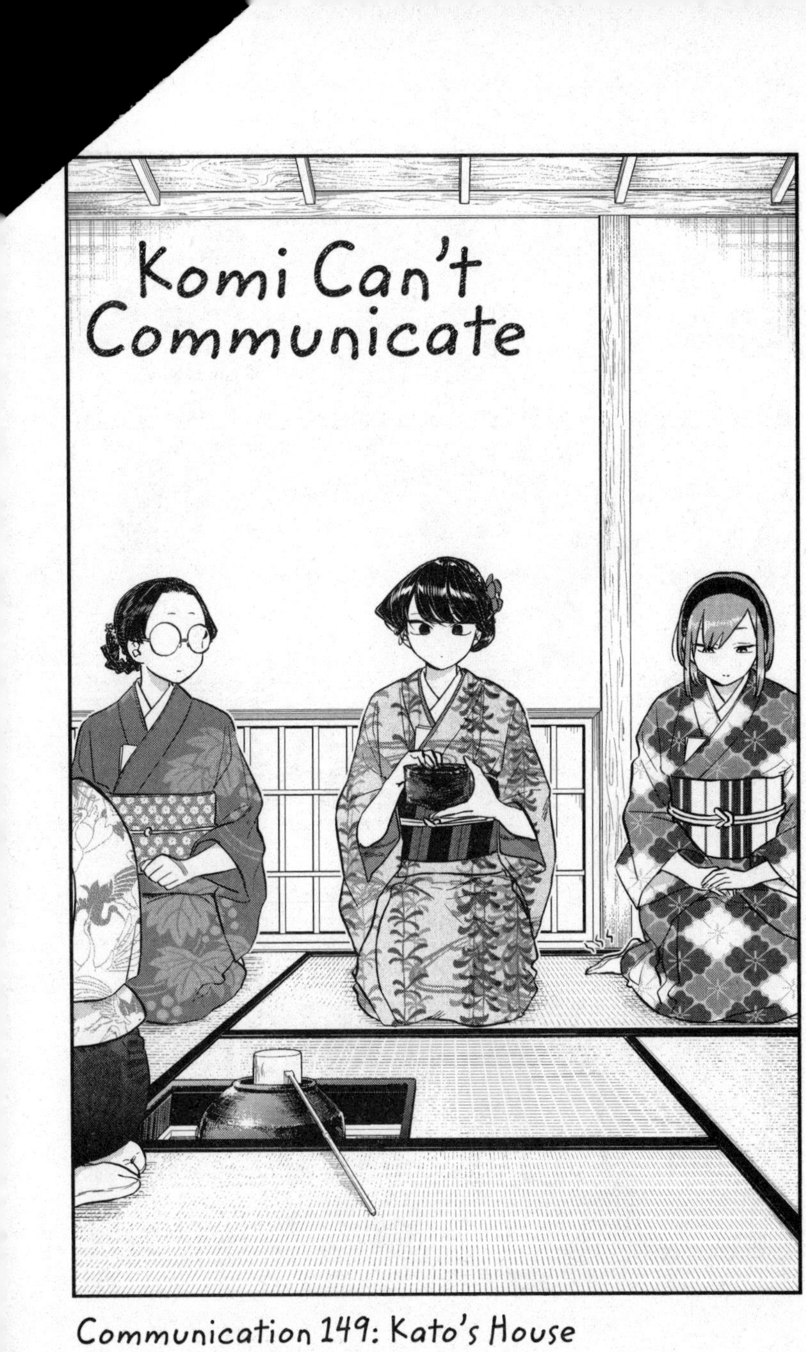
Komi Can't Communicate

Communication 149: Kato's House

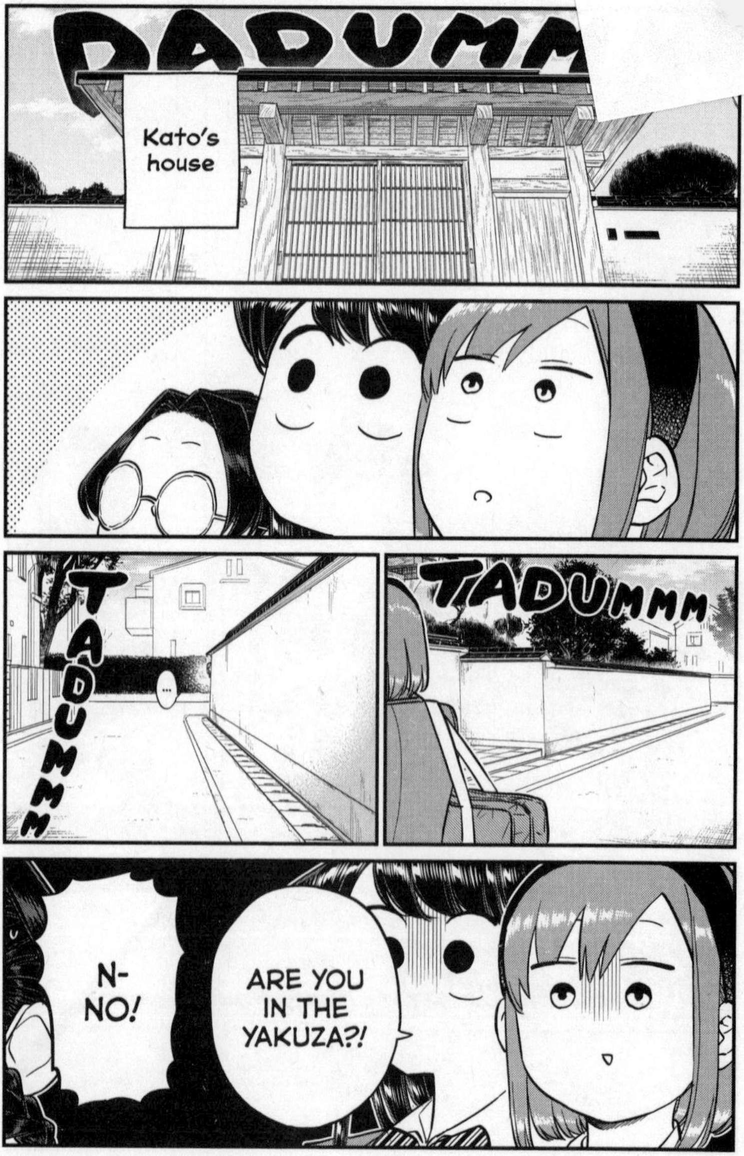
DADUMM
Kato's house
TADUMMM
TADUMMM
...
ARE YOU IN THE YAKUZA?!
N-NO!

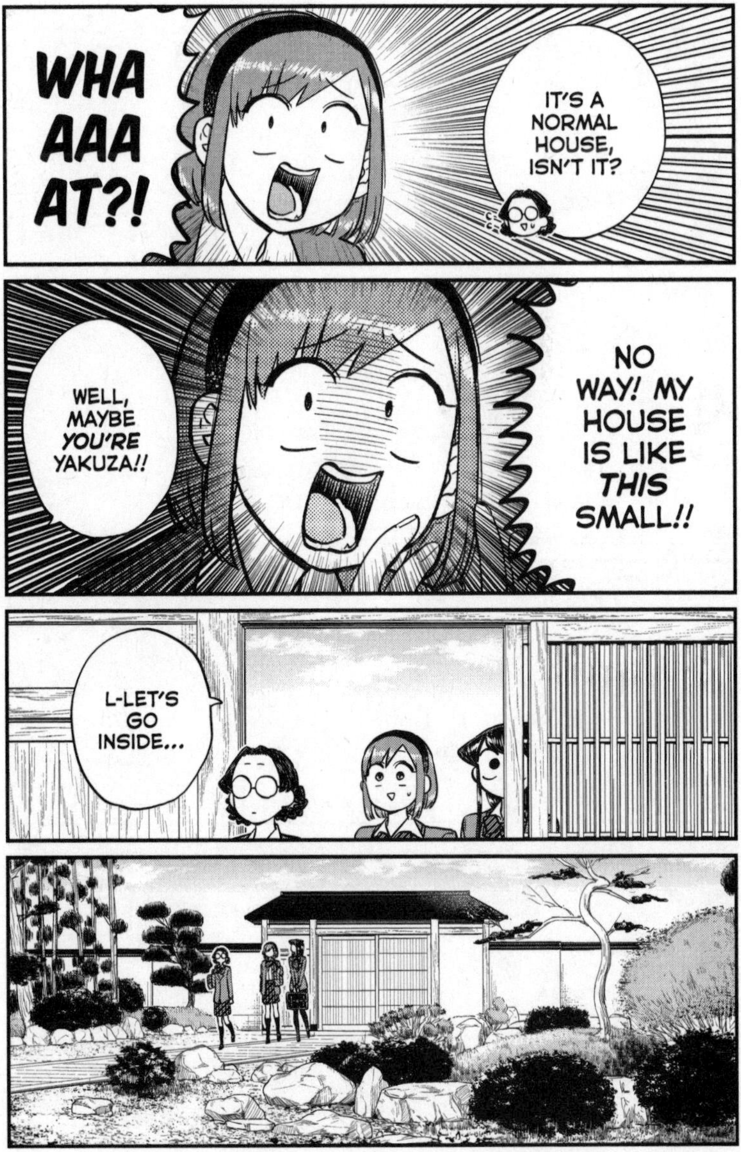
IT'S A NORMAL HOUSE, ISN'T IT?
WHA AAA AT?!
NO WAY! MY HOUSE IS LIKE THIS SMALL!!
WELL, MAYBE YOU'RE YAKUZA!!
L-LET'S GO INSIDE...

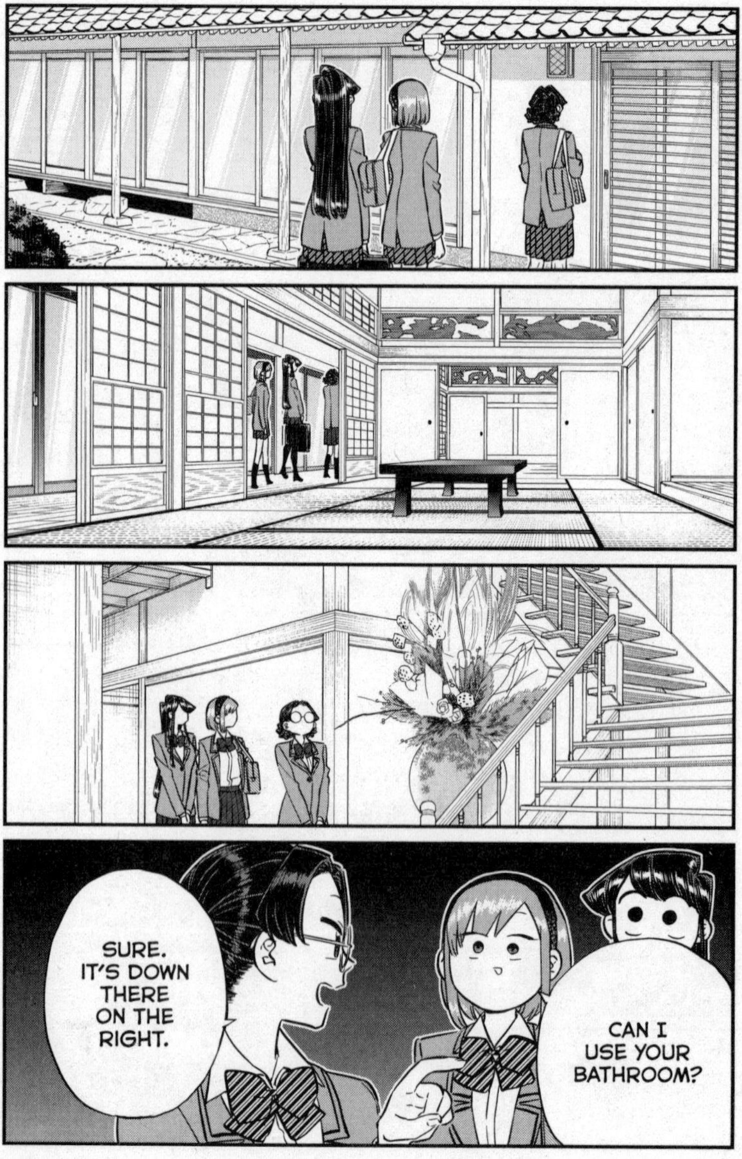
CAN I USE YOUR BATHROOM?
SURE. IT'S DOWN THERE ON THE RIGHT.

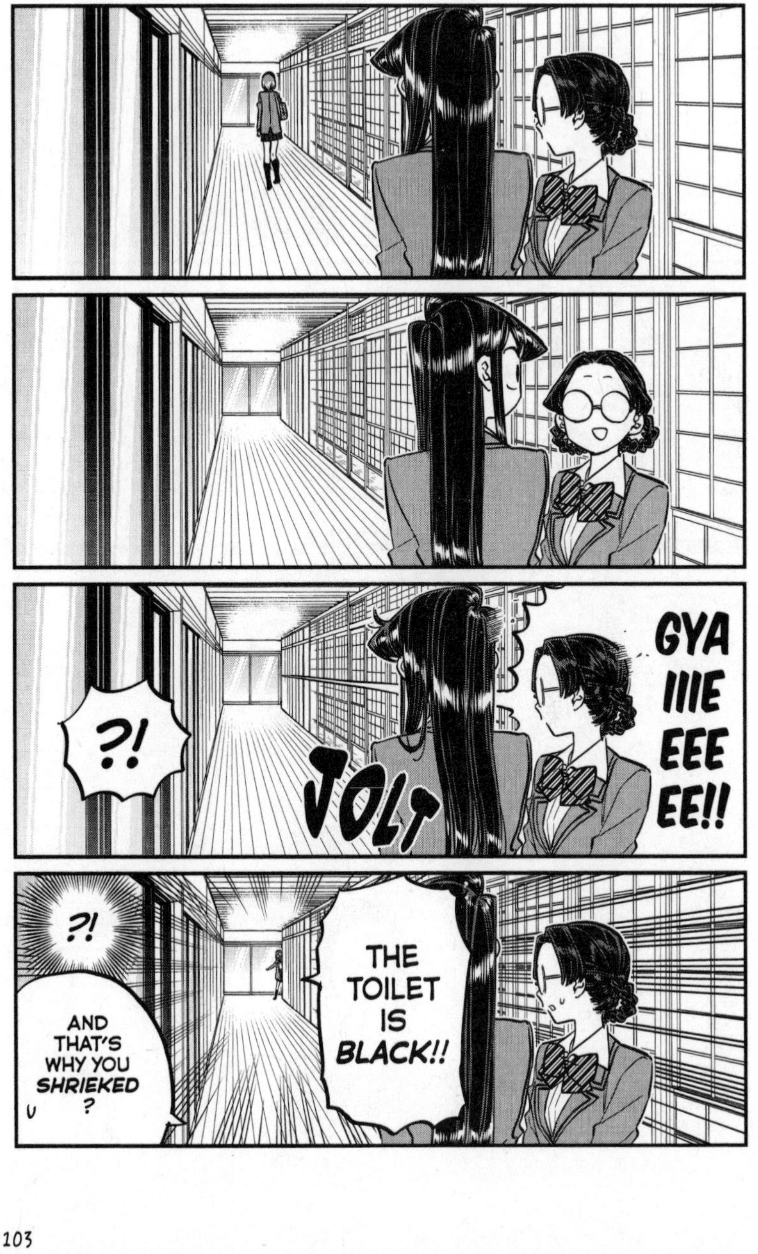
GYA IIIE EEE EE!!
JOLT
?!
THE TOILET IS BLACK!!
?!
AND THAT'S WHY YOU SHRIEKED?

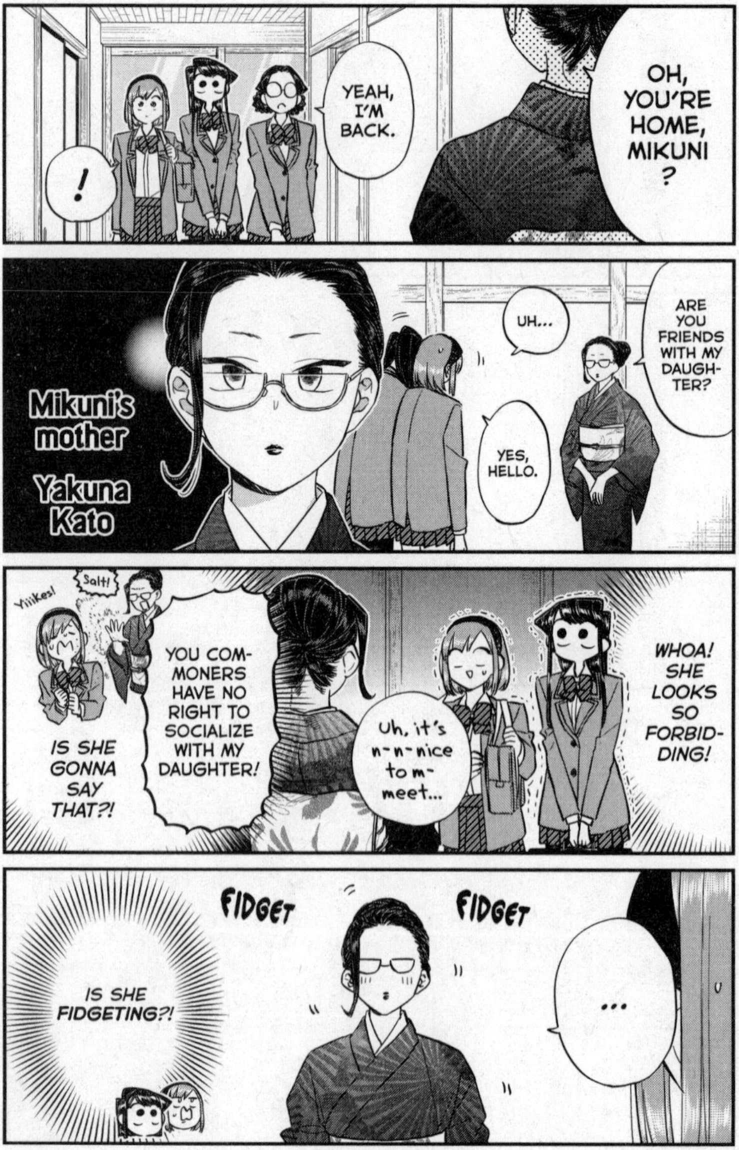
OH, YOU'RE HOME, MIKUNI?
YEAH, I'M BACK.
!
ARE YOU FRIENDS WITH MY DAUGHTER?
UH...
YES, HELLO.
Mikuni's mother
Yakuna Kato
WHOA! SHE LOOKS SO FORBIDDING!
Uh, it's n-n-nice to m-meet...
YOU COMMONERS HAVE NO RIGHT TO SOCIALIZE WITH MY DAUGHTER!
Salt!
Yiiikes!
IS SHE GONNA SAY THAT?!
...
FIDGET
FIDGET
IS SHE FIDGETING?!

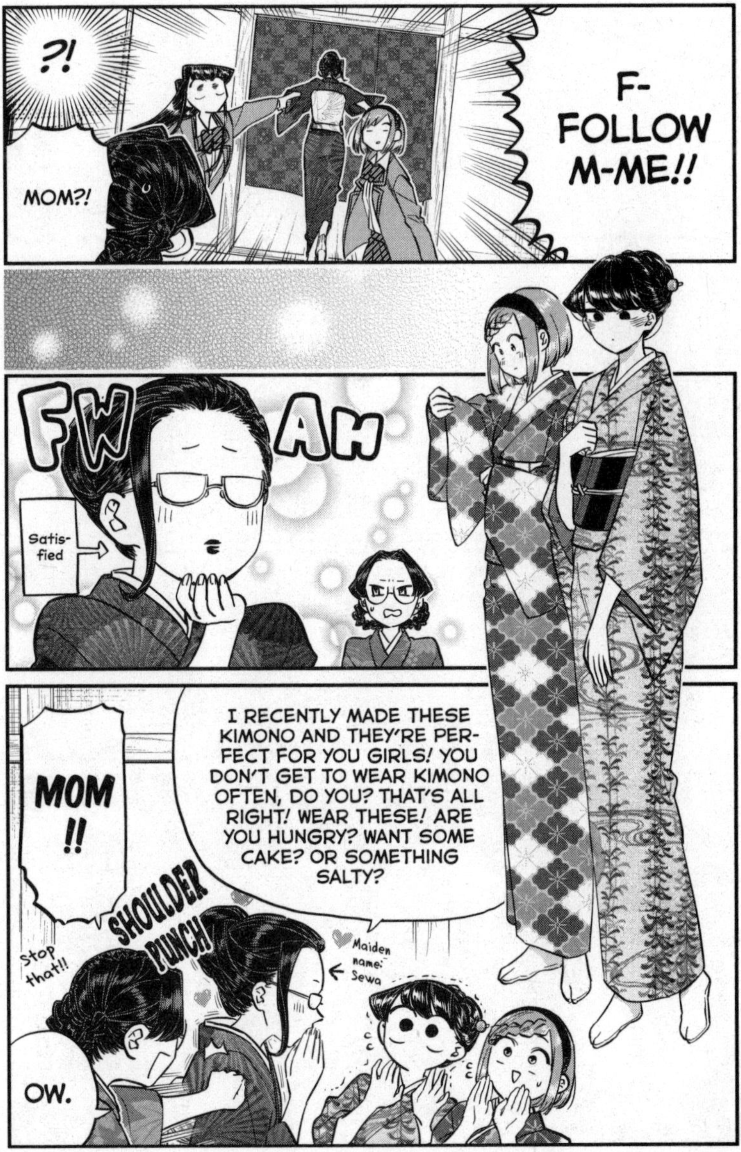
F-
FOLLOW
M-ME!!
?!
MOM?!
FWAH
Satis-
fied
I RECENTLY MADE THESE KIMONO AND THEY'RE PERFECT FOR YOU GIRLS! YOU DON'T GET TO WEAR KIMONO OFTEN, DO YOU? THAT'S ALL RIGHT! WEAR THESE! ARE YOU HUNGRY? WANT SOME CAKE? OR SOMETHING SALTY?
MOM !!
Maiden name: Sewa
SHOULDER PUNCH
Stop that!!
OW.

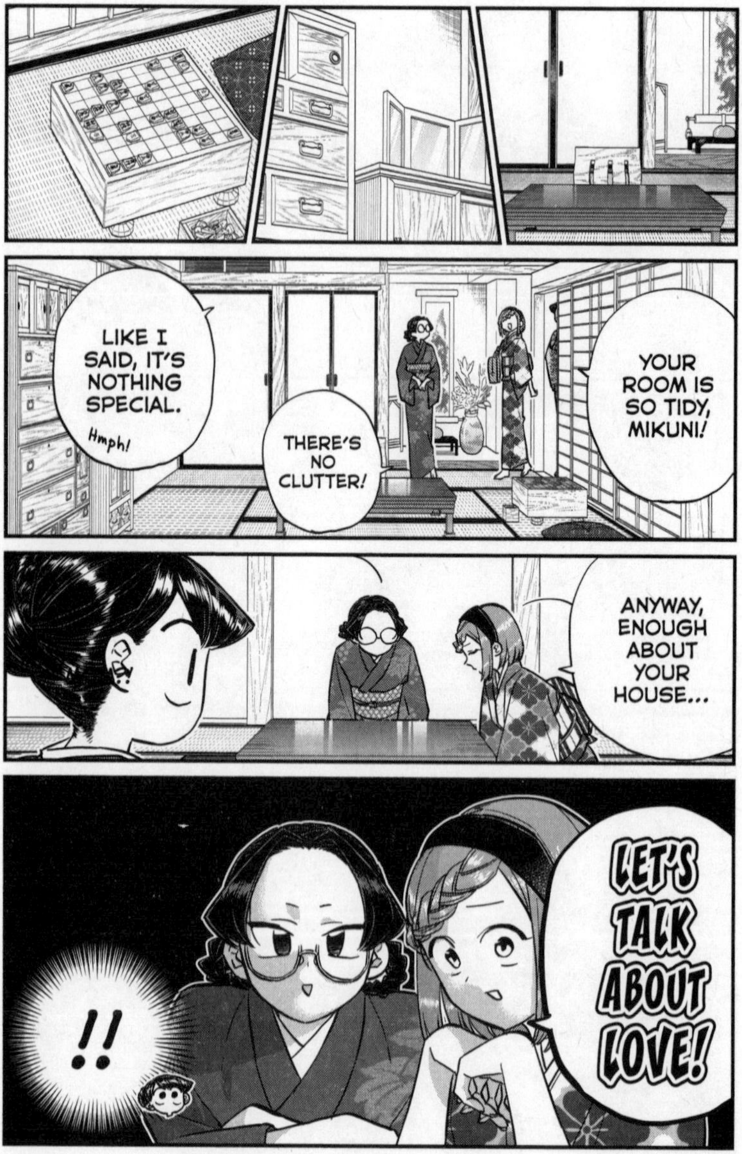
YOUR ROOM IS SO TIDY, MIKUNI!
THERE'S NO CLUTTER!
LIKE I SAID, IT'S NOTHING SPECIAL.
Hmph!
ANYWAY, ENOUGH ABOUT YOUR HOUSE...
LET'S TALK ABOUT LOVE!
!!

GIVE US THE LOWDOWN! YOU AND TADANO DID VALENTINE'S DAY AND WHITE DAY, RIGHT?!
?!
AND YOU'RE IN THE SAME CLASS AGAIN!
ANY PROG-RESS?!
?!
?!
...
...
...
SKRK SKRK SKRK
...
"Prog-ress? I don't think so."
GYARRRGH!
?!

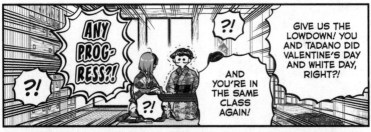

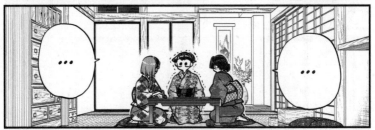

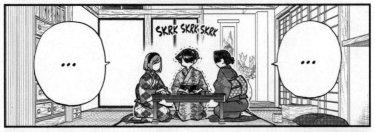

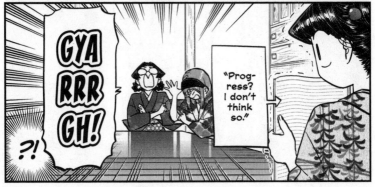

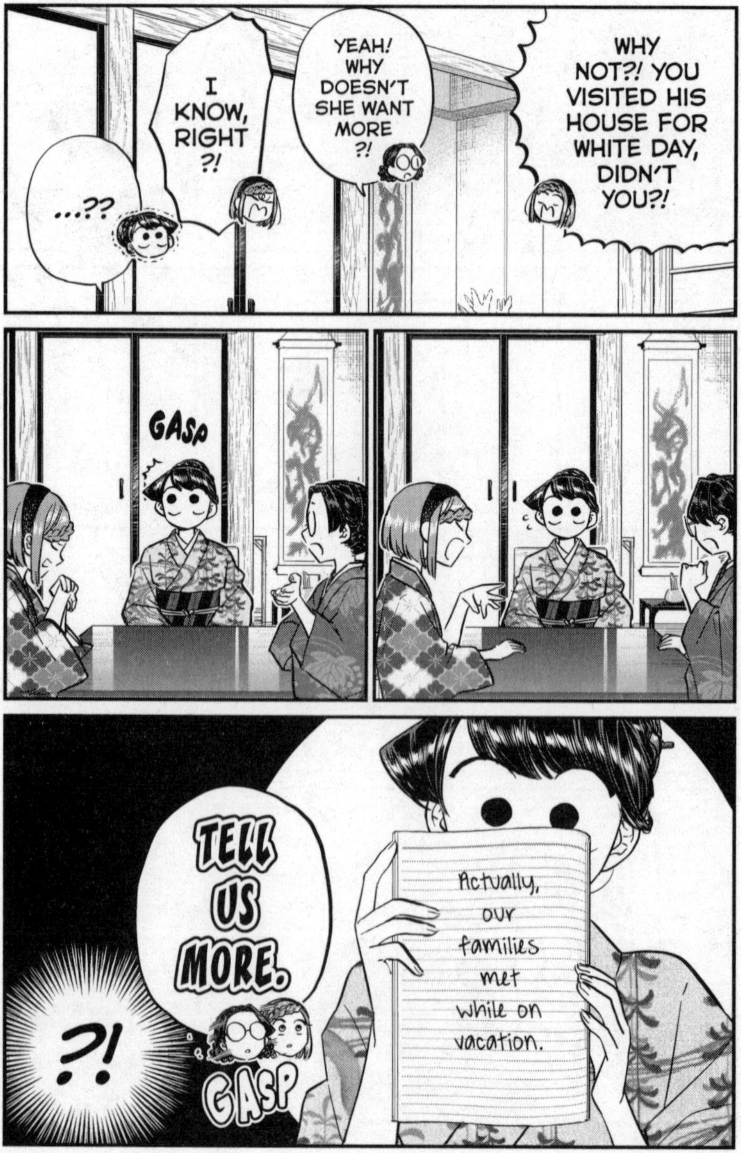
WHY NOT?! YOU VISITED HIS HOUSE FOR WHITE DAY, DIDN'T YOU?!
YEAH! WHY DOESN'T SHE WANT MORE ?!
I KNOW, RIGHT ?!
...??
GASP
Actually, our families met while on vacation.
TELL US MORE.
GASP
?!

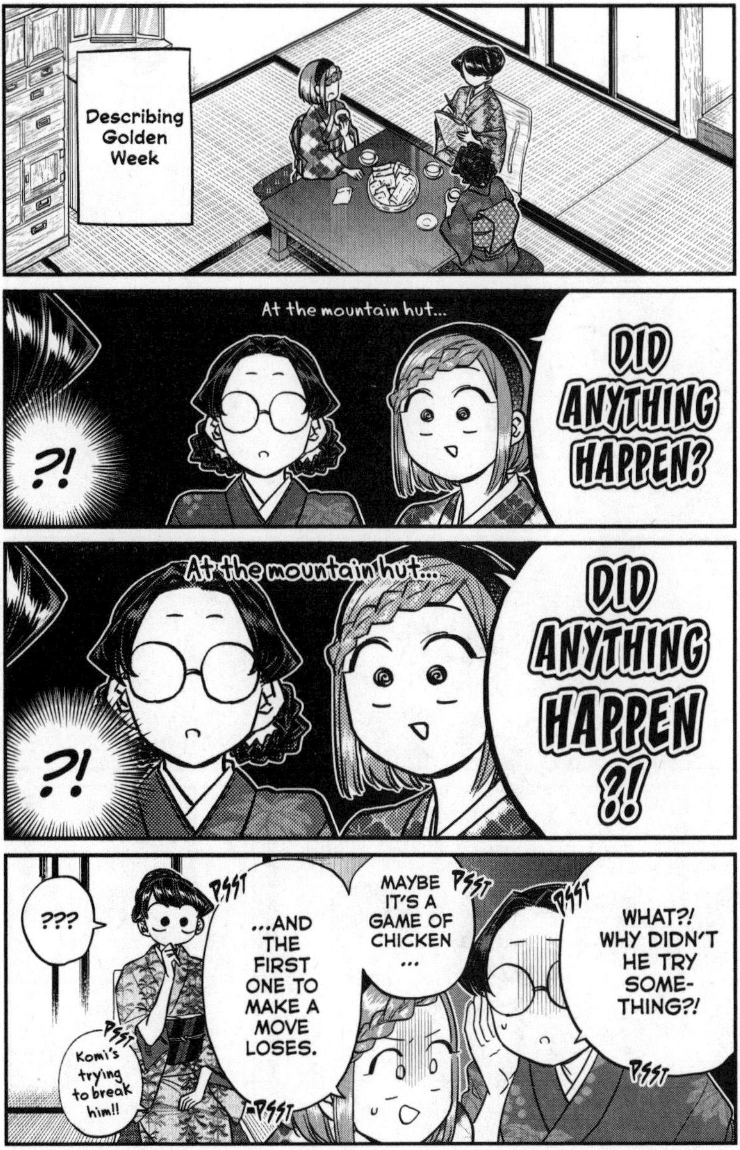
Describing Golden Week
DID ANYTHING HAPPEN?
At the mountain hut...
?!
DID ANYTHING HAPPEN ?!
At the mountain hut...
?!
PSST
WHAT?! WHY DIDN'T HE TRY SOME-THING?!
PSST
PSST
MAYBE IT'S A GAME OF CHICKEN ...
PSST
...AND THE FIRST ONE TO MAKE A MOVE LOSES.
PSST
???
PSST
Komi's trying to break him!!

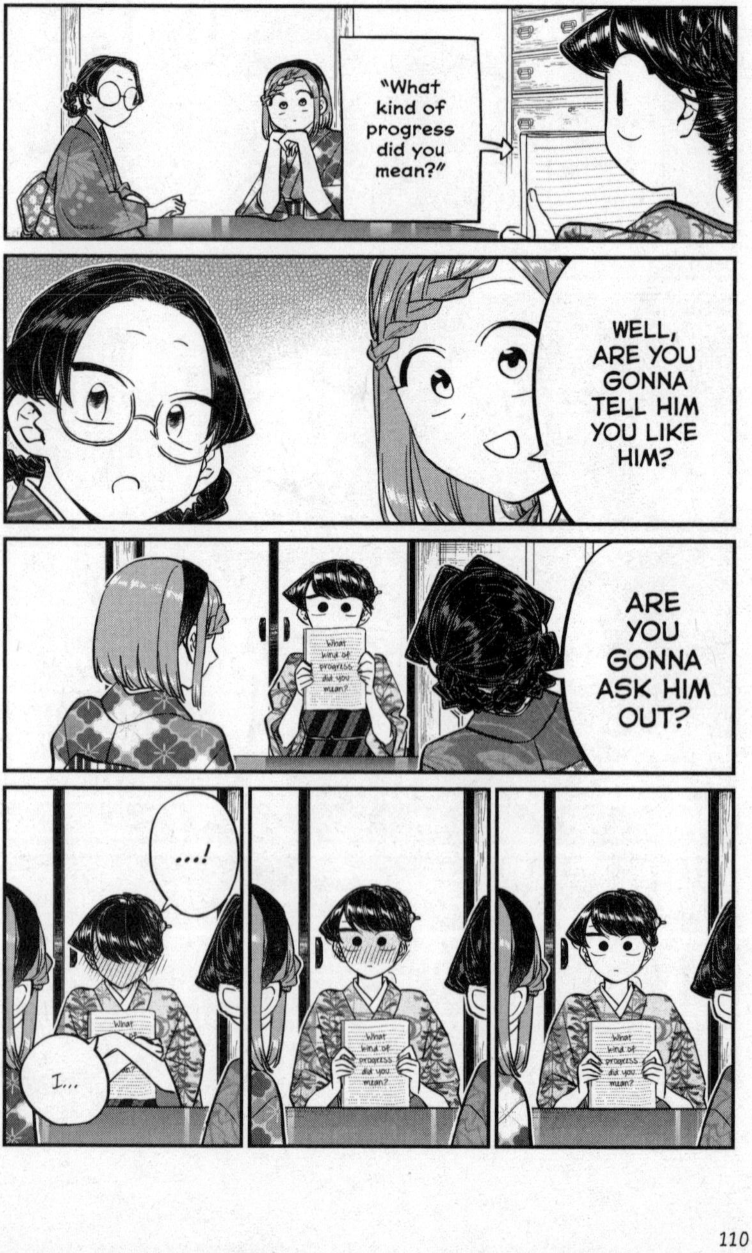
"What kind of progress did you mean?"
WELL, ARE YOU GONNA TELL HIM YOU LIKE HIM?
ARE YOU GONNA ASK HIM OUT?
What kind of progress did you mean?
What kind of progress did you mean?
What kind of progress did you mean?
...!
I...

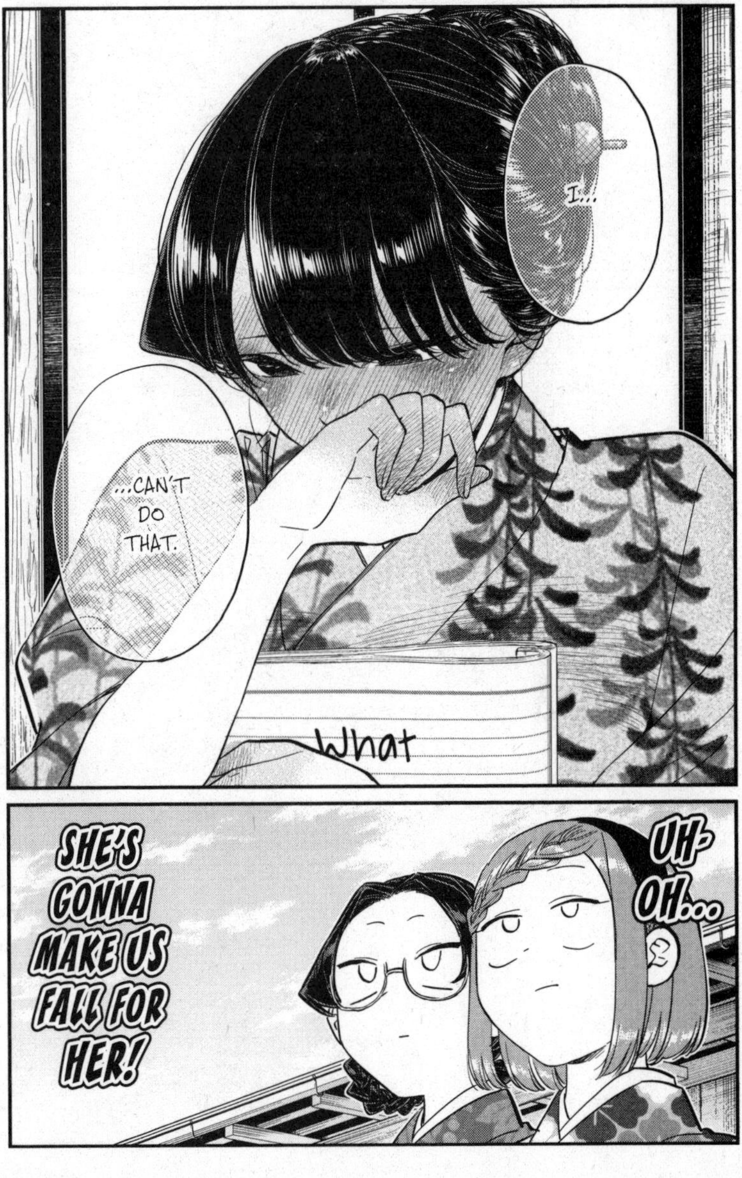
I...
...CAN'T DO THAT.
What
UH-OH...
SHE'S GONNA MAKE US FALL FOR HER!

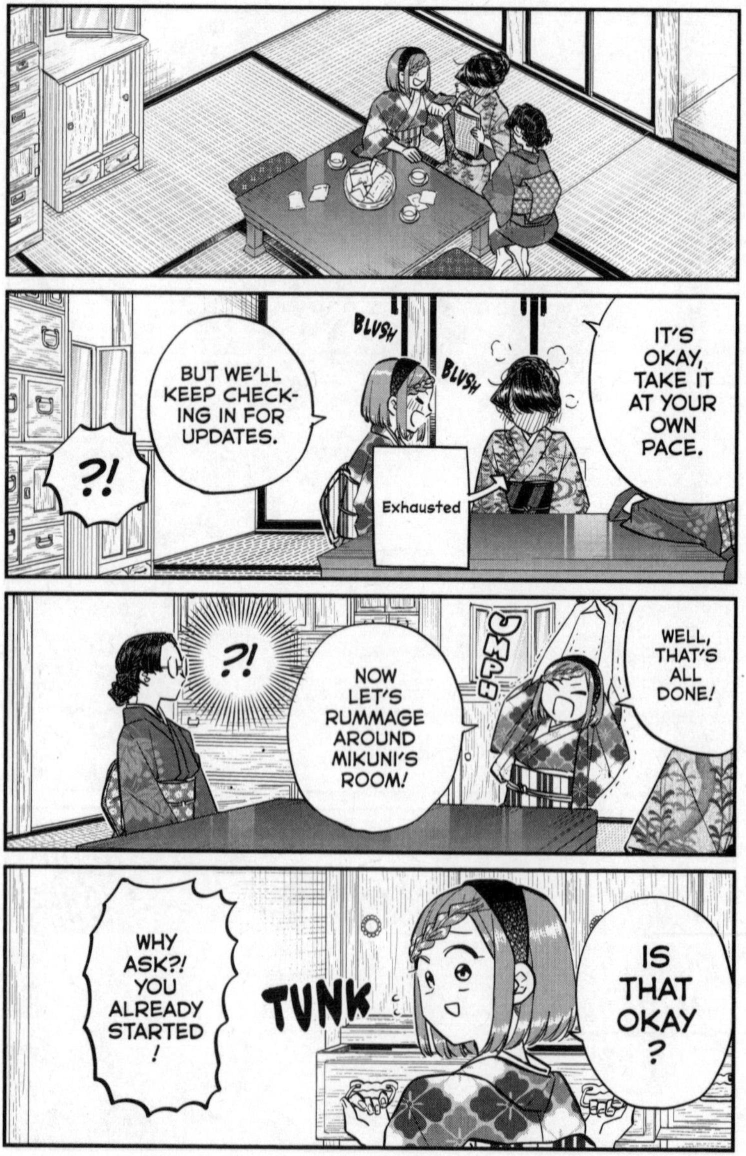
IT'S OKAY, TAKE IT AT YOUR OWN PACE.
BLUSH
BLUSH
Exhausted
BUT WE'LL KEEP CHECKING IN FOR UPDATES.
?!
WELL, THAT'S ALL DONE!
UMPH
NOW LET'S RUMMAGE AROUND MIKUNI'S ROOM!
?!
IS THAT OKAY?
TUNK
WHY ASK?! YOU ALREADY STARTED!

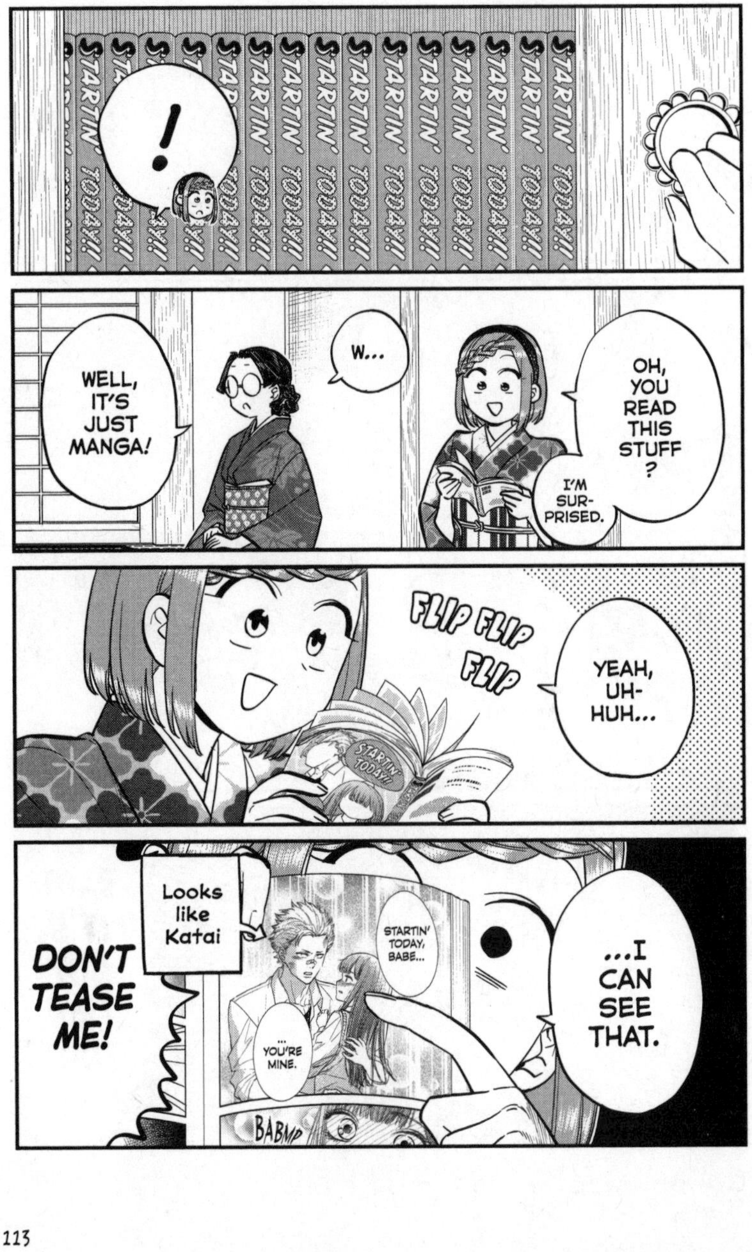
STARTIN' TODAY!!
!
OH, YOU READ THIS STUFF?
I'M SURPRISED.
W...
WELL, IT'S JUST MANGA!
YEAH, UH-HUH...
FLIP FLIP FLIP
STARTIN' TODAY!!
...I CAN SEE THAT.
STARTIN' TODAY, BABE...
...YOU'RE MINE.
BABMP
Looks like Katai
DON'T TEASE ME!

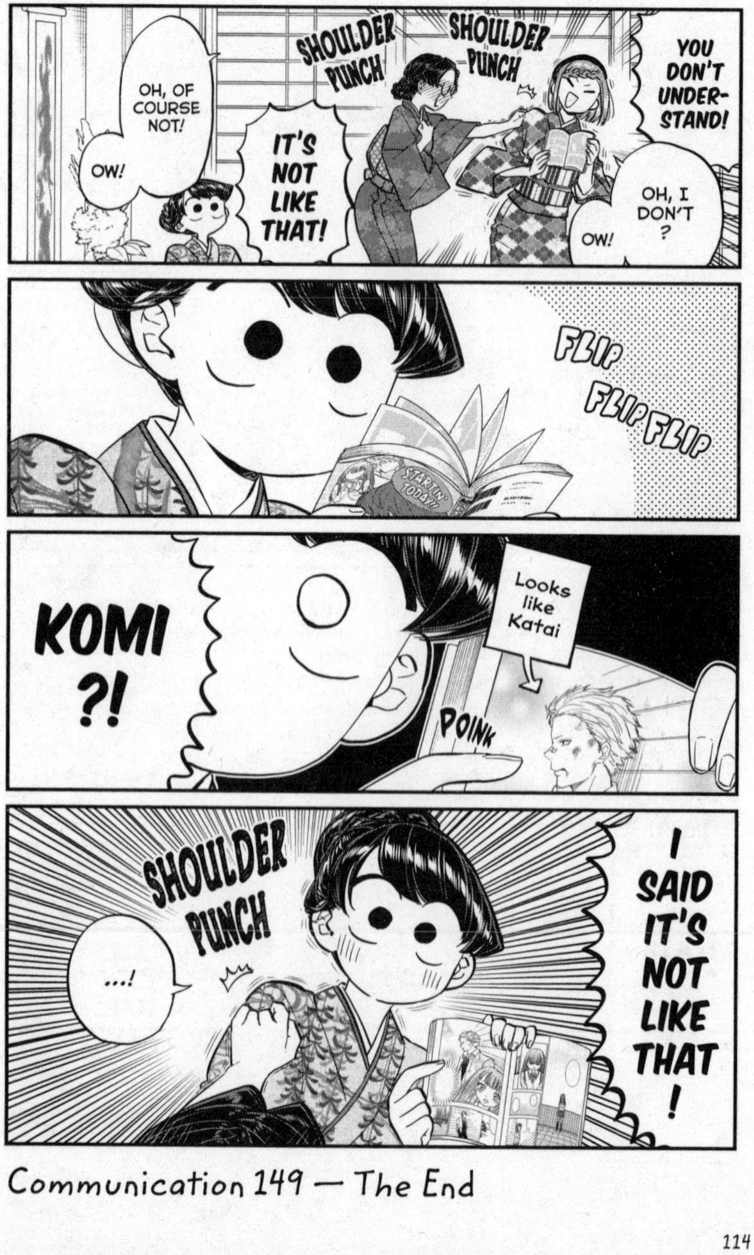
YOU DON'T UNDERSTAND!
OH, I DON'T ?
OW!
SHOULDER PUNCH
SHOULDER PUNCH
IT'S NOT LIKE THAT!
OH, OF COURSE NOT!
OW!
FLIP
FLIP FLIP
STARTIN' TODAY!!
Looks like Katai
POINK
KOMI ?!
I SAID IT'S NOT LIKE THAT!
SHOULDER PUNCH
...!

Communication 149 — The End

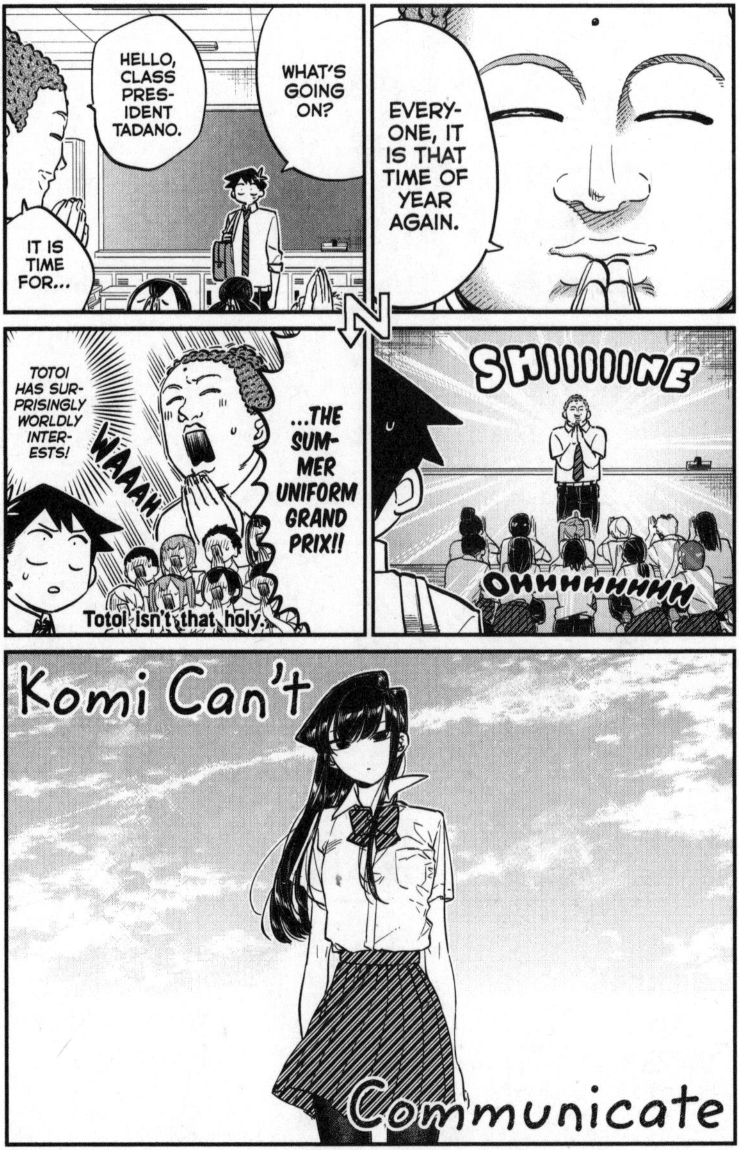
EVERYONE, IT IS THAT TIME OF YEAR AGAIN.
WHAT'S GOING ON?
HELLO, CLASS PRESIDENT TADANO.
IT IS TIME FOR...
SHIIIIIINE
OHHHHHHHH
...THE SUMMER UNIFORM GRAND PRIX!!
WAAAAH
TOTOI HAS SURPRISINGLY WORLDLY INTERESTS!
Totoi isn't that holy.
Komi Can't
Communicate

Communication 150: Summer Uniform Grand Prix?

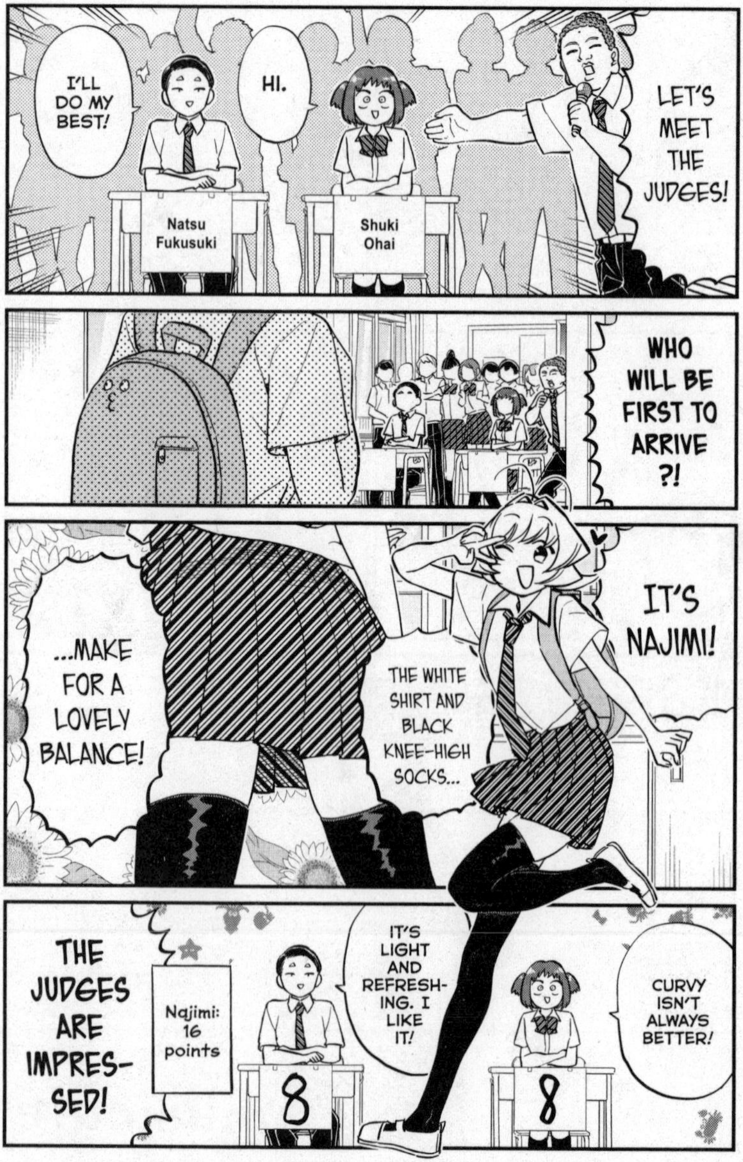
LET'S MEET THE JUDGES!
HI.
I'LL DO MY BEST!
Shuki Ohai
Natsu Fukusuki
WHO WILL BE FIRST TO ARRIVE ?!
IT'S NAJIMI!
THE WHITE SHIRT AND BLACK KNEE-HIGH SOCKS...
...MAKE FOR A LOVELY BALANCE!
CURVY ISN'T ALWAYS BETTER!
8
IT'S LIGHT AND REFRESHING. I LIKE IT!
8
Najimi: 16 points
THE JUDGES ARE IMPRESSED!

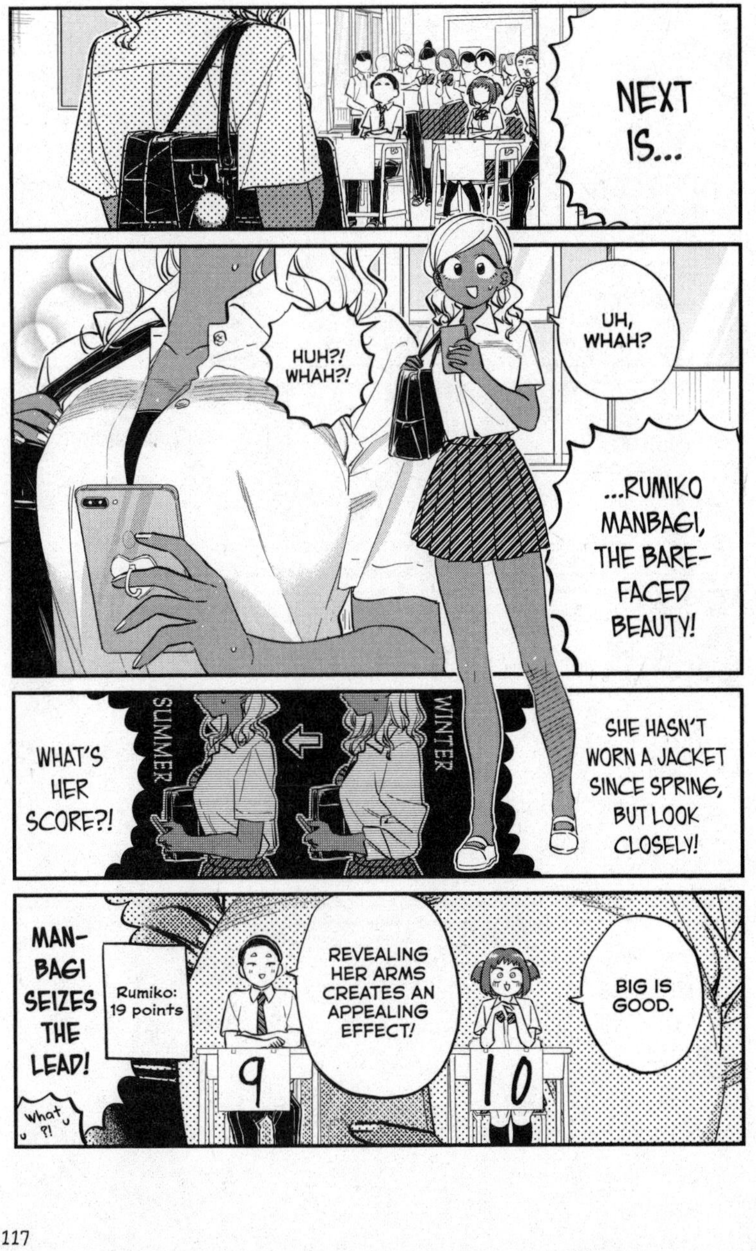
NEXT IS...
UH, WHAH?
HUH?! WHAH?!
...RUMIKO MANBAGI, THE BARE-FACED BEAUTY!
SHE HASN'T WORN A JACKET SINCE SPRING, BUT LOOK CLOSELY!
WINTER
SUMMER
WHAT'S HER SCORE?!
BIG IS GOOD.
10
REVEALING HER ARMS CREATES AN APPEALING EFFECT!
9
Rumiko: 19 points
MAN-BAGI SEIZES THE LEAD!
what ?!

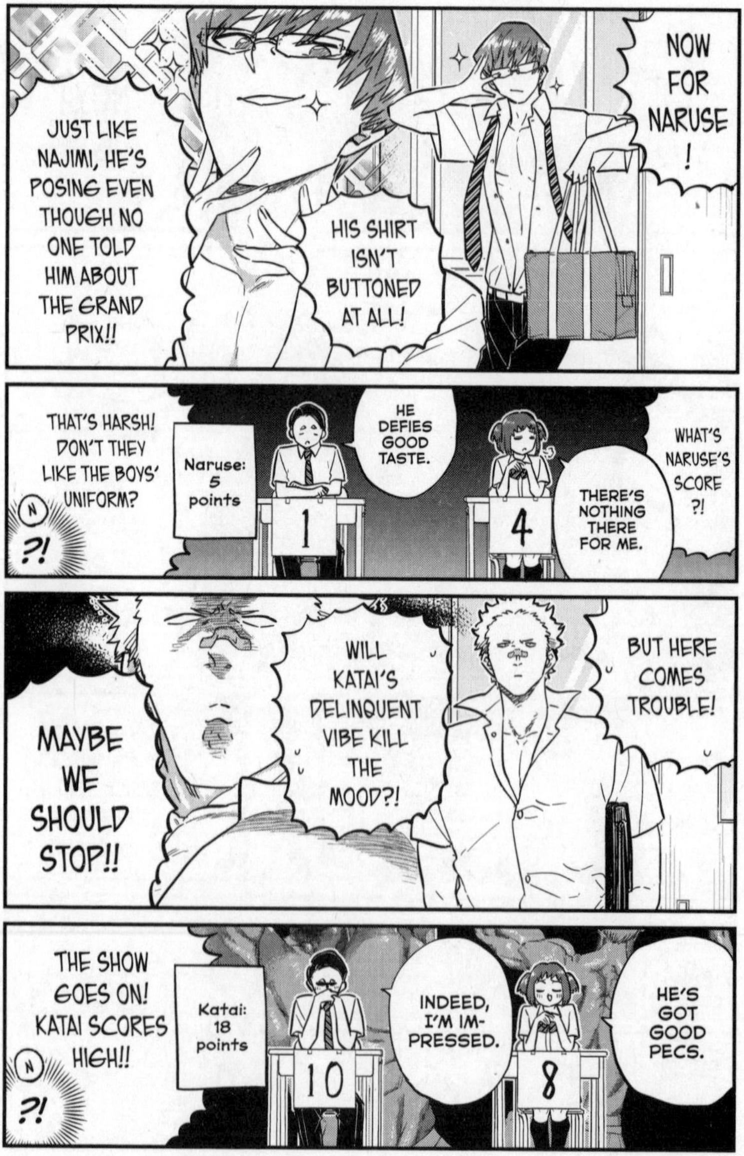
NOW FOR NARUSE!
HIS SHIRT ISN'T BUTTONED AT ALL!
JUST LIKE NAJIMI, HE'S POSING EVEN THOUGH NO ONE TOLD HIM ABOUT THE GRAND PRIX!!
WHAT'S NARUSE'S SCORE?!
THERE'S NOTHING THERE FOR ME.
4
HE DEFIES GOOD TASTE.
1
Naruse: 5 points
THAT'S HARSH! DON'T THEY LIKE THE BOYS' UNIFORM?
N
?!
BUT HERE COMES TROUBLE!
WILL KATAI'S DELINQUENT VIBE KILL THE MOOD?!
MAYBE WE SHOULD STOP!!
HE'S GOT GOOD PECS.
8
INDEED, I'M IMPRESSED.
10
Katai: 18 points
THE SHOW GOES ON! KATAI SCORES HIGH!!
N
?!

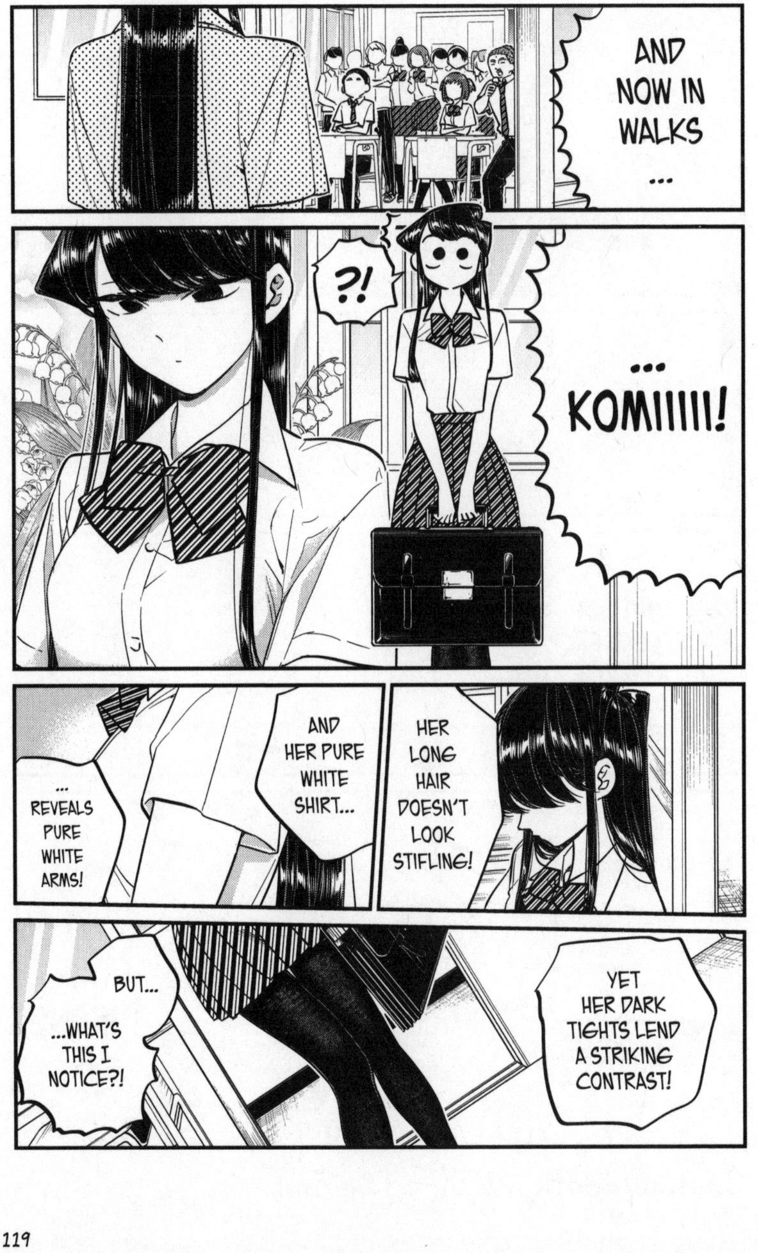
AND NOW IN WALKS ...
... KOMIIIII!
?!
HER LONG HAIR DOESN'T LOOK STIFLING!
AND HER PURE WHITE SHIRT...
... REVEALS PURE WHITE ARMS!
YET HER DARK TIGHTS LEND A STRIKING CONTRAST!
BUT...
...WHAT'S THIS I NOTICE?!

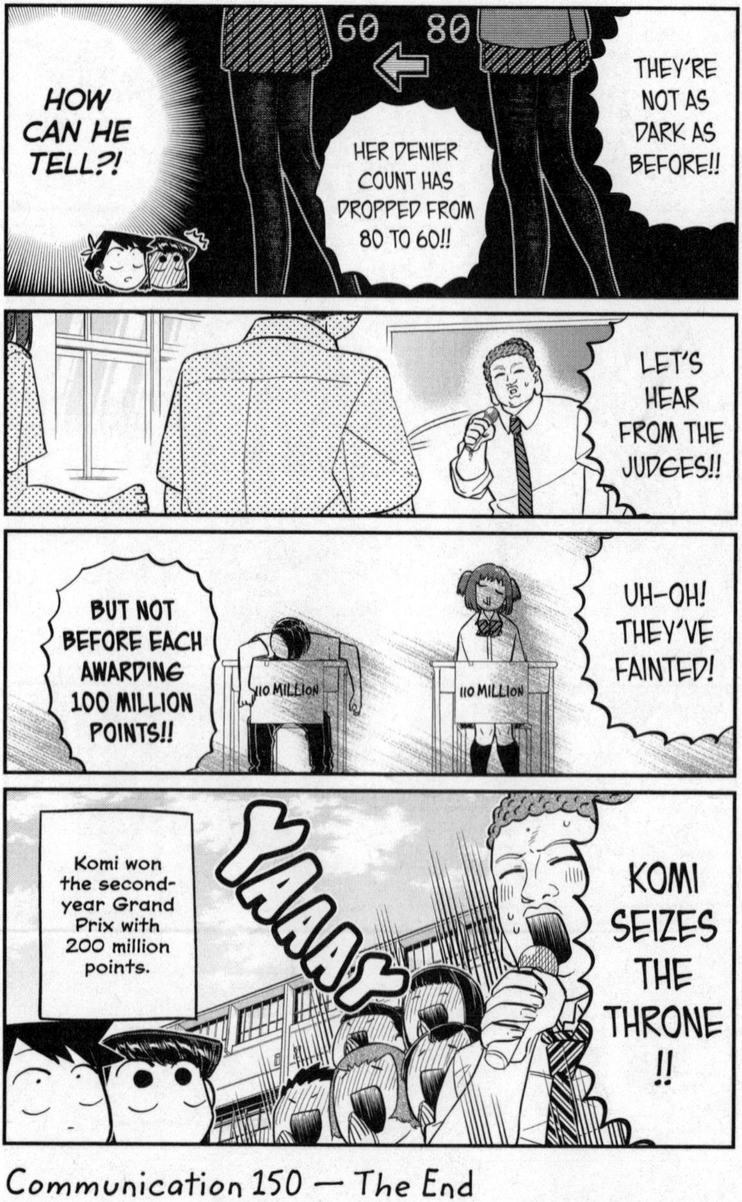
THEY'RE NOT AS DARK AS BEFORE!!
60 80
HER DENIER COUNT HAS DROPPED FROM 80 TO 60!!
HOW CAN HE TELL?!
LET'S HEAR FROM THE JUDGES!!
UH-OH! THEY'VE FAINTED!
110 MILLION
110 MILLION
BUT NOT BEFORE EACH AWARDING 100 MILLION POINTS!!
KOMI SEIZES THE THRONE!!
YAAAY
Komi won the second-year Grand Prix with 200 million points.

Communication 150 — The End

Komi Can't Communicate

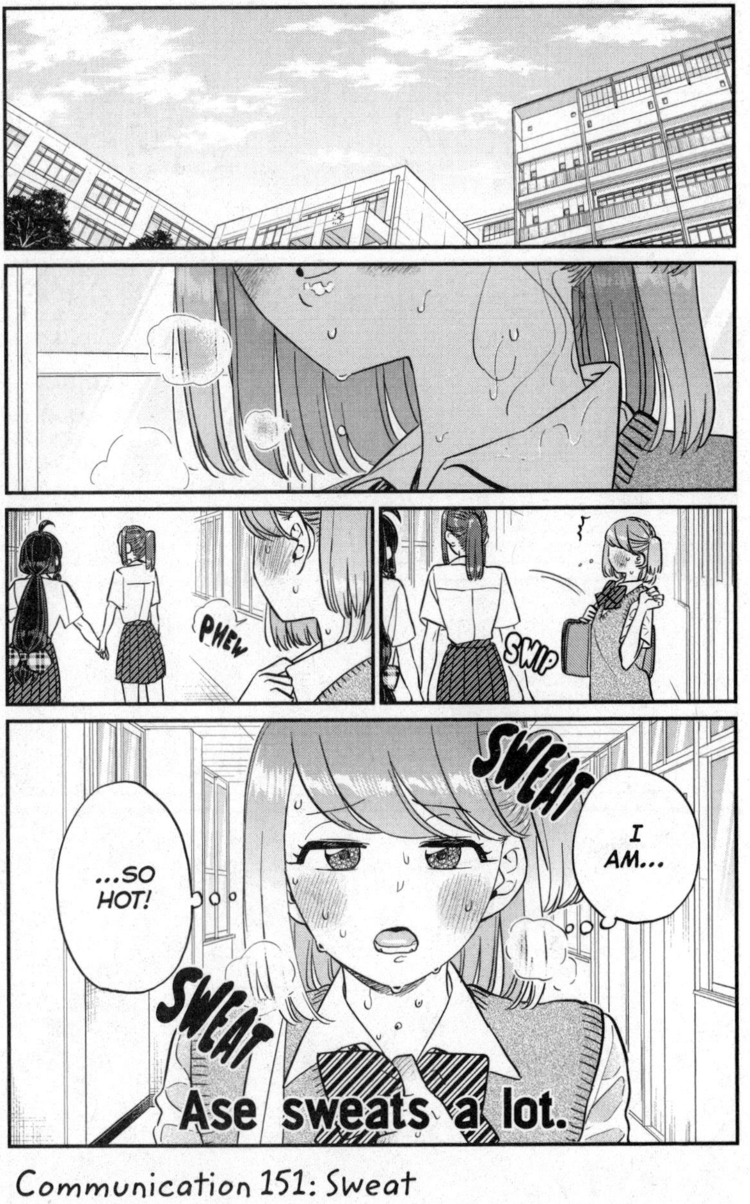
SWIP
PHEW
SWEAT
I AM...
...SO HOT!
SWEAT
Ase sweats a lot.

Communication 151: Sweat

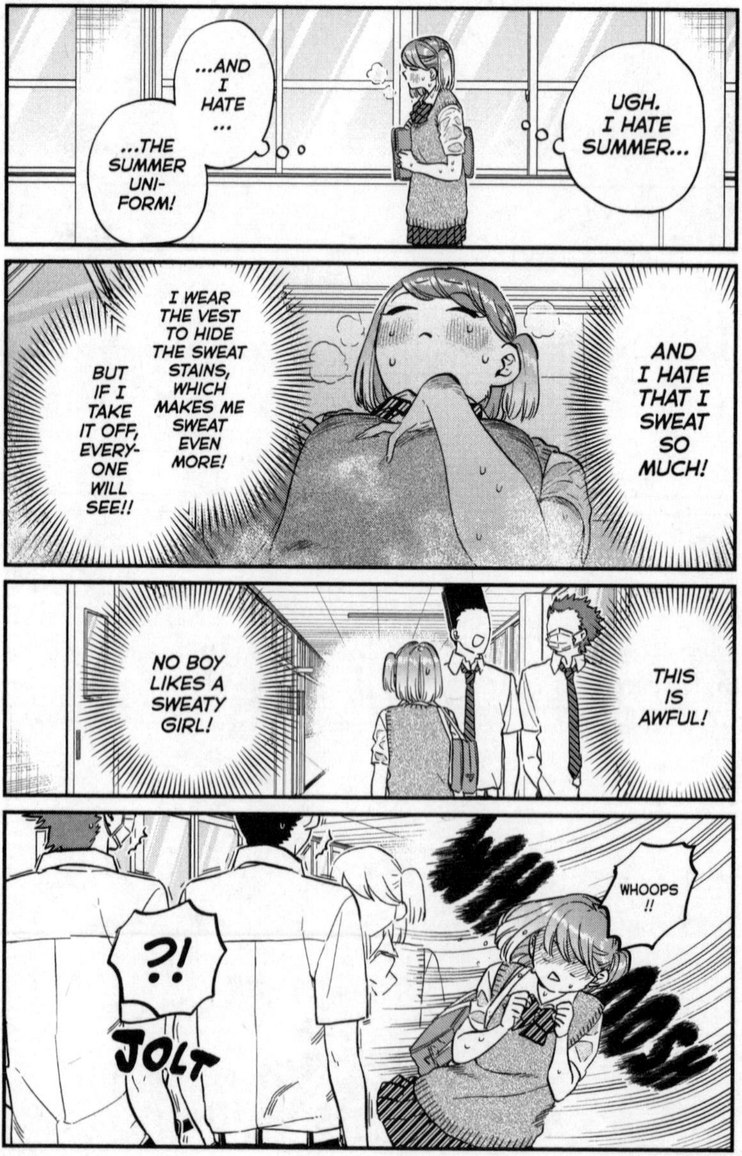
UGH. I HATE SUMMER...
...AND I HATE ...
...THE SUMMER UNI-FORM!
AND I HATE THAT I SWEAT SO MUCH!
I WEAR THE VEST TO HIDE THE SWEAT STAINS, WHICH MAKES ME SWEAT EVEN MORE!
BUT IF I TAKE IT OFF, EVERYONE WILL SEE!!
THIS IS AWFUL!
NO BOY LIKES A SWEATY GIRL!
WHOOSH
WHOOPS !!
?!
JOLT

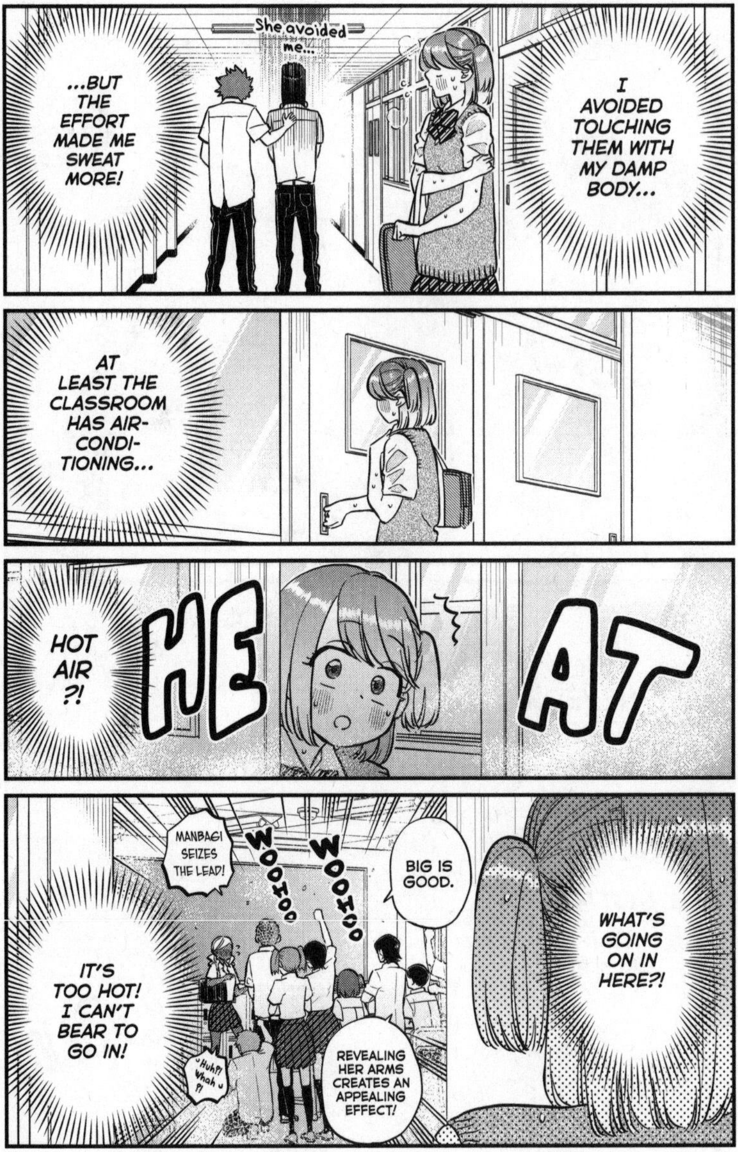
I AVOIDED TOUCHING THEM WITH MY DAMP BODY...
She avoided me...
...BUT THE EFFORT MADE ME SWEAT MORE!
AT LEAST THE CLASSROOM HAS AIR-CONDITIONING...
HE AT
HOT AIR?!
WHAT'S GOING ON IN HERE?!
BIG IS GOOD.
WOOHOO
WOOHOO
MANBAGI SEIZES THE LEAD!
REVEALING HER ARMS CREATES AN APPEALING EFFECT!
Huh?! Whah?!
IT'S TOO HOT! I CAN'T BEAR TO GO IN!

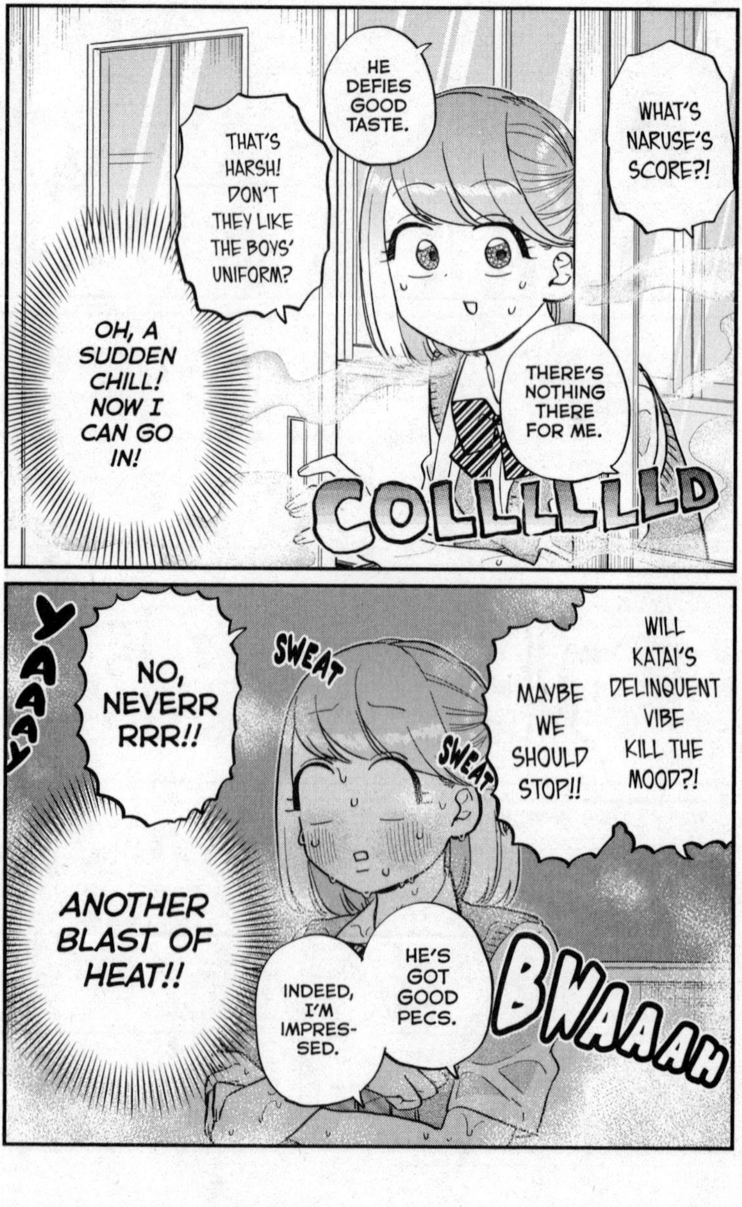
WHAT'S NARUSE'S SCORE?!
HE DEFIES GOOD TASTE.
THAT'S HARSH! DON'T THEY LIKE THE BOYS' UNIFORM?
THERE'S NOTHING THERE FOR ME.
OH, A SUDDEN CHILL! NOW I CAN GO IN!
COLLLLLLD
WILL KATAI'S DELINQUENT VIBE KILL THE MOOD?!
MAYBE WE SHOULD STOP!!
SWEAT
SWEAT
NO, NEVERR RRR!!
YAAAY
HE'S GOT GOOD PECS.
INDEED, I'M IMPRES-SED.
BWAAAAH
ANOTHER BLAST OF HEAT!!

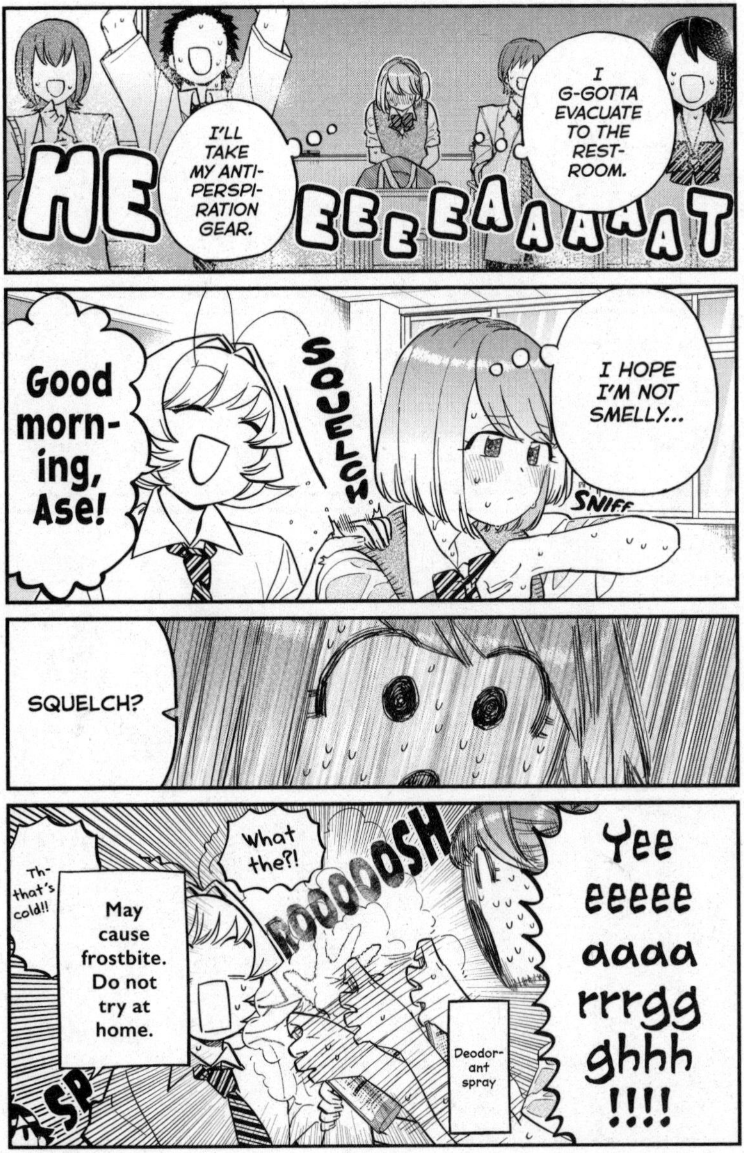
I G-GOTTA EVACUATE TO THE REST-ROOM.
I'LL TAKE MY ANTI-PERSPI-RATION GEAR.
HEEEEEAAAAAT
I HOPE I'M NOT SMELLY...
SNIFF
SQUELCH
Good morn-ing, Ase!
SQUELCH?
Yeeeeeeeaaaarrrggghhh!!!!
Deodor-ant spray
What the?!
OOOOOSH
Th-that's cold!!
May cause frostbite. Do not try at home.
SP

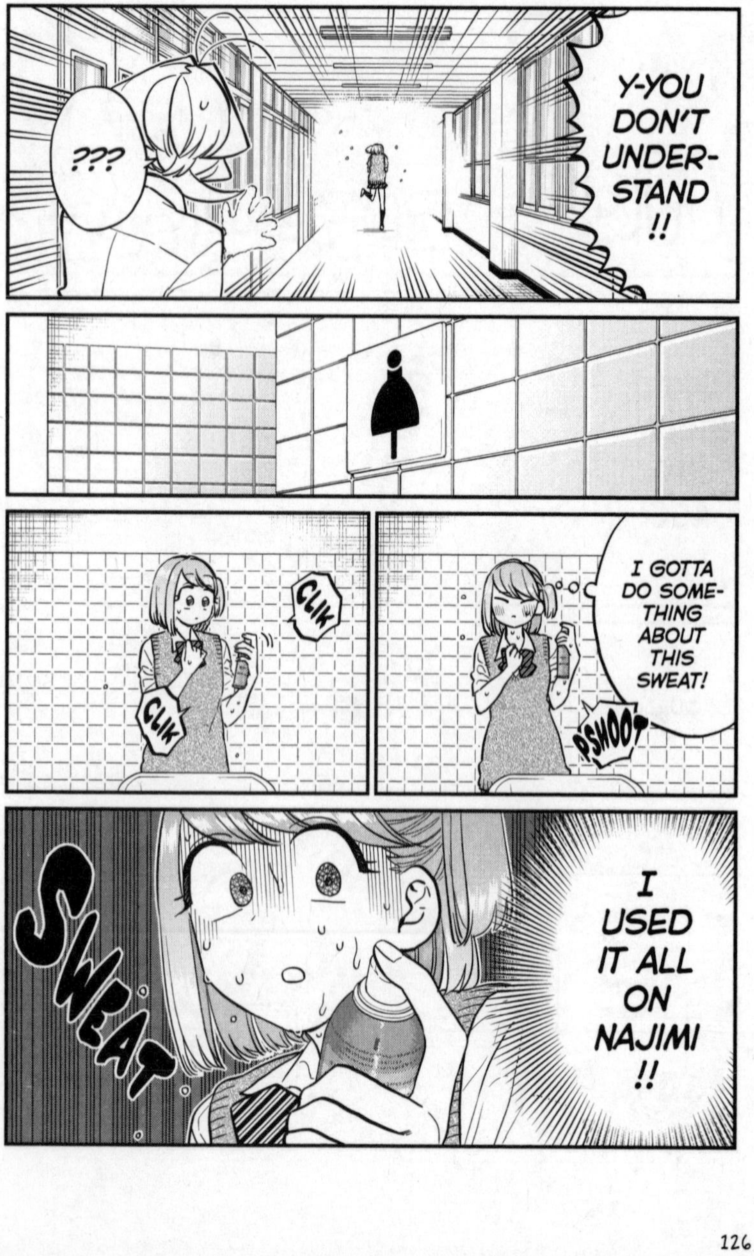
Y-YOU DON'T UNDER-STAND!!
???
I GOTTA DO SOME-THING ABOUT THIS SWEAT!
PSHOOT
CLIK
CLIK
I USED IT ALL ON NAJIMI!!
SWEAT

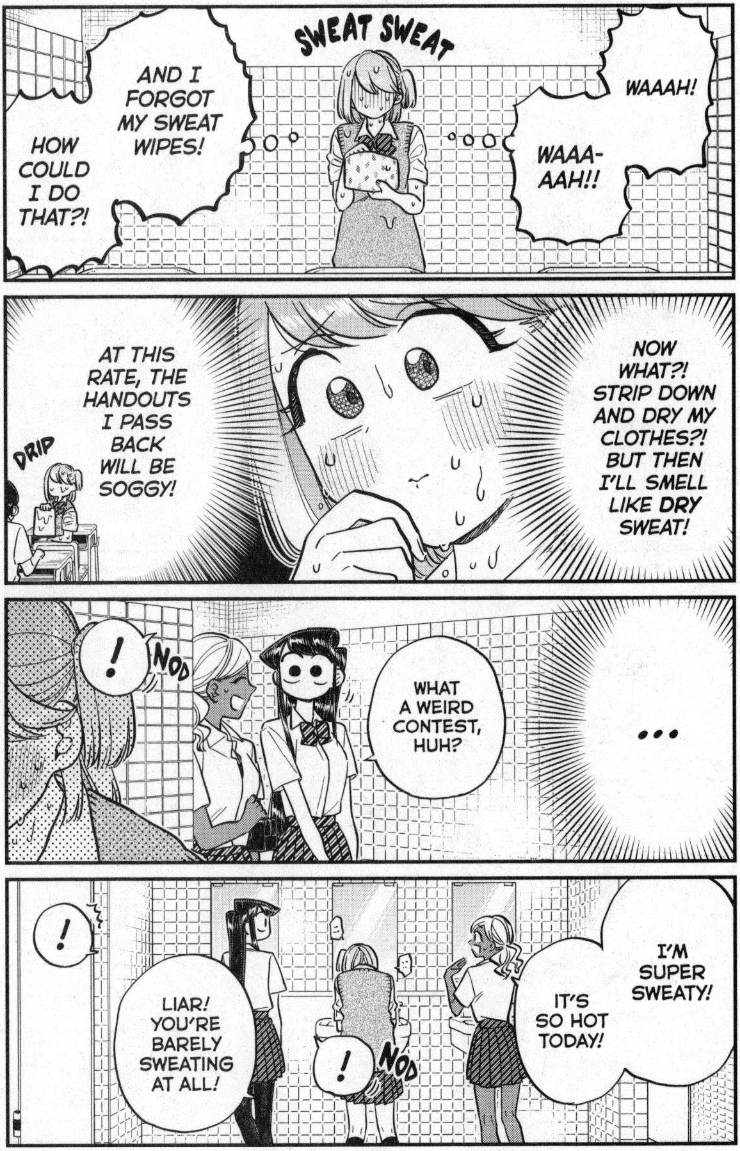
SWEAT SWEAT
WAAAH!
WAAA-AAH!!
AND I FORGOT MY SWEAT WIPES!
HOW COULD I DO THAT?!
NOW WHAT?! STRIP DOWN AND DRY MY CLOTHES?! BUT THEN I'LL SMELL LIKE DRY SWEAT!
AT THIS RATE, THE HANDOUTS I PASS BACK WILL BE SOGGY!
DRIP
...
WHAT A WEIRD CONTEST, HUH?
NOD
!
I'M SUPER SWEATY!
IT'S SO HOT TODAY!
NOD
!
LIAR! YOU'RE BARELY SWEATING AT ALL!
!

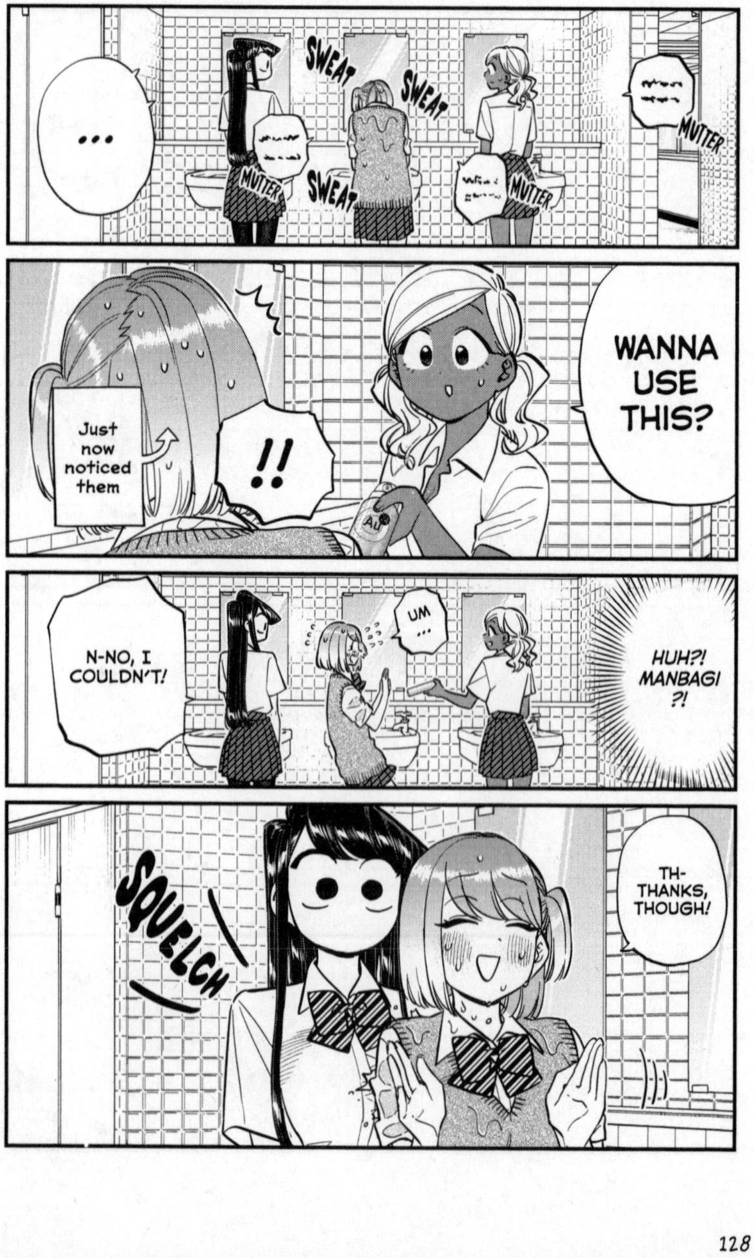
MUTTER
MUTTER
SWEAT
SWEAT
SWEAT
MUTTER
...
WANNA USE THIS?
!!
Just now noticed them
HUH?! MANBAGI ?!
UM ...
N-NO, I COULDN'T!
TH-THANKS, THOUGH!
SQUELCH

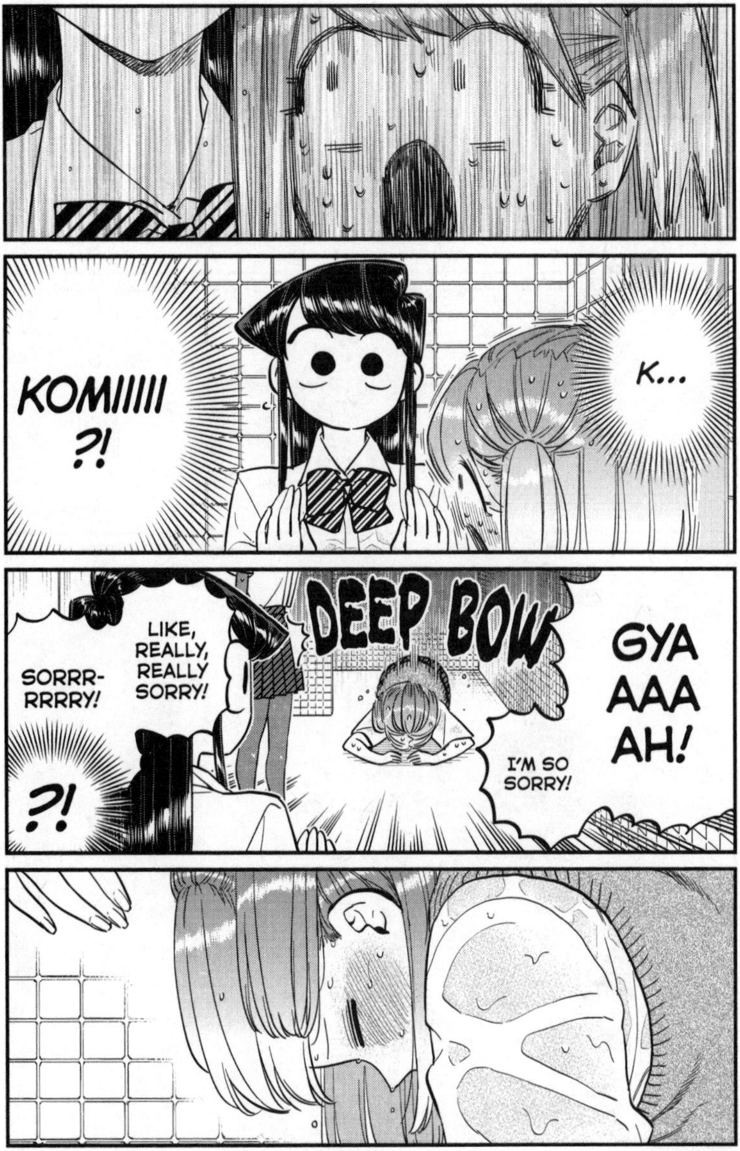
K...
KOMIIIIII ?!
GYA AAA AH!
I'M SO SORRY!
DEEP BOW
LIKE, REALLY, REALLY SORRY!
SORRR-RRRRY!
?!

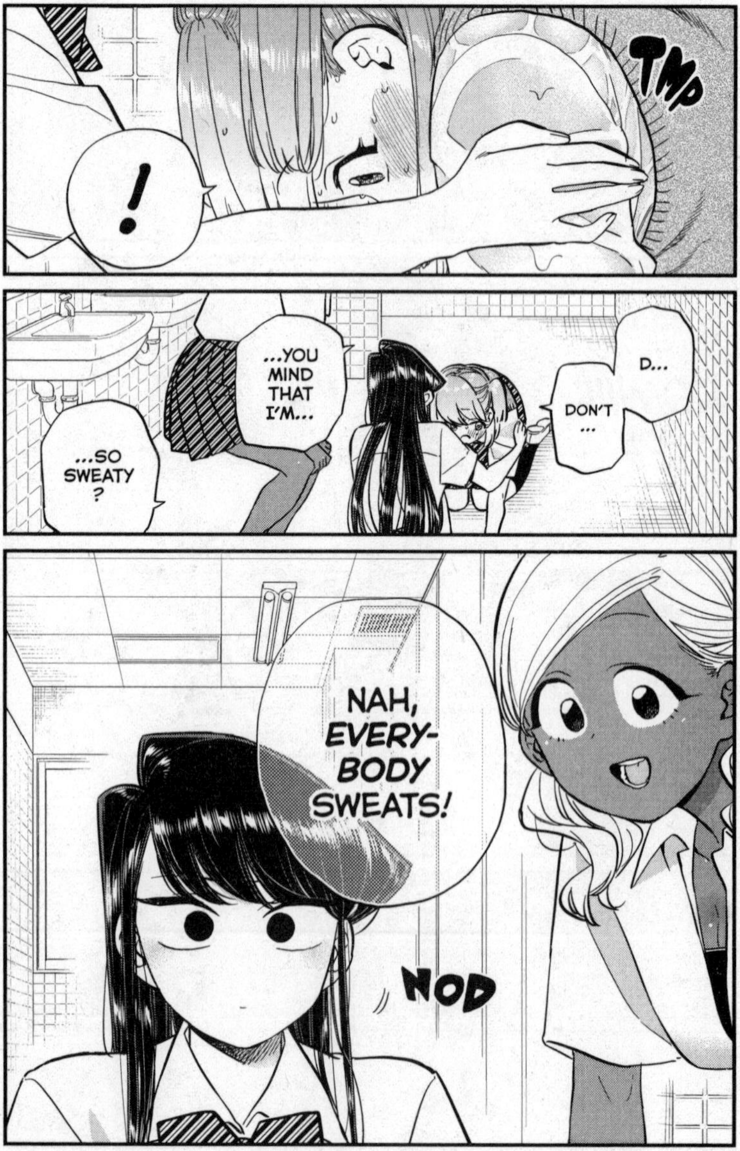
TMP
!
D...
DON'T ...
...YOU MIND THAT I'M...
...SO SWEATY ?
NAH, EVERY-BODY SWEATS!
NOD

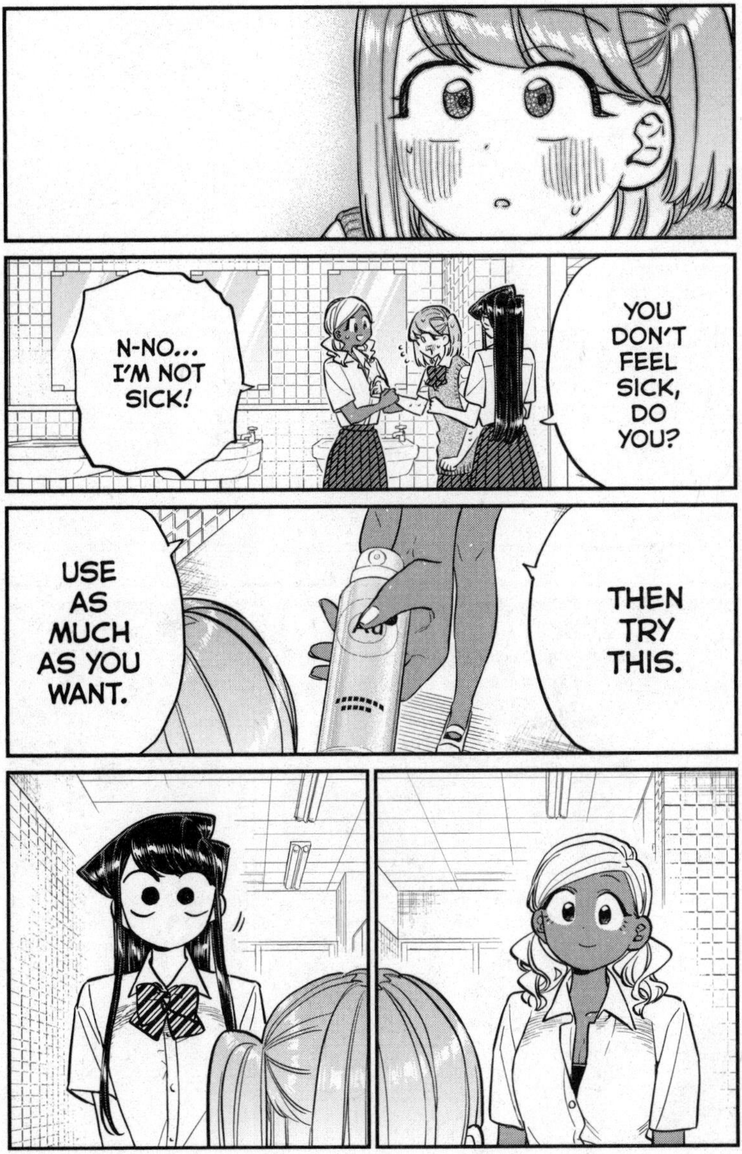
YOU DON'T FEEL SICK, DO YOU?
N-NO... I'M NOT SICK!
THEN TRY THIS.
USE AS MUCH AS YOU WANT.

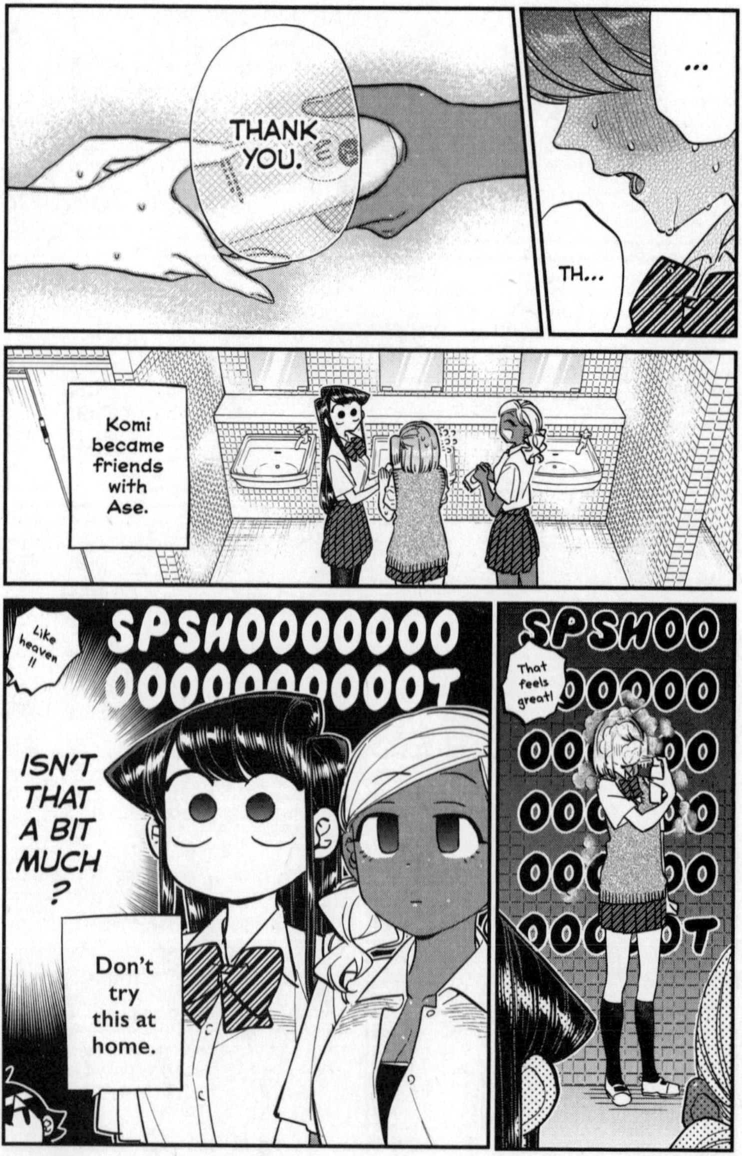
...
TH...
THANK YOU.
Komi became friends with Ase.
SPSHOOOOOOOOOOOOOOOOOOOOOOOOOT
That feels great!
SPSHOOOOOOO
OOOOOOOOOT
Like heaven!!
ISN'T THAT A BIT MUCH?
Don't try this at home.

Communication 151 — The End

Komi Can't Communicate

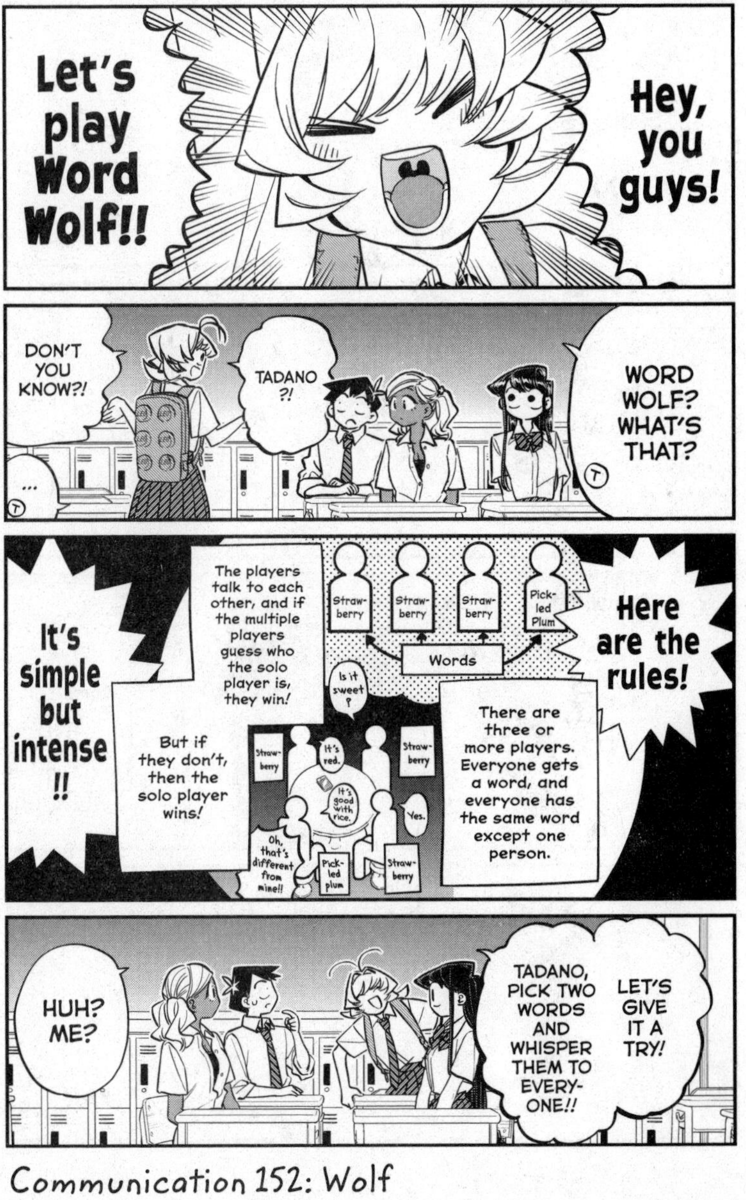

Hey, you guys!
Let's play Word Wolf!!
WORD WOLF? WHAT'S THAT?
TADANO ?!
DON'T YOU KNOW?!
...
Here are the rules!
There are three or more players. Everyone gets a word, and everyone has the same word except one person.
Straw-berry
Straw-berry
Straw-berry
Pick-led Plum
Words
The players talk to each other, and if the multiple players guess who the solo player is, they win!
Is it sweet?
Straw-berry
It's red.
Straw-berry
It's good with rice.
Yes.
Straw-berry
Pick-led plum
Oh, that's different from mine!!
But if they don't, then the solo player wins!
It's simple but intense!!
LET'S GIVE IT A TRY!
TADANO, PICK TWO WORDS AND WHISPER THEM TO EVERY-ONE!!
HUH? ME?

Communication 152: Wolf

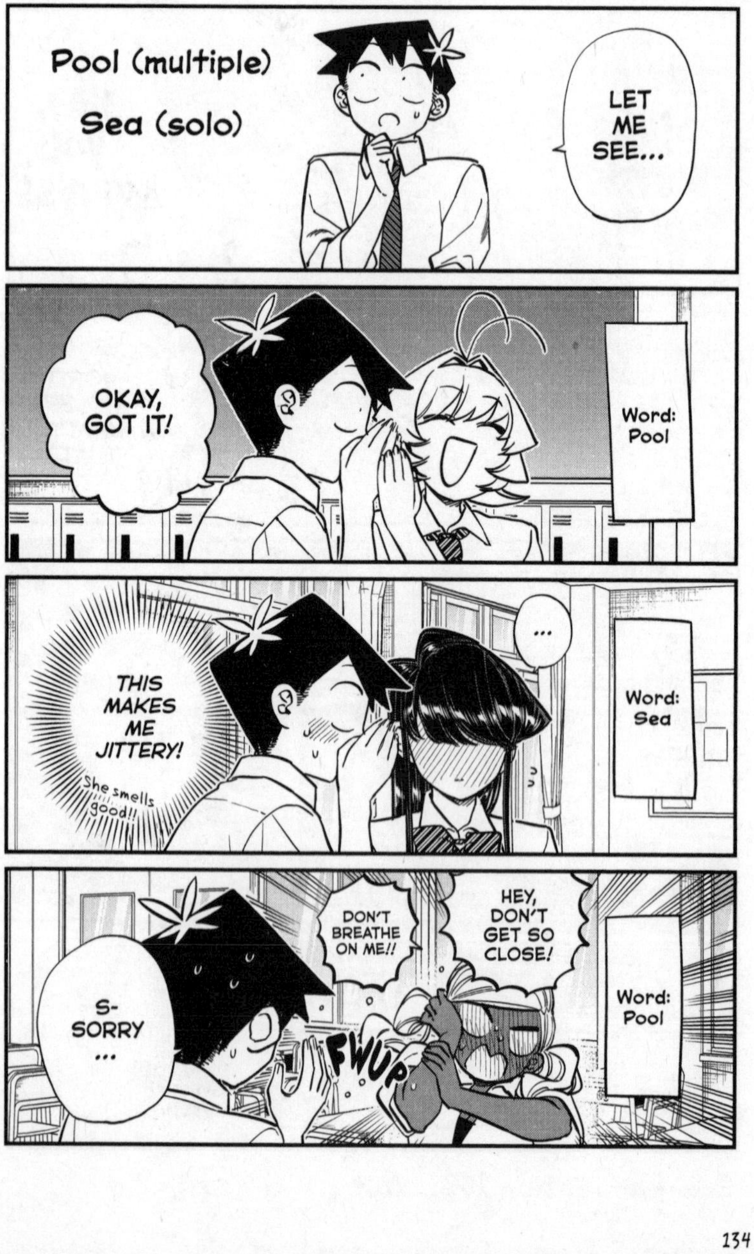
LET ME SEE...
Pool (multiple)
Sea (solo)
Word: Pool
OKAY, GOT IT!
Word: Sea
...
THIS MAKES ME JITTERY!
She smells good!!
Word: Pool
HEY, DON'T GET SO CLOSE!
DON'T BREATHE ON ME!!
FWUP
S-SORRY...

Okay, let's start!!
Talk for three minutes!
Pool
NOD NOD
Sea
YOU CAN SWIM IN IT, RIGHT?
!
Pool
YEAH!
IS IT REPRESEN-TATIVE OF SUMMER?
Pool
WE DEFINITELY GOTTA GO AGAIN THIS YEAR!
Sea
!
Pool
UM, HOW BIG IS IT?
Pool
"Very big."
Very big.
Sea
HM?
Pool
UH, MINE SORT OF IS, BUT...
Sea
Is it salty?
HUH?
Komi's side loses.
?!
Pro tip! Don't ask anything that gives away your word!

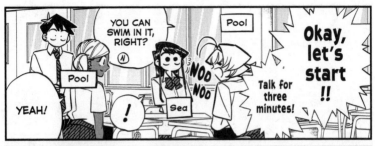

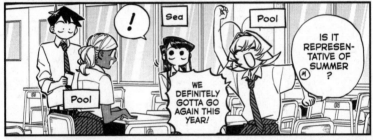

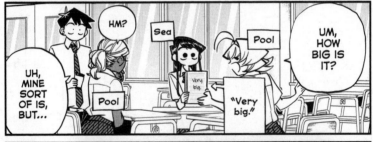

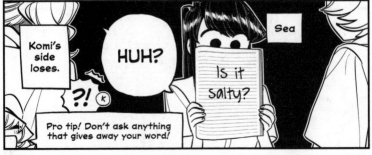

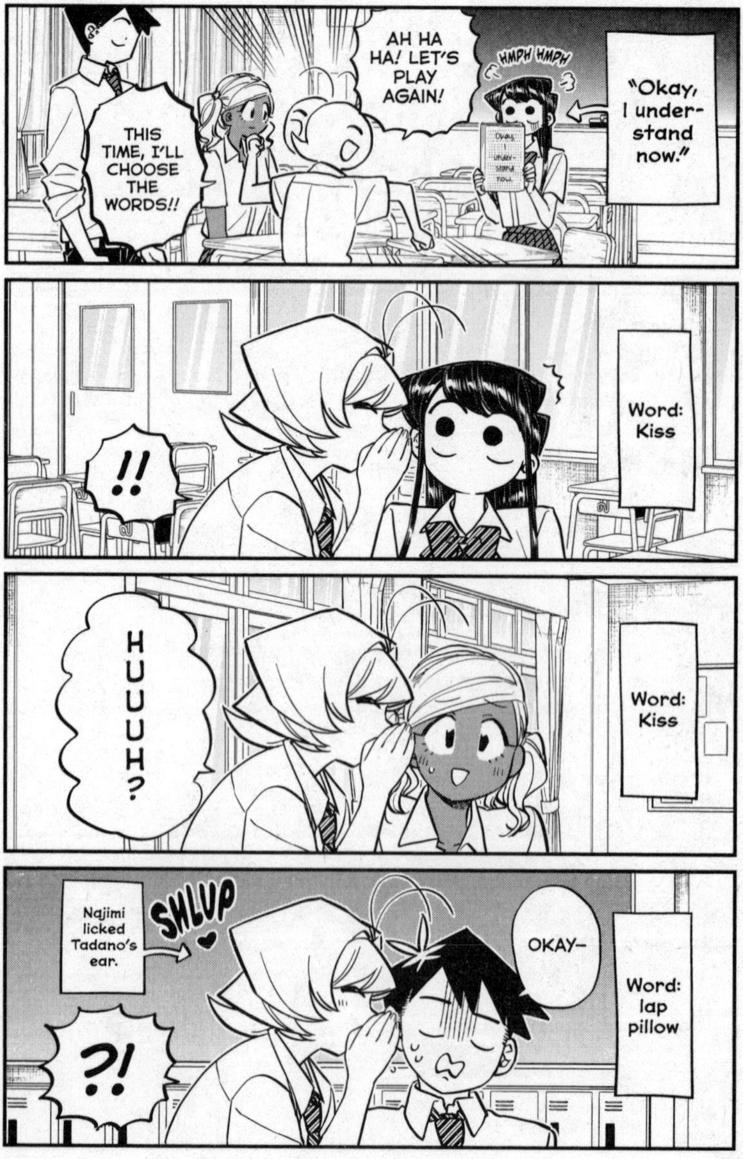
"Okay, I understand now."
HMPH HMPH
Okay, I under-stand now.
AH HA HA! LET'S PLAY AGAIN!
THIS TIME, I'LL CHOOSE THE WORDS!!
Word: Kiss
!!
Word: Kiss
HUUUH?
Word: lap pillow
OKAY–
SHLUP
Najimi licked Tadano's ear.
?!

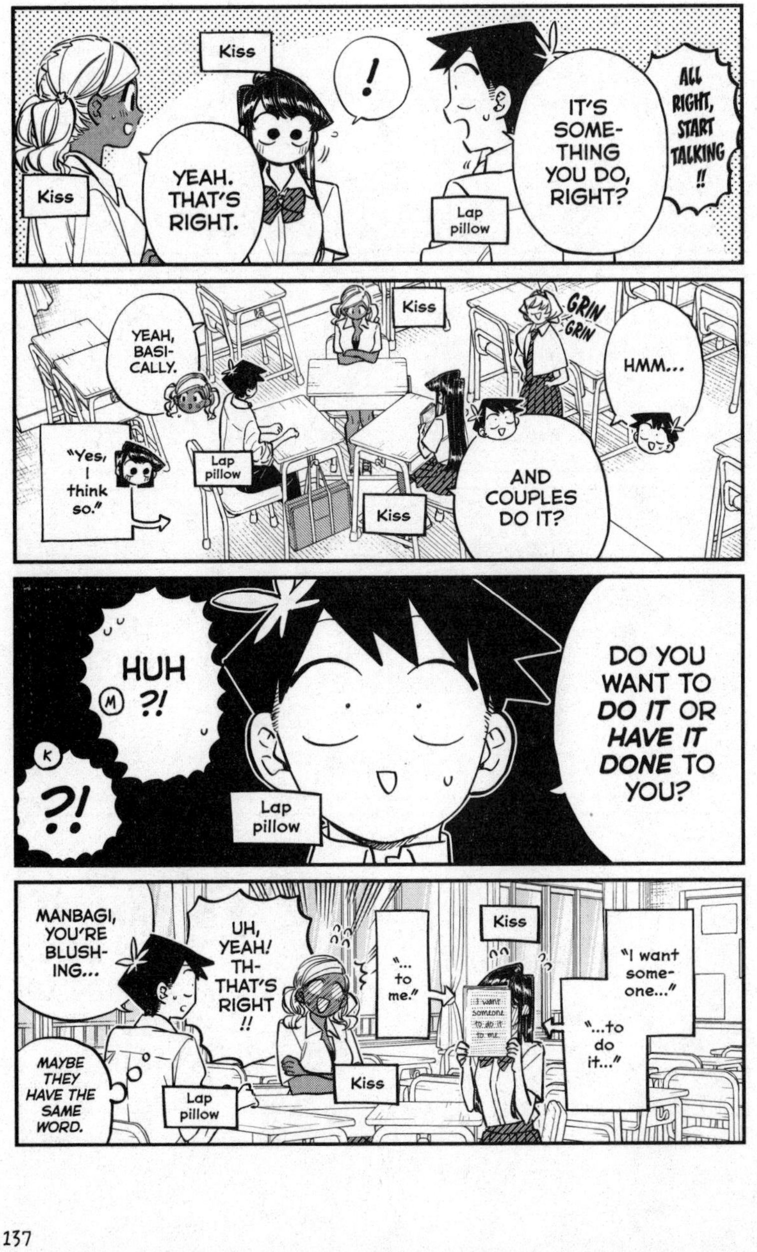
ALL RIGHT, START TALKING!!
IT'S SOME-THING YOU DO, RIGHT?
Lap pillow
!
Kiss
YEAH. THAT'S RIGHT.
Kiss
GRIN GRIN
HMM...
Kiss
AND COUPLES DO IT?
Kiss
YEAH, BASI-CALLY.
Lap pillow
"Yes, I think so."
DO YOU WANT TO *DO IT* OR *HAVE IT DONE* TO YOU?
Lap pillow
HUH ?!
?!
"I want some-one..."
"...to do it..."
Kiss
"... to me."
I want someone to do it to me.
UH, YEAH! TH-THAT'S RIGHT!!
Kiss
MANBAGI, YOU'RE BLUSH-ING...
Lap pillow
MAYBE THEY HAVE THE SAME WORD.

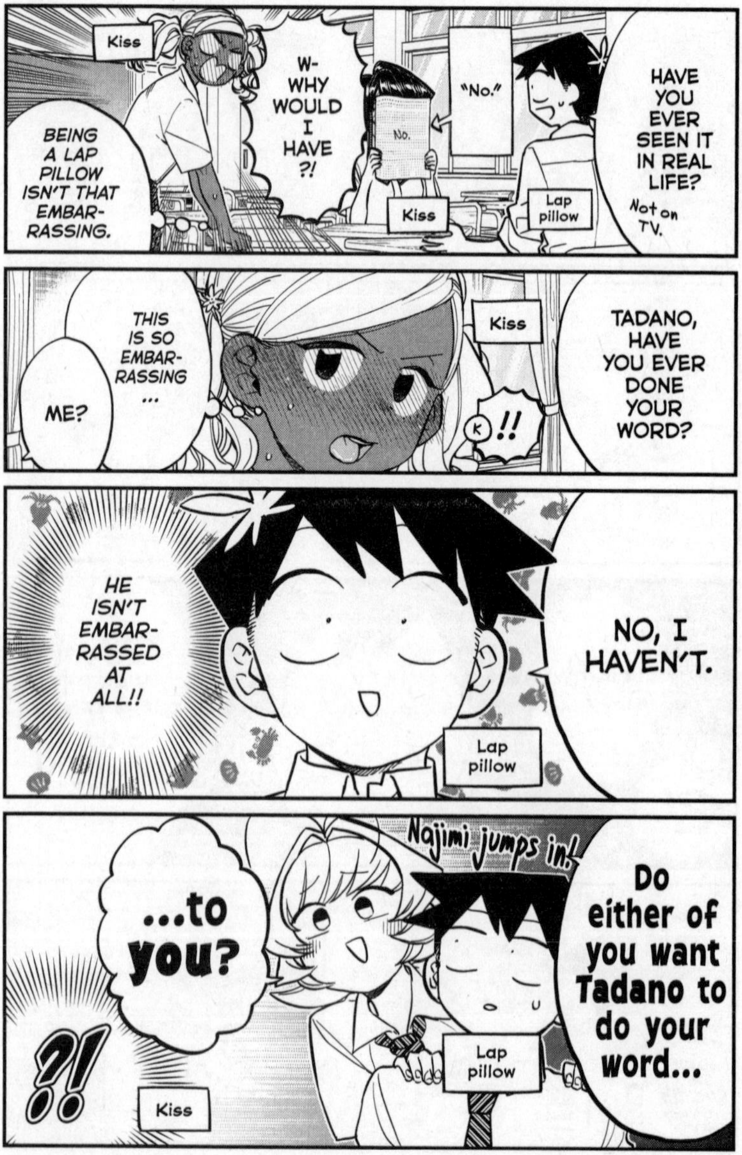

HAVE YOU EVER SEEN IT IN REAL LIFE?
Not on TV.
Lap pillow
"No."
No.
W-WHY WOULD I HAVE ?!
Kiss
Kiss
BEING A LAP PILLOW ISN'T THAT EMBARRASSING.
TADANO, HAVE YOU EVER DONE YOUR WORD?
Kiss
K !!
THIS IS SO EMBARRASSING...
ME?
NO, I HAVEN'T.
Lap pillow
HE ISN'T EMBARRASSED AT ALL!!
Do either of you want Tadano to do your word...
Najimi jumps in!
Lap pillow
...to you?
?!
Kiss

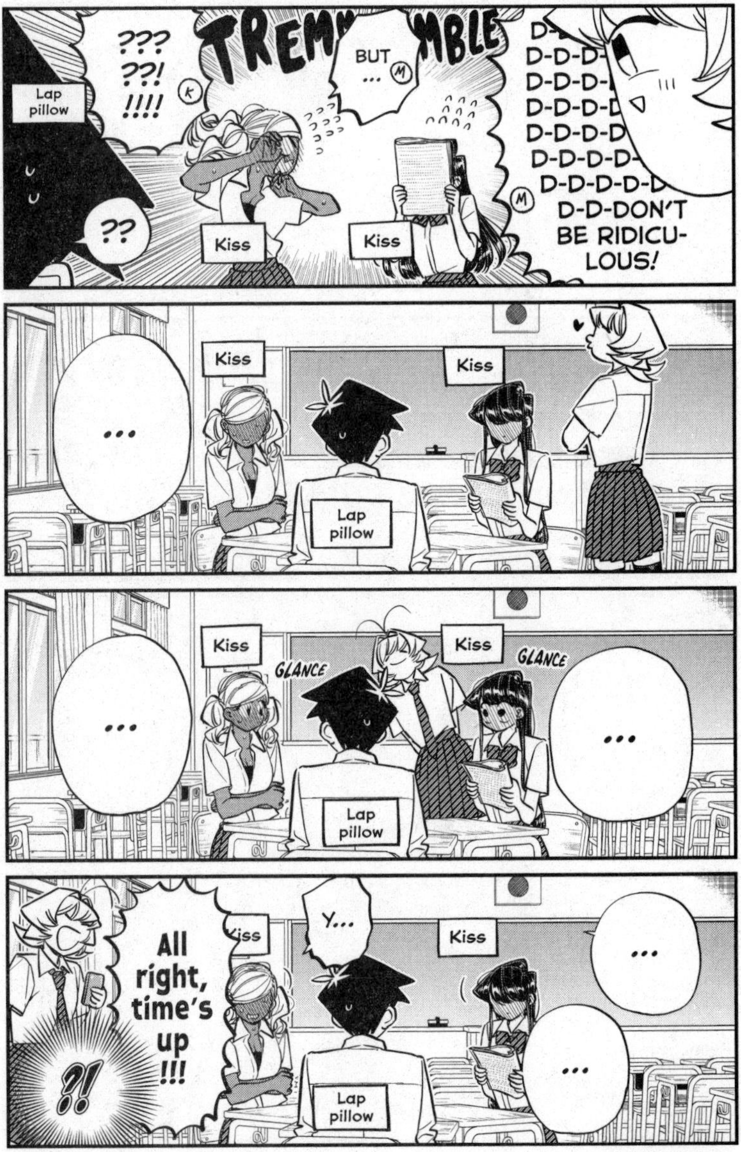

D-D-D-D-D-D-D-D-D-D-D-D-D-D-D-D-D-D-D-D-D-D-D-D-D-DON'T BE RIDICULOUS!
BUT ...
TREMM MBLE
Kiss
Kiss
???
??!
!!!!
Lap pillow
??
Kiss
Kiss
...
Lap pillow
...
GLANCE
Kiss
GLANCE
Kiss
...
Lap pillow
...
...
Kiss
Y...
iss
All right, time's up!!!
?!
Lap pillow

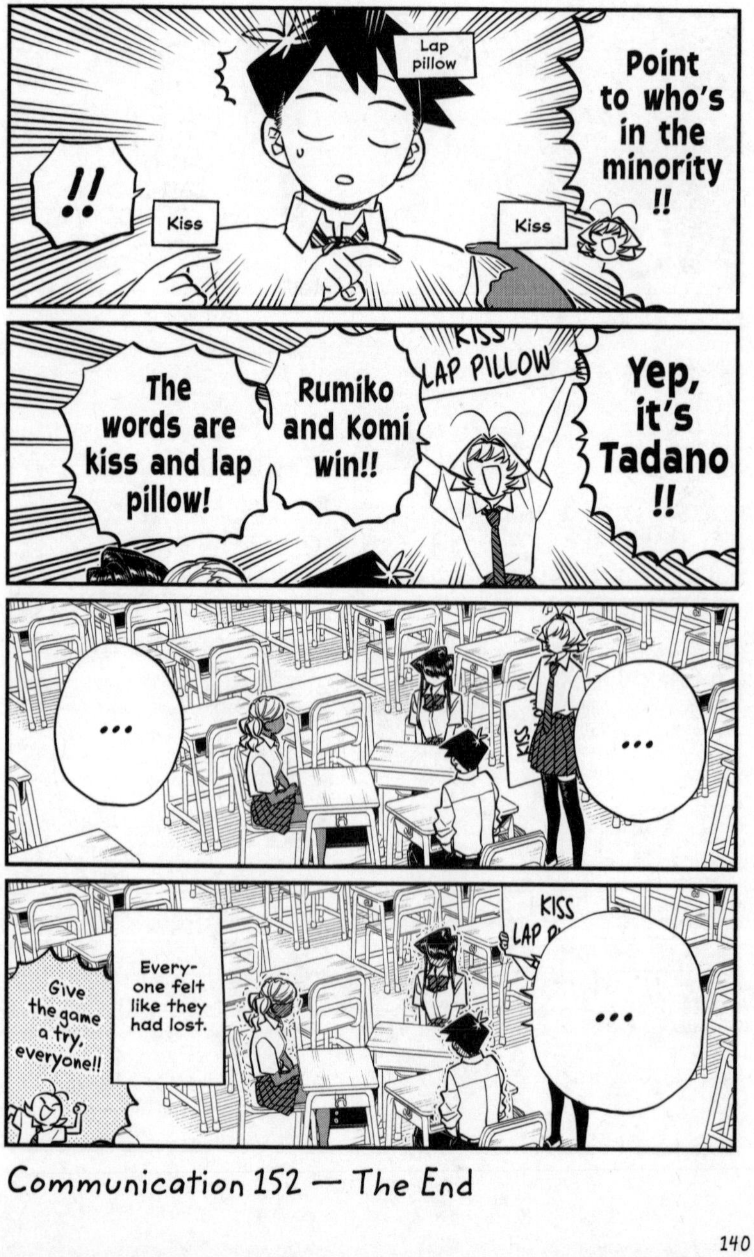
Point to who's in the minority!!
Lap pillow
Kiss
Kiss
!!
Yep, it's Tadano!!
KISS
LAP PILLOW
Rumiko and Komi win!!
The words are kiss and lap pillow!
...
KISS
...
...
KISS
Every-one felt like they had lost.
Give the game a try, everyone!!

Communication 152 — The End

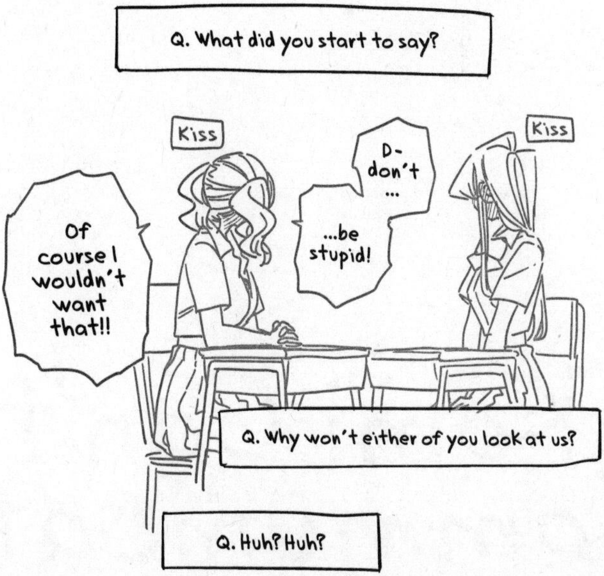
Q. What did you start to say?
Kiss
D-don't...
...be stupid!
Kiss
Of course I wouldn't want that!!
Q. Why won't either of you look at us?
Q. Huh? Huh?

Komi Can't
Communicate

Komi Can't Communicate

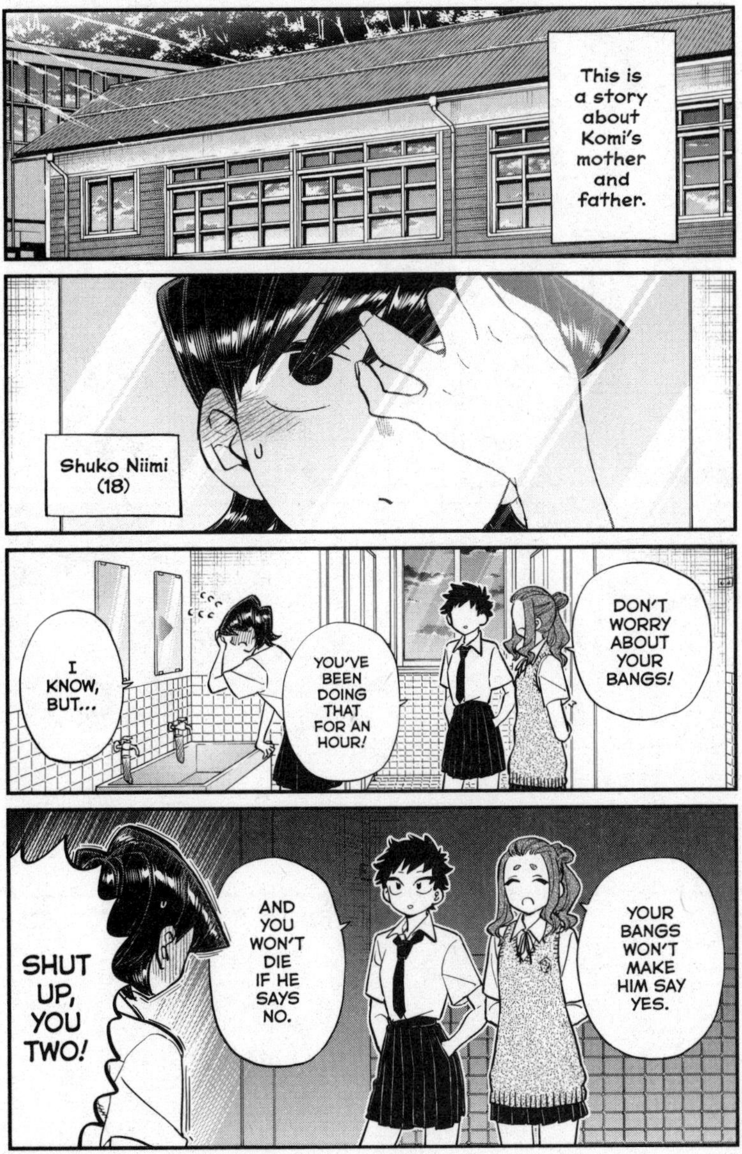
This is a story about Komi's mother and father.
Shuko Niimi (18)
DON'T WORRY ABOUT YOUR BANGS!
YOU'VE BEEN DOING THAT FOR AN HOUR!
I KNOW, BUT...
YOUR BANGS WON'T MAKE HIM SAY YES.
AND YOU WON'T DIE IF HE SAYS NO.
SHUT UP, YOU TWO!

Communication 153: Mom and Dad Confess Their Feelings

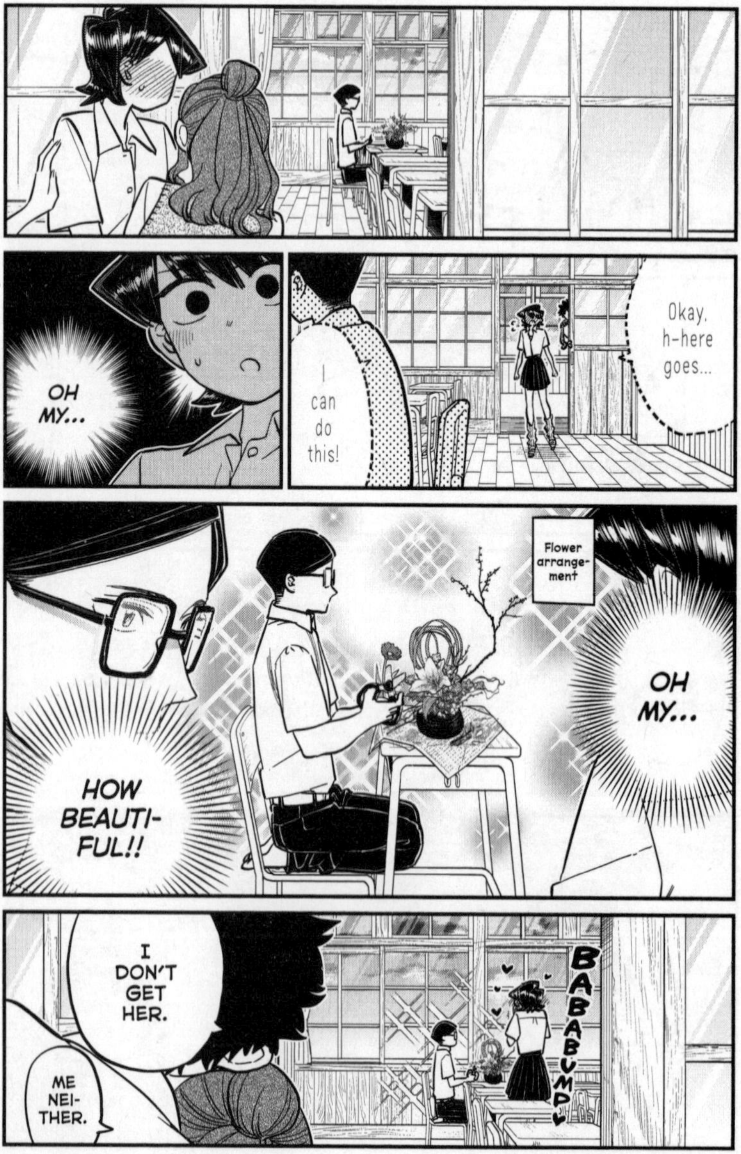
Okay, h-here goes...
I can do this!
OH MY...
Flower arrangement
OH MY...
HOW BEAUTIFUL!!
BABABUMP
I DON'T GET HER.
ME NEITHER.

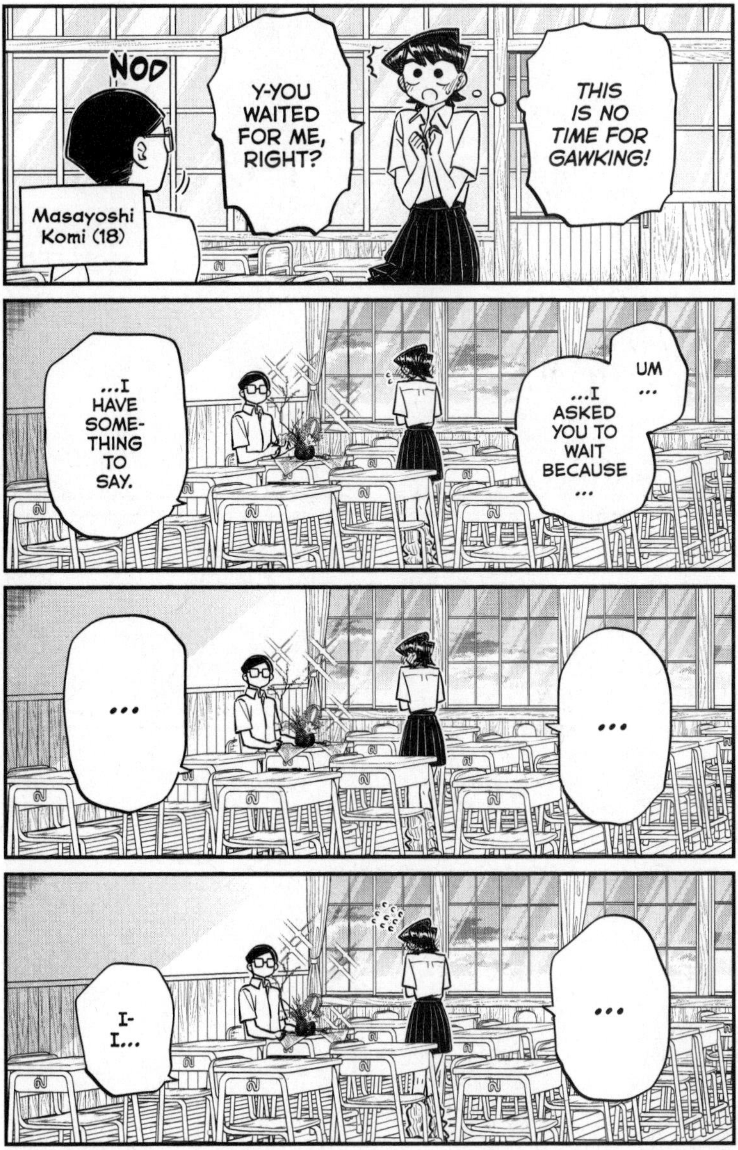
THIS IS NO TIME FOR GAWKING!
Y-YOU WAITED FOR ME, RIGHT?
NOD
Masayoshi Komi (18)
UM ...
...I ASKED YOU TO WAIT BECAUSE ...
...I HAVE SOME-THING TO SAY.
...
...
...
I- I...

BLUSH HHHH
I CAAA-AAN'T!!
I CAN'T DO IT!!!
NEVER MIND! IT'S NOTHING!!
WHOOSH
S-SEE YA!!
CLASP
!!
HM?
Y-YES?
YOU WANT TO WALK HOME TOGETHER?
NOD

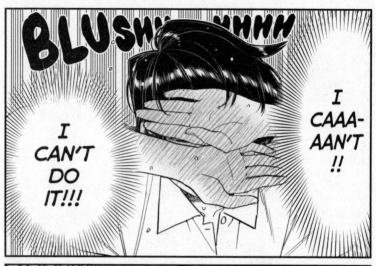

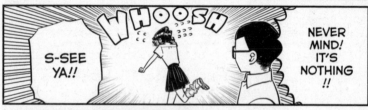

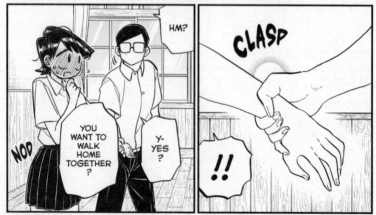

Are those two following us?
...delays on the Hokuriku Express-way...
...today's high tempera-ture...
Now for the national–
CLIK
BOOM SHAKKA
BABOP
BABOP
BOP
?!
BOOM BAP
BABOP
SHAKKA BOOM
?!

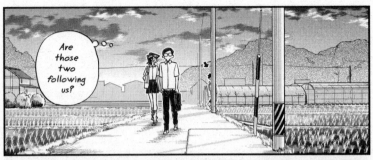

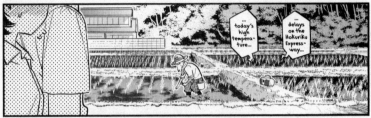

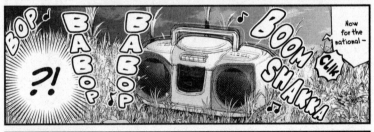

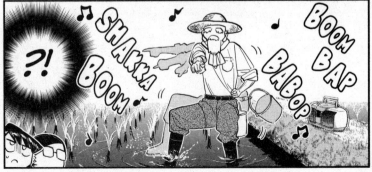

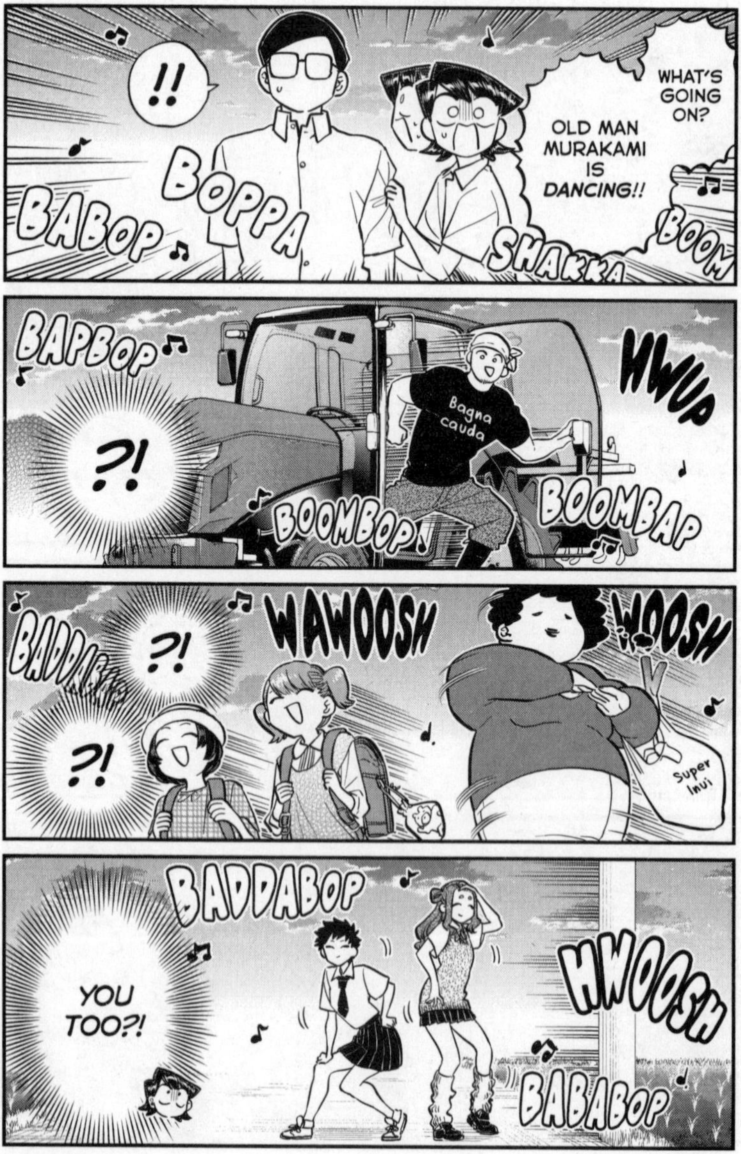
WHAT'S GOING ON?
OLD MAN MURAKAMI IS DANCING!!
BOOM
SHAKKA
!!
BOPPA
BABOP
HWUP
BOOMBAP
Bagna cauda
BOOMBOP
?!
BAPBOP
WOOSH
Super Inui
WAWOOSH
?!
?!
HWOOSH
BABABOP
BADDABOP
YOU TOO?!

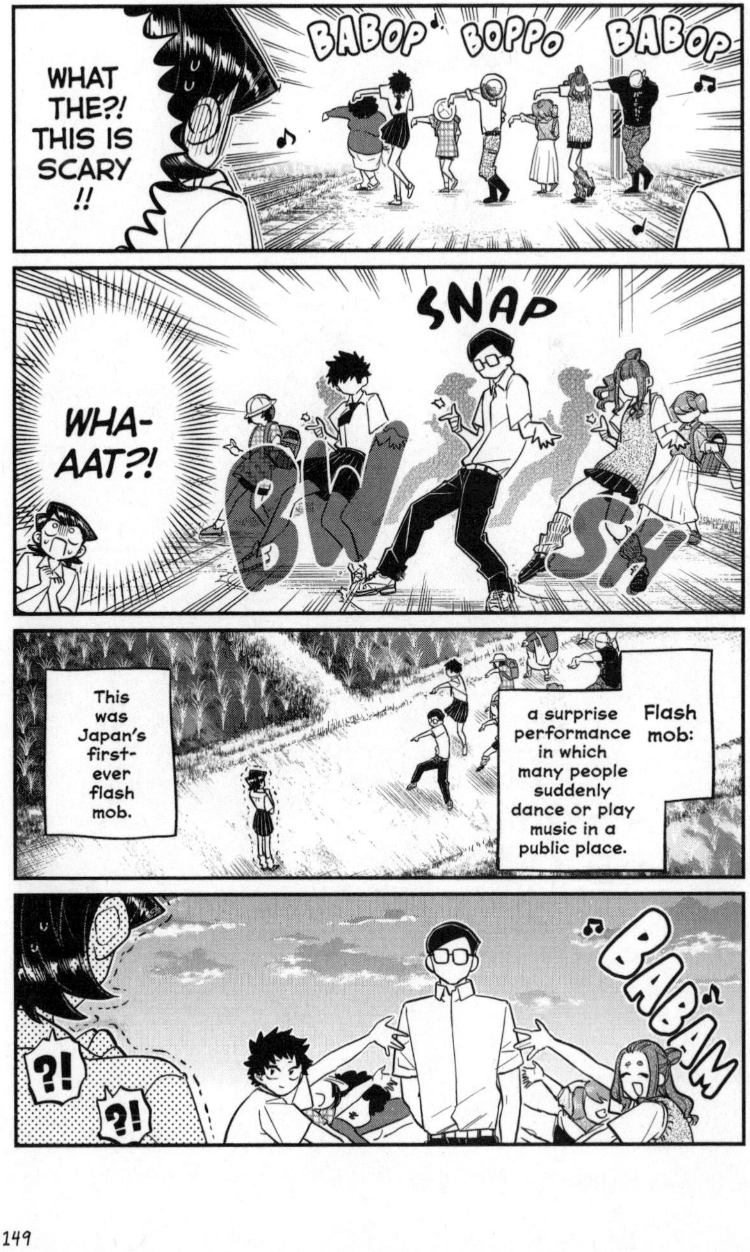
BABOP
BOPPO
BABOP
WHAT THE?! THIS IS SCARY!!
SNAP
WHA-AAT?!
Flash mob: a surprise performance in which many people suddenly dance or play music in a public place.
This was Japan's first-ever flash mob.
BABAM
?!
?!

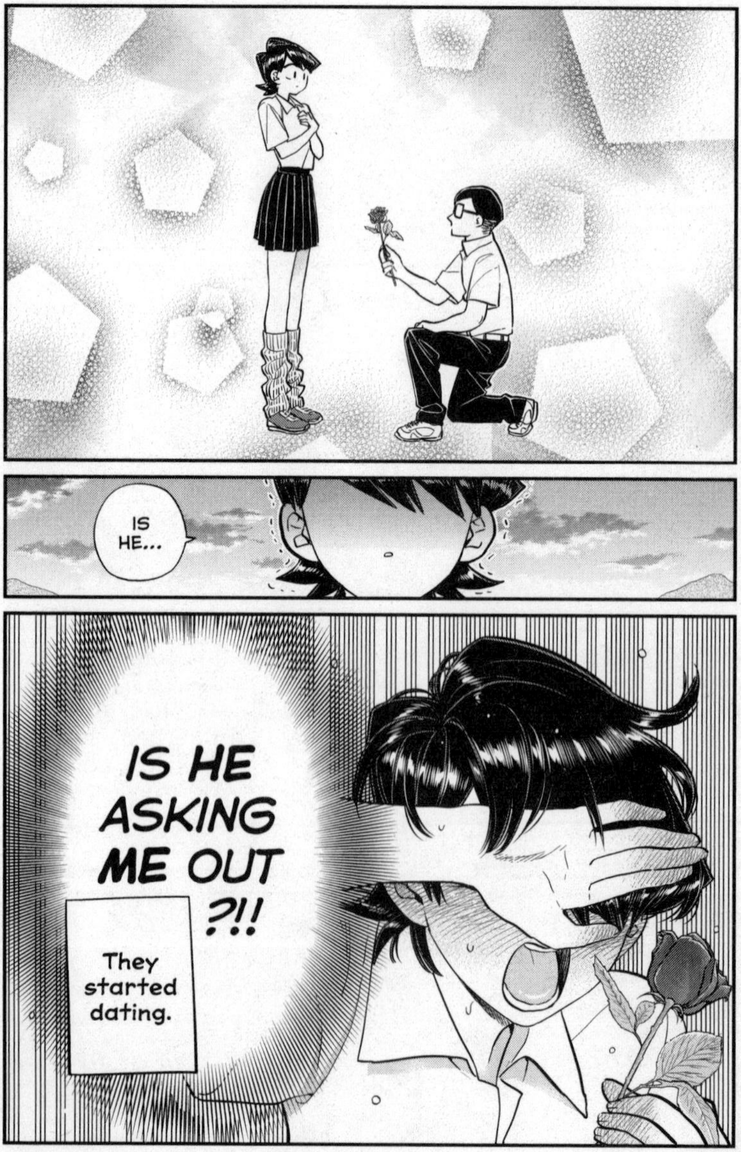
IS HE...
IS HE ASKING ME OUT ?!!
They started dating.

Communication 153 — The End

Komi Can't Communicate

One day in June...
2 – 3
CHATTER
CHATTER
CHATTER
Ah ha ha!
And then...
Huh?!
Wa ha ha!
...
Ha ha ha!
Nakanaka still doesn't fit in!!
Gimme a break!

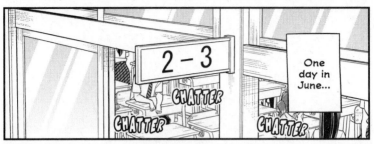

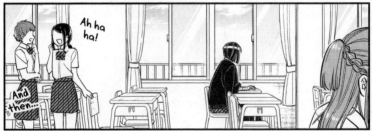

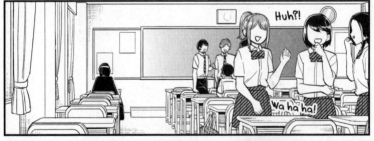

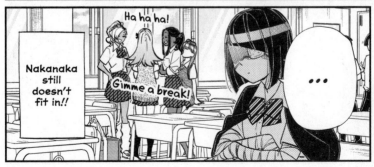

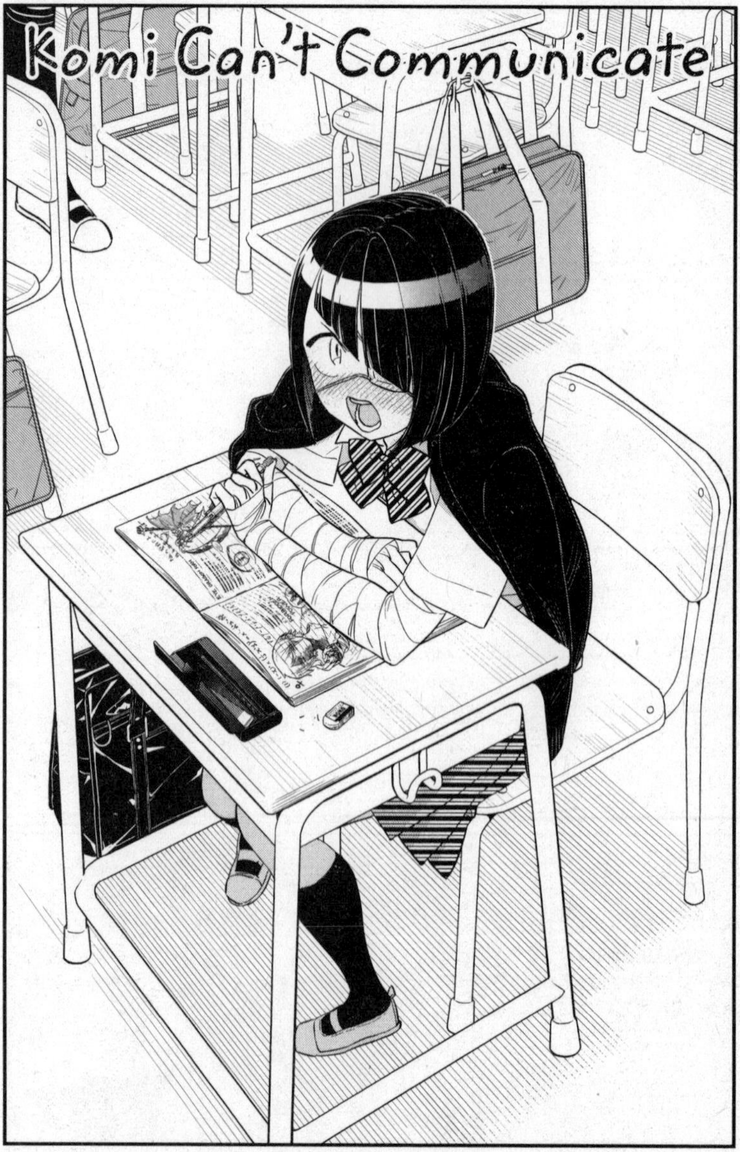
Komi Can't Communicate

Communication 154: Nakanaka's Story

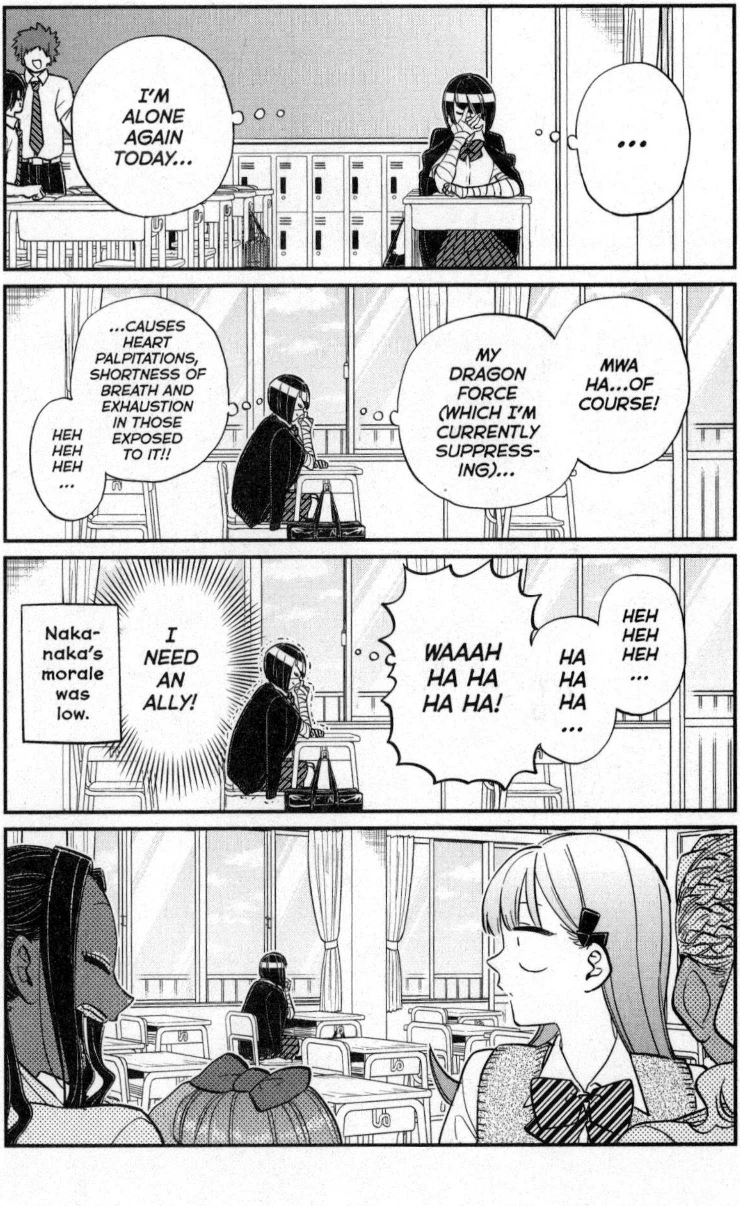
...
I'M ALONE AGAIN TODAY...
MWA HA...OF COURSE!
MY DRAGON FORCE (WHICH I'M CURRENTLY SUPPRESS-ING)...
...CAUSES HEART PALPITATIONS, SHORTNESS OF BREATH AND EXHAUSTION IN THOSE EXPOSED TO IT!!
HEH HEH HEH ...
HEH HEH HEH ...
HA HA HA ...
WAAAH HA HA HA HA!
I NEED AN ALLY!
Naka-naka's morale was low.

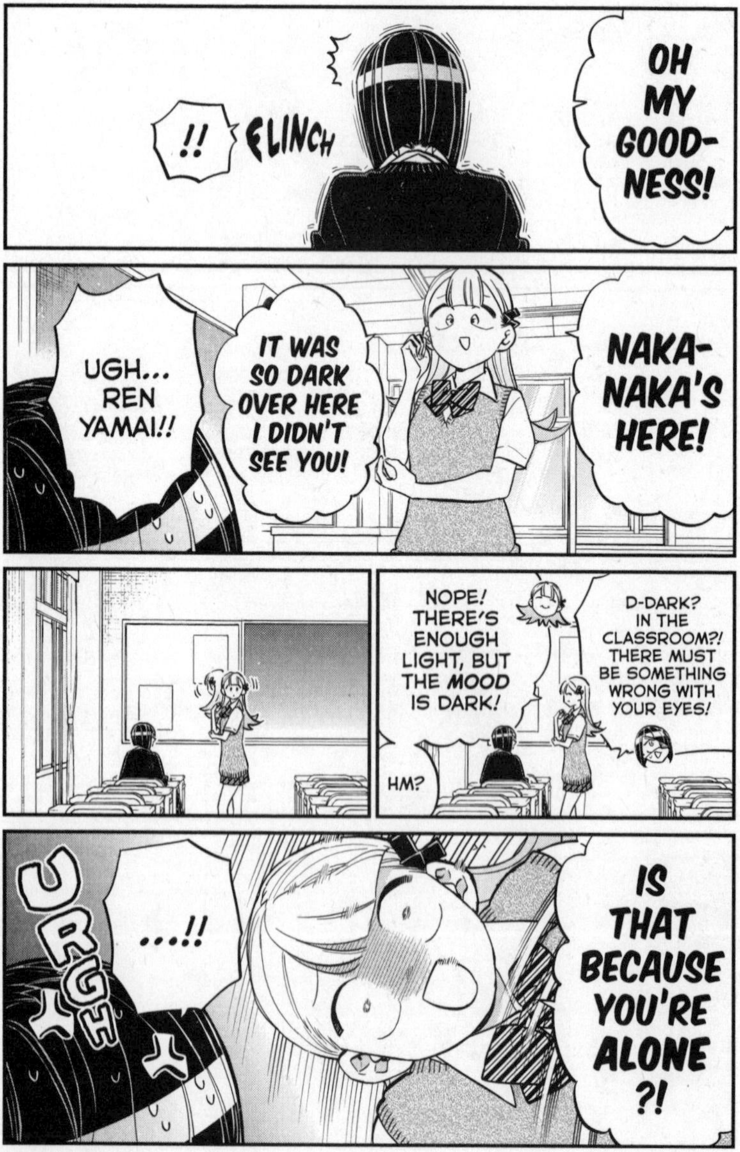
OH MY GOOD-NESS!
!!
FLINCH
NAKA-NAKA'S HERE!
IT WAS SO DARK OVER HERE I DIDN'T SEE YOU!
UGH... REN YAMAI!!
D-DARK? IN THE CLASSROOM?! THERE MUST BE SOMETHING WRONG WITH YOUR EYES!
NOPE! THERE'S ENOUGH LIGHT, BUT THE *MOOD* IS DARK!
HM?
IS THAT BECAUSE YOU'RE ALONE ?!
...!!
URGH

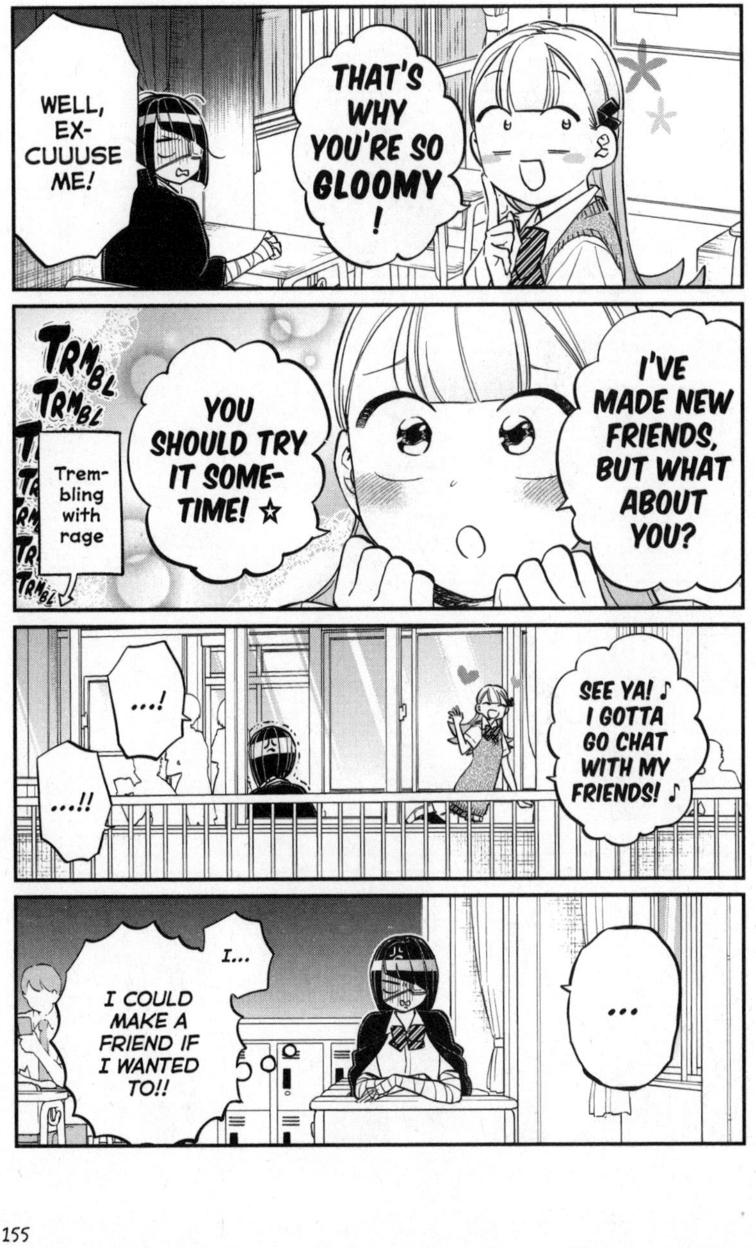
THAT'S WHY YOU'RE SO GLOOMY!
WELL, EX-CUUUSE ME!
I'VE MADE NEW FRIENDS, BUT WHAT ABOUT YOU?
YOU SHOULD TRY IT SOMETIME! ☆
TRMBL TRMBL
Trembling with rage
TRMBL
SEE YA! ♪ I GOTTA GO CHAT WITH MY FRIENDS! ♪
...!
...!!
...
I...
I COULD MAKE A FRIEND IF I WANTED TO!!

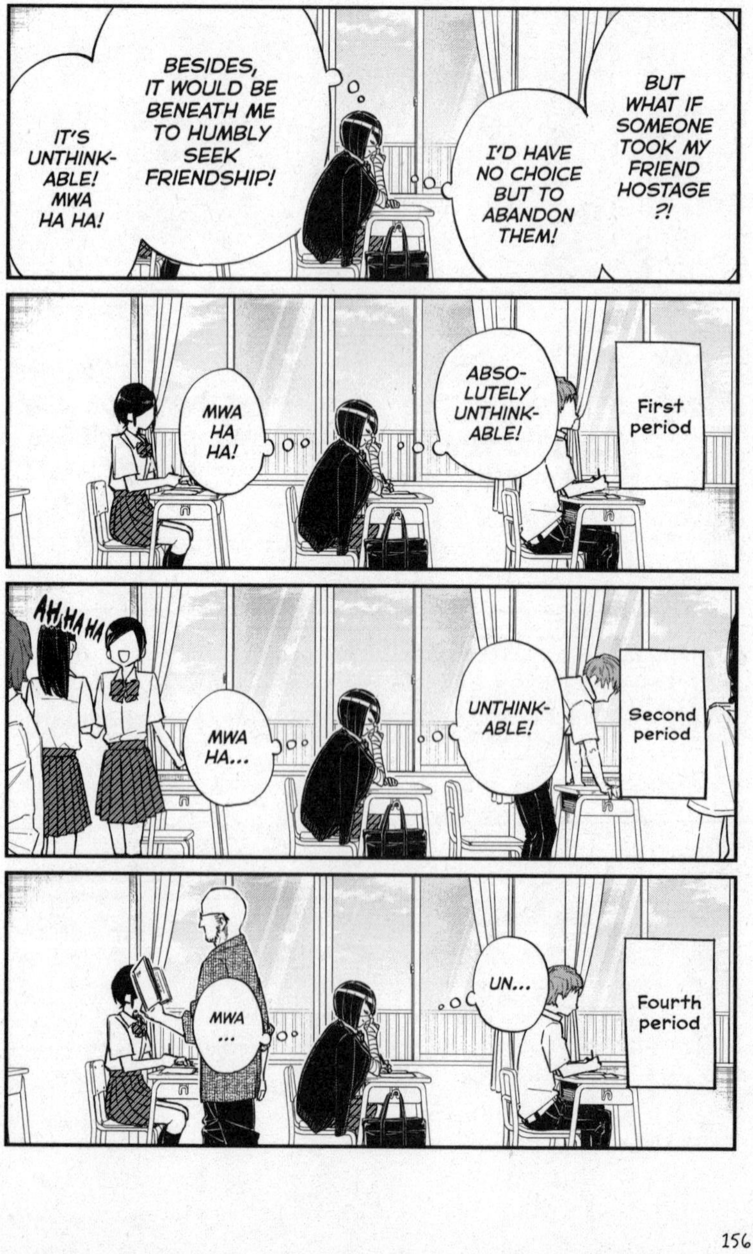
BUT WHAT IF SOMEONE TOOK MY FRIEND HOSTAGE?!
I'D HAVE NO CHOICE BUT TO ABANDON THEM!
BESIDES, IT WOULD BE BENEATH ME TO HUMBLY SEEK FRIENDSHIP!
IT'S UNTHINK-ABLE! MWA HA HA!
First period
ABSO-LUTELY UNTHINK-ABLE!
MWA HA HA!
Second period
UNTHINK-ABLE!
MWA HA...
AH HA HA
Fourth period
UN...
MWA ...

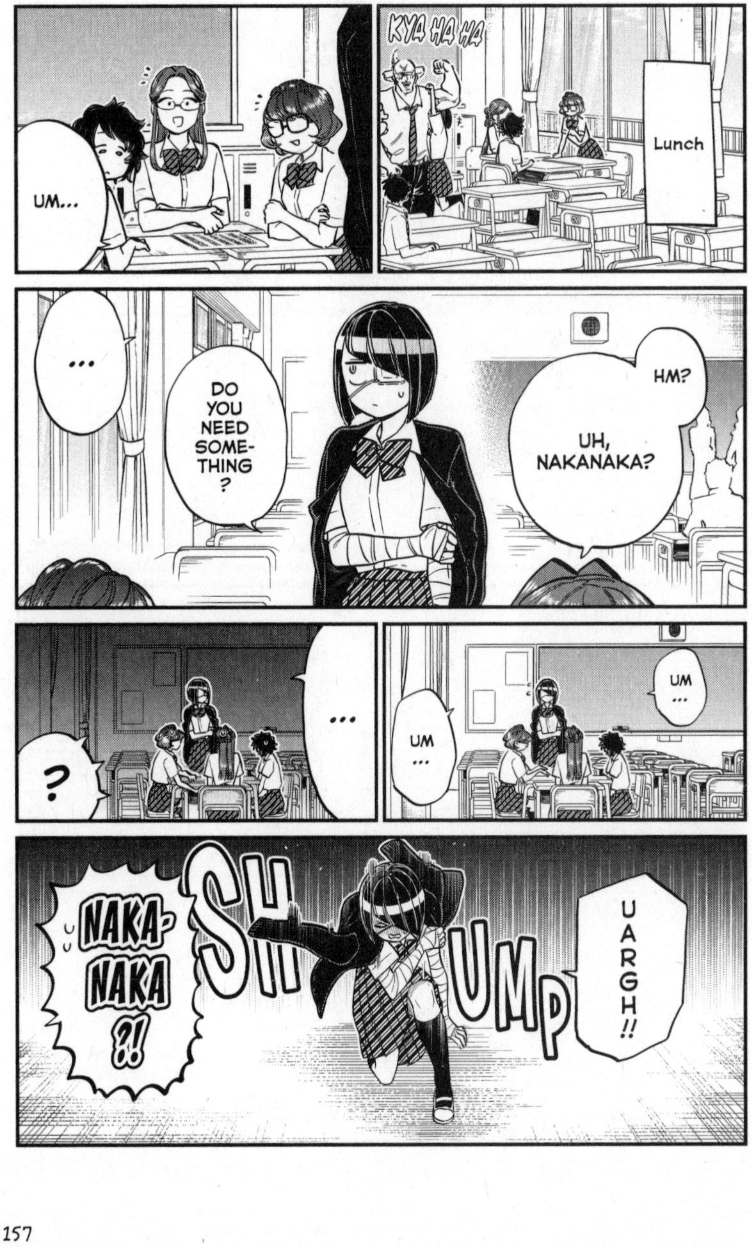

Lunch
KYA HA HA
UM...
HM?
UH, NAKANAKA?
DO YOU NEED SOMETHING?
...
UM...
UM...
...
?
UARGH!!
SHUMP
NAKA-NAKA?!

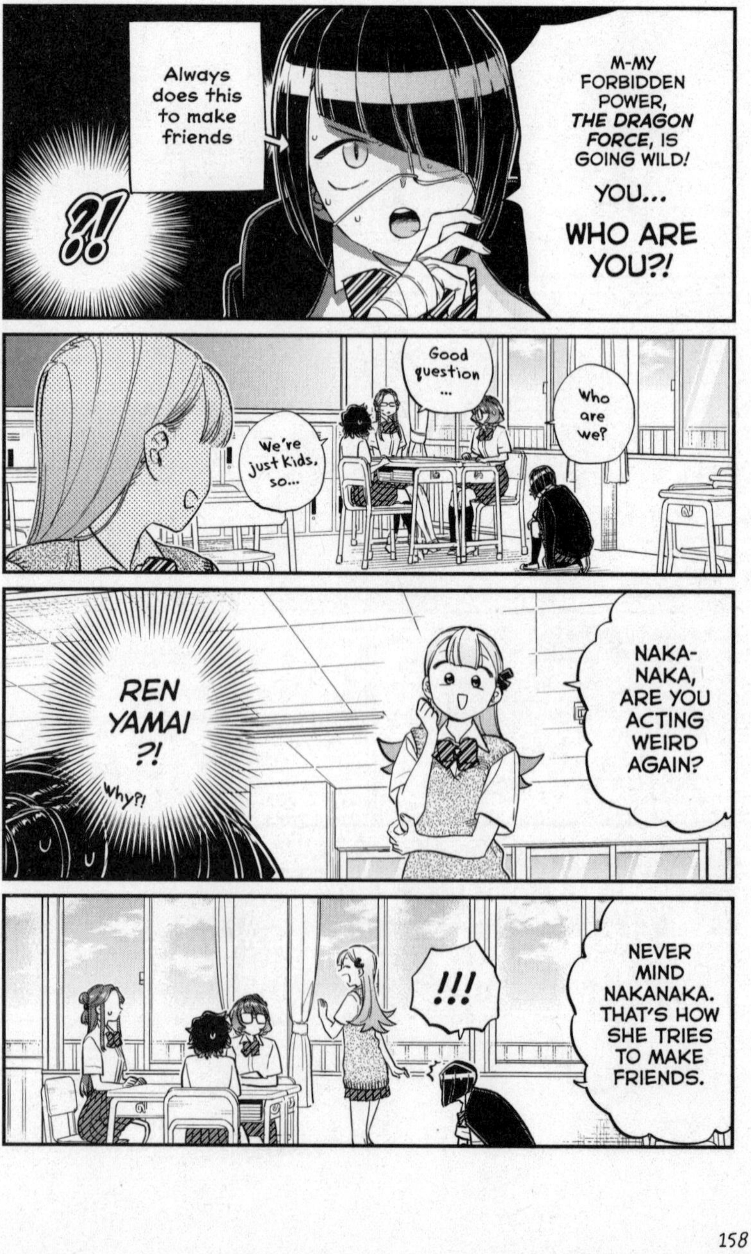
M-MY FORBIDDEN POWER, THE DRAGON FORCE, IS GOING WILD!
YOU...
WHO ARE YOU?!
Always does this to make friends
?!
Who are we?
Good question...
We're just kids, so...
NAKA-NAKA, ARE YOU ACTING WEIRD AGAIN?
REN YAMAI ?!
Why?!
NEVER MIND NAKANAKA. THAT'S HOW SHE TRIES TO MAKE FRIENDS.
!!!

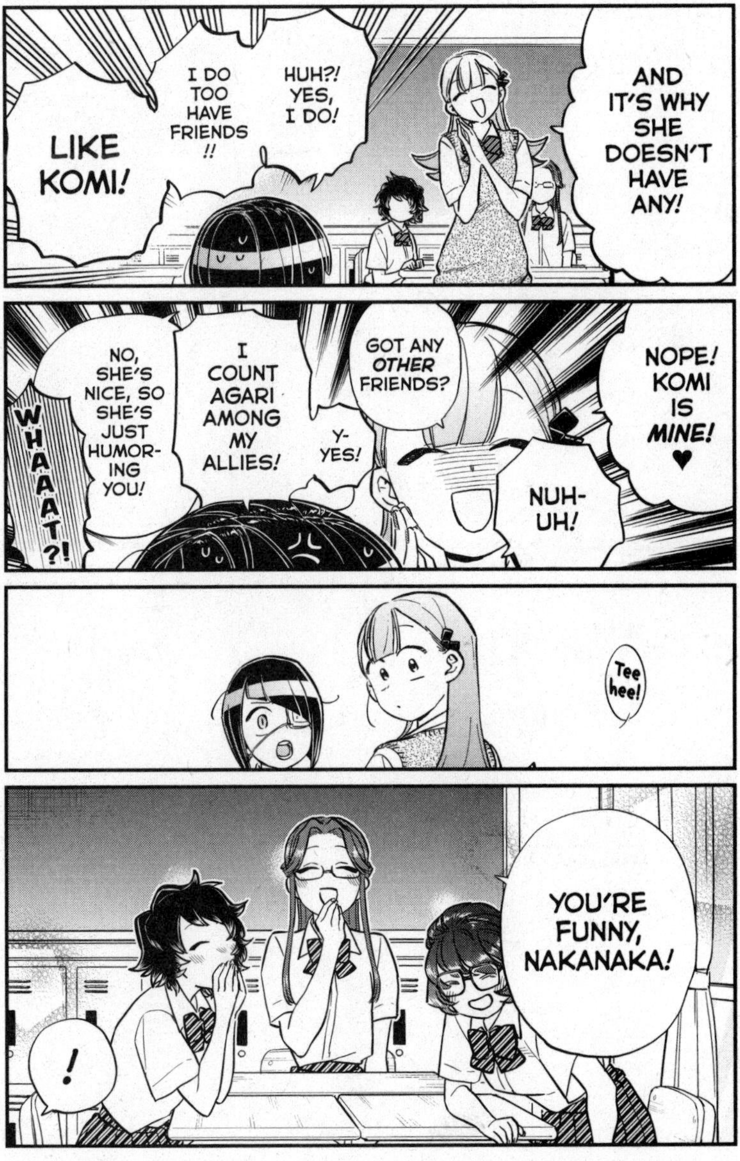
AND IT'S WHY SHE DOESN'T HAVE ANY!
HUH?! YES, I DO!
I DO TOO HAVE FRIENDS!!
LIKE KOMI!
NOPE! KOMI IS MINE! ♥
NUH-UH!
GOT ANY OTHER FRIENDS?
Y-YES!
I COUNT AGARI AMONG MY ALLIES!
NO, SHE'S NICE, SO SHE'S JUST HUMORING YOU!
WHAAAAT?!
Tee hee!
YOU'RE FUNNY, NAKANAKA!
!

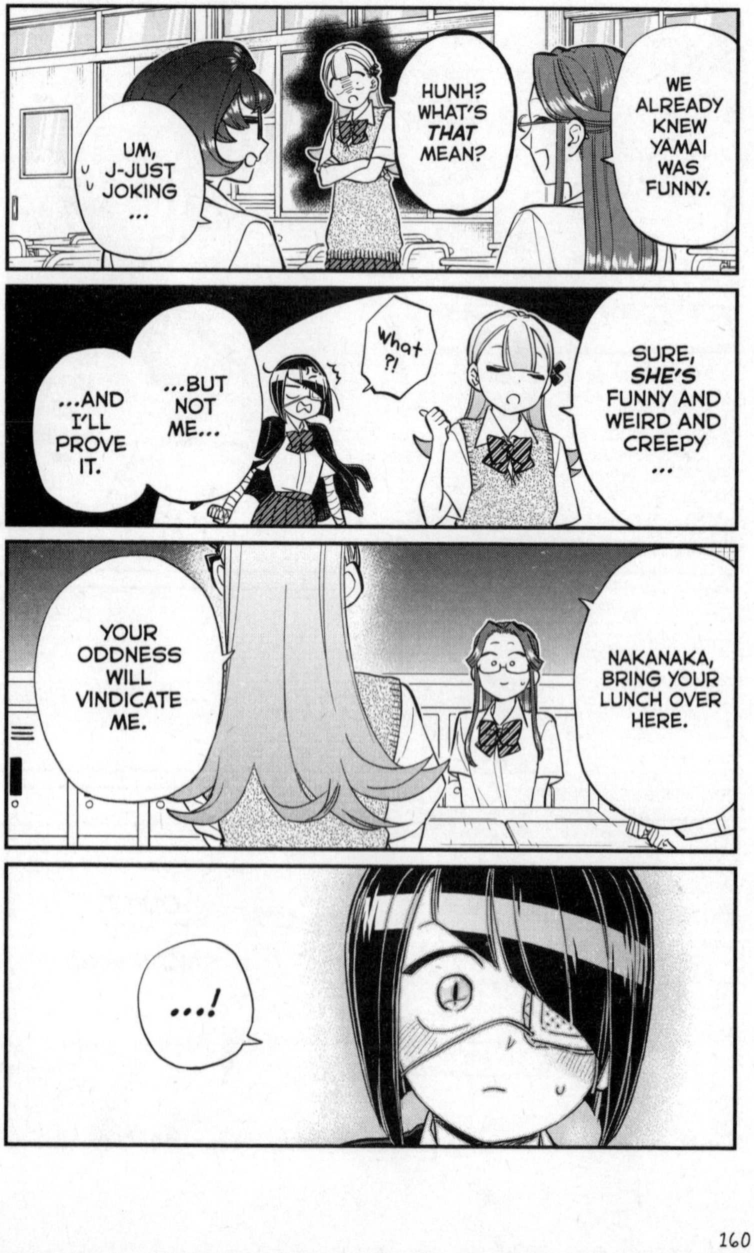
WE ALREADY KNEW YAMAI WAS FUNNY.
HUNH? WHAT'S *THAT* MEAN?
UM, J-JUST JOKING ...
SURE, *SHE'S* FUNNY AND WEIRD AND CREEPY ...
What ?!
...BUT NOT ME...
...AND I'LL PROVE IT.
NAKANAKA, BRING YOUR LUNCH OVER HERE.
YOUR ODDNESS WILL VINDICATE ME.
...!

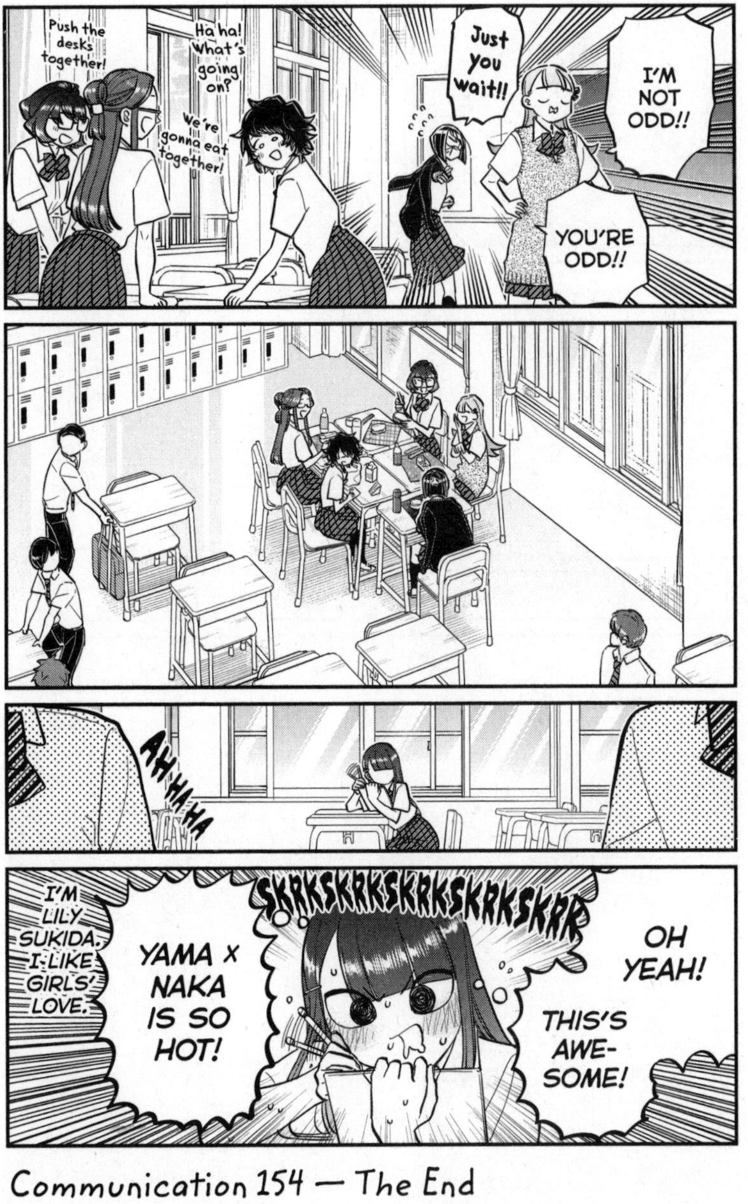
I'M NOT ODD!!
YOU'RE ODD!!
Just you wait!!
Ha ha! What's going on?
We're gonna eat together!
Push the desks together!
AH HA HA HA
OH YEAH!
THIS'S AWE-SOME!
SKRKSKRKSKRKSKRKSKRK
YAMA x NAKA IS SO HOT!
I'M LILY SUKIDA. I LIKE GIRLS' LOVE.

Communication 154 — The End

Komi Can't Communicate

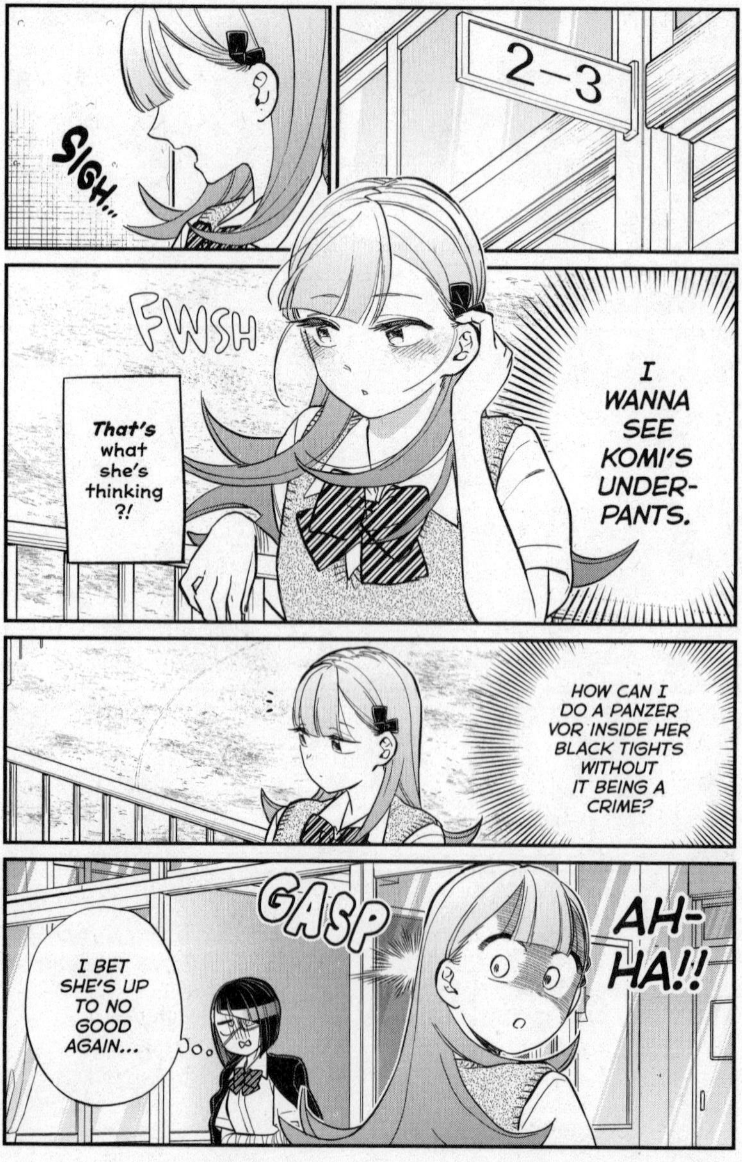
2-3
SIGH...
I WANNA SEE KOMI'S UNDER-PANTS.
FWSH
That's what she's thinking ?!
HOW CAN I DO A PANZER VOR INSIDE HER BLACK TIGHTS WITHOUT IT BEING A CRIME?
AH-HA!!
GASP
I BET SHE'S UP TO NO GOOD AGAIN...

Communication 155: Backward Flip

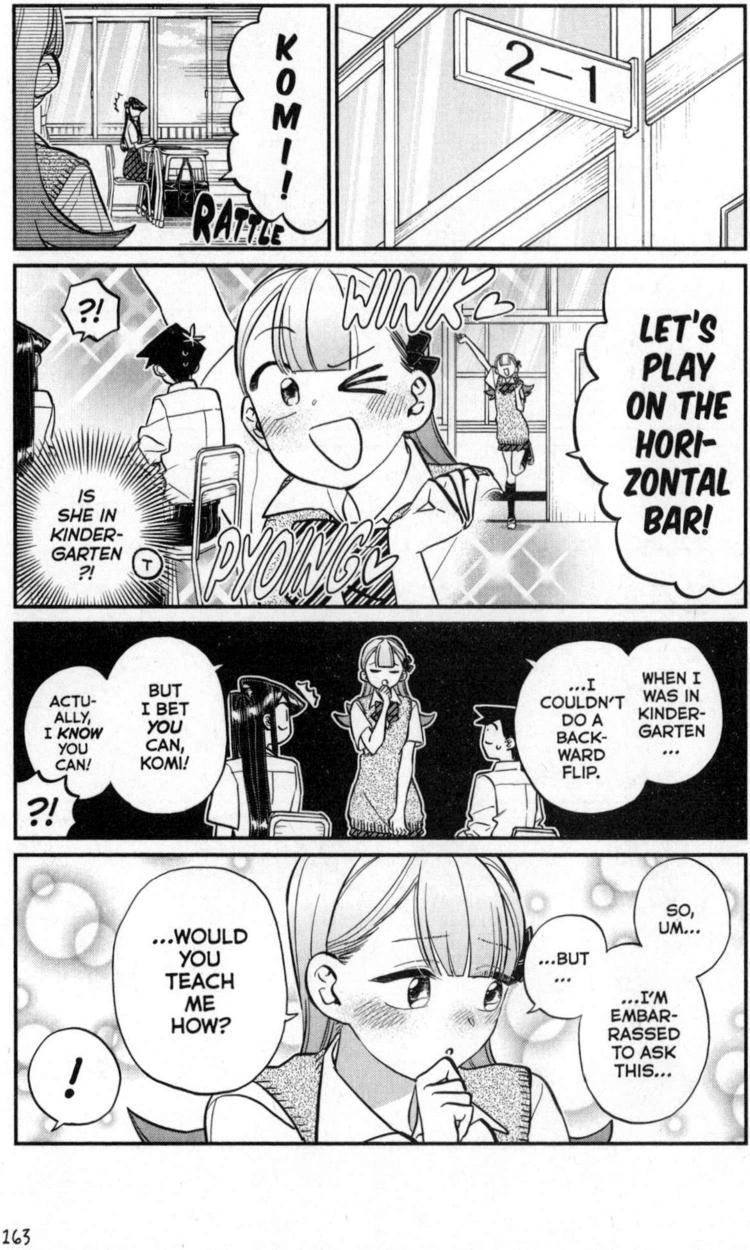
2-1
KOMI!
RATTLE
LET'S PLAY ON THE HORIZONTAL BAR!
WINK
PYONG
?!
IS SHE IN KINDERGARTEN?!
T
WHEN I WAS IN KINDERGARTEN...
...I COULDN'T DO A BACKWARD FLIP.
BUT I BET YOU CAN, KOMI!
ACTUALLY, I KNOW YOU CAN!
?!
SO, UM...
...BUT...
...I'M EMBARRASSED TO ASK THIS...
...WOULD YOU TEACH ME HOW?
!

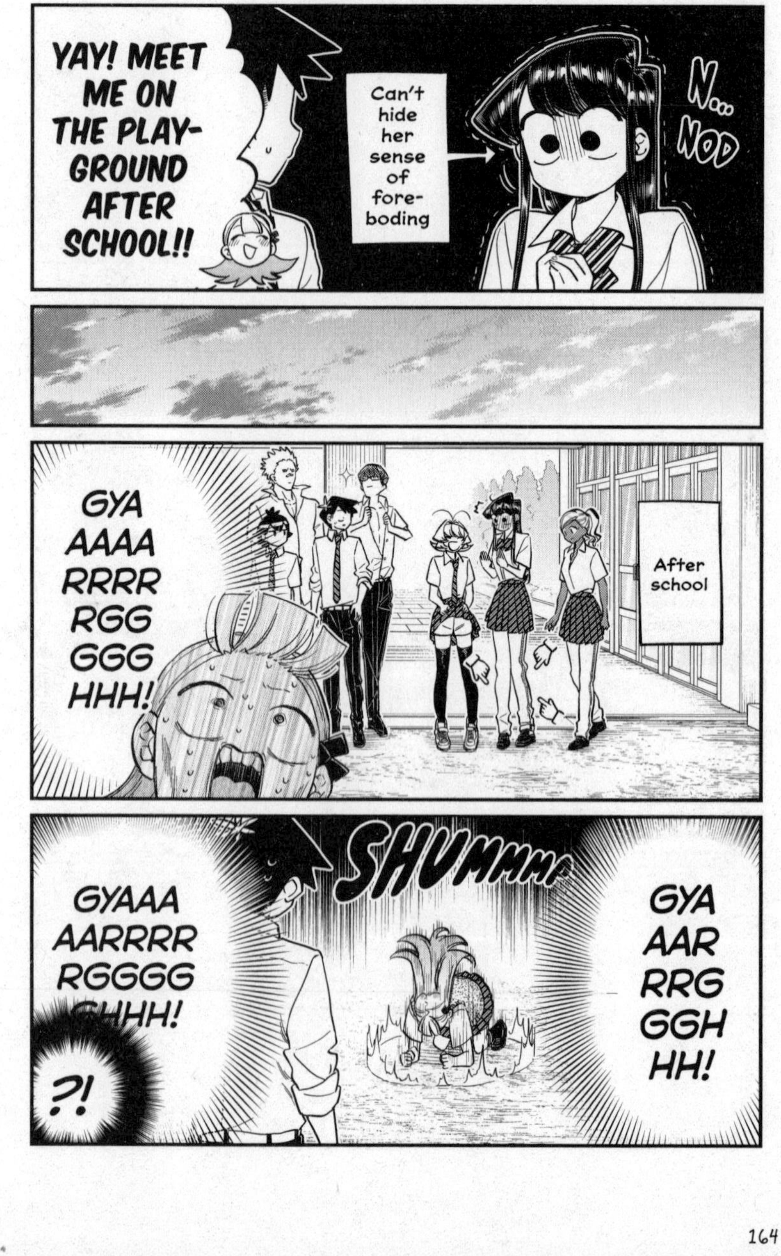
N... NOD
Can't hide her sense of foreboding
YAY! MEET ME ON THE PLAY-GROUND AFTER SCHOOL!!
After school
GYAAAAARRRRRGGGGGHHH!
GYAAARRRGGGHHH!
SHUMMMM
GYAAAAARRRRRGGGGGHHH!
?!

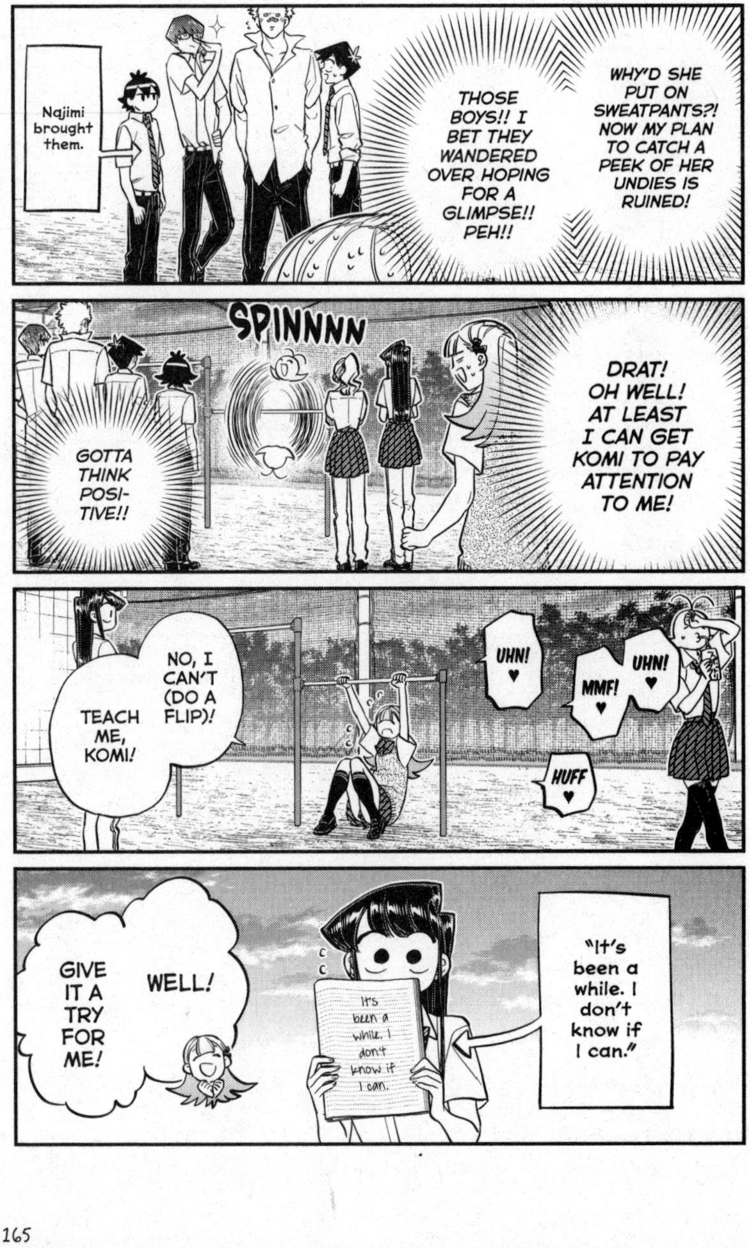
WHY'D SHE PUT ON SWEATPANTS?! NOW MY PLAN TO CATCH A PEEK OF HER UNDIES IS RUINED!
THOSE BOYS!! I BET THEY WANDERED OVER HOPING FOR A GLIMPSE!! PEH!!
Najimi brought them.
DRAT! OH WELL! AT LEAST I CAN GET KOMI TO PAY ATTENTION TO ME!
SPINNNNN
GOTTA THINK POSI-TIVE!!
UHN! ♥
UHN! ♥
MMF! ♥
HUFF ♥
NO, I CAN'T (DO A FLIP)!
TEACH ME, KOMI!
"It's been a while. I don't know if I can."
It's been a while. I don't know if I can.
WELL!
GIVE IT A TRY FOR ME!

Komi's Backwards Flip

TOMP
WOOOOOW!
WHOOOOOO AAA
FWEET
CLAP
CLAP CLAP
CLAP
CLAP
CLAP
CLAP
CLAP
?!
CLAP

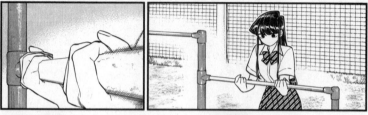

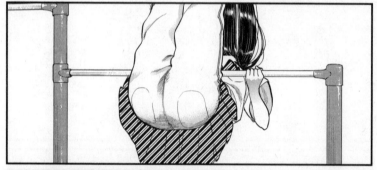

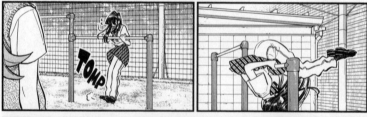

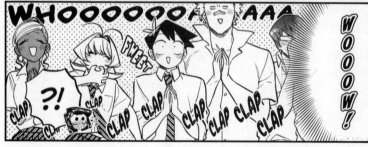

Komi's Backwards Flip: Yamai's Gaze

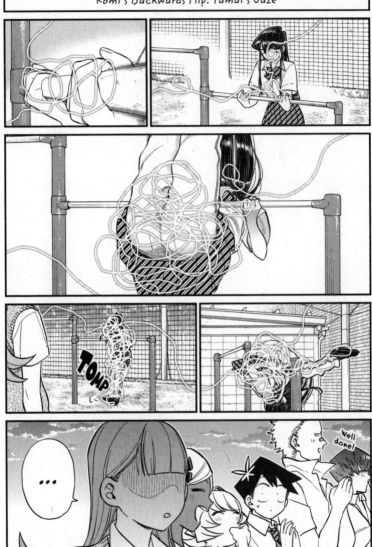

Well done!

···

TOMP

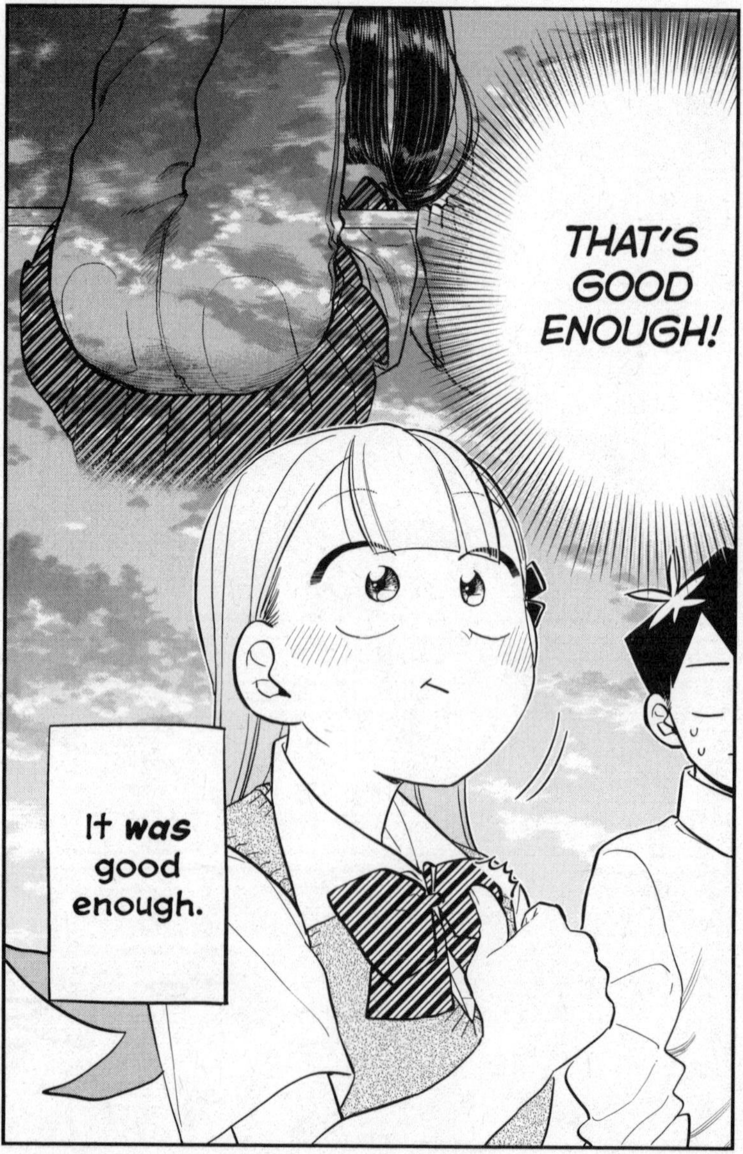
THAT'S GOOD ENOUGH!
It *was* good enough.

Communication 155 — The End

Komi Can't Communicate

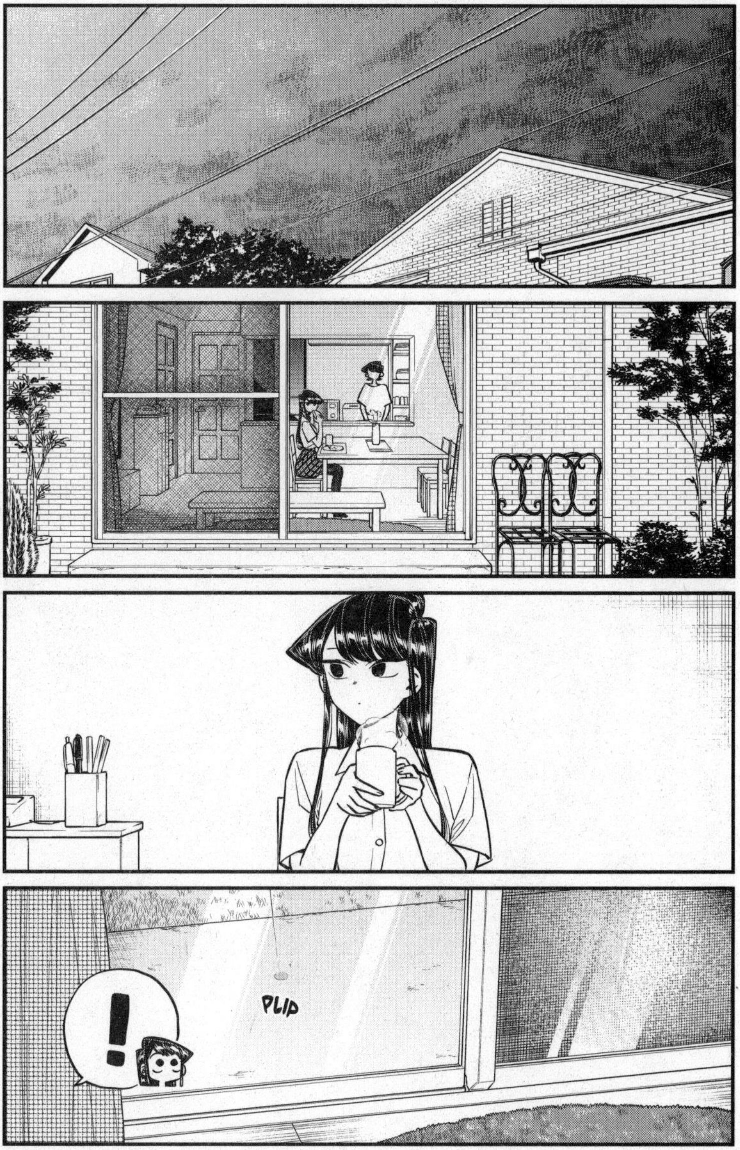

!
PLIP

Communication 156: Rainy Season

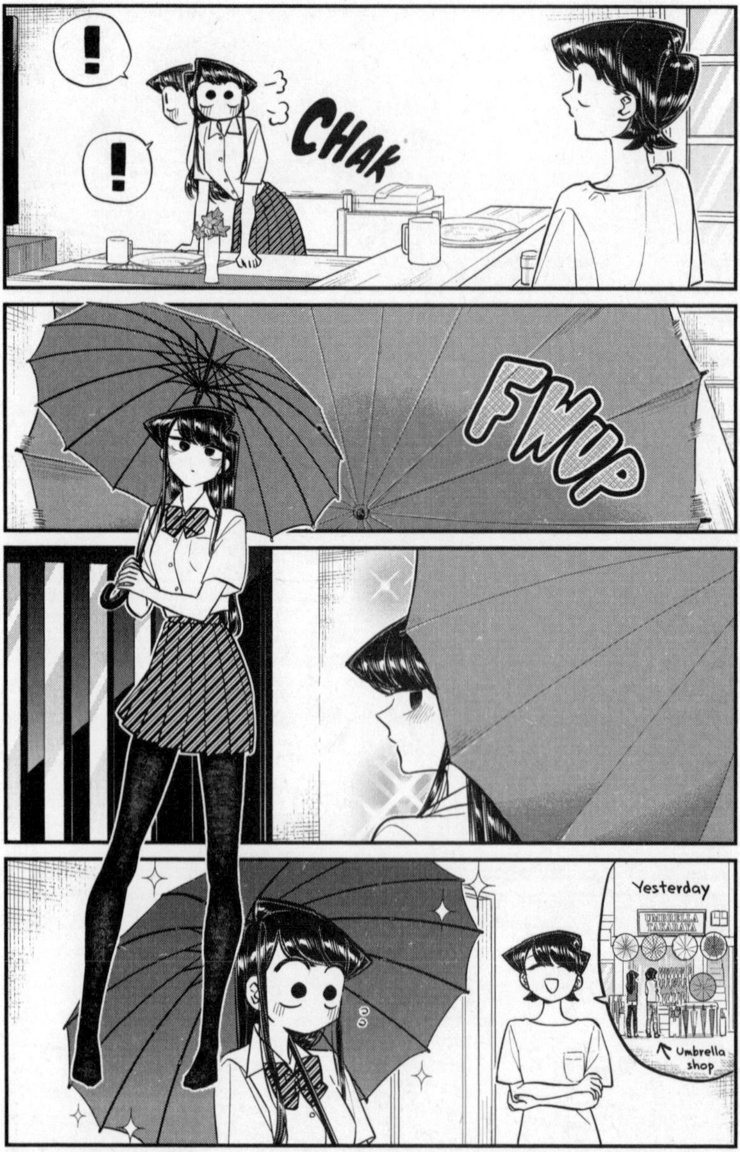
CHAK
!
!
FWUP
Yesterday
UMBRELLA TAKARAYA
Umbrella shop

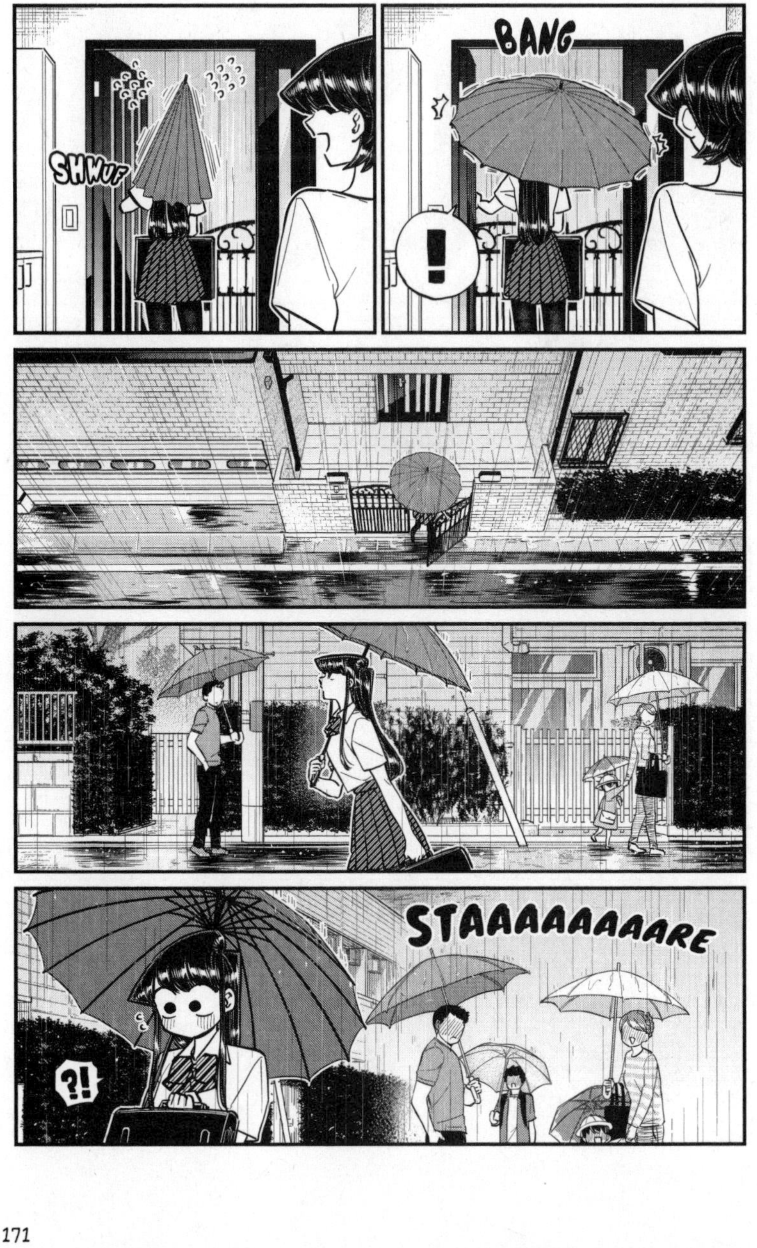
BANG
!
SHWUF
STAAAAAAAARE
?!

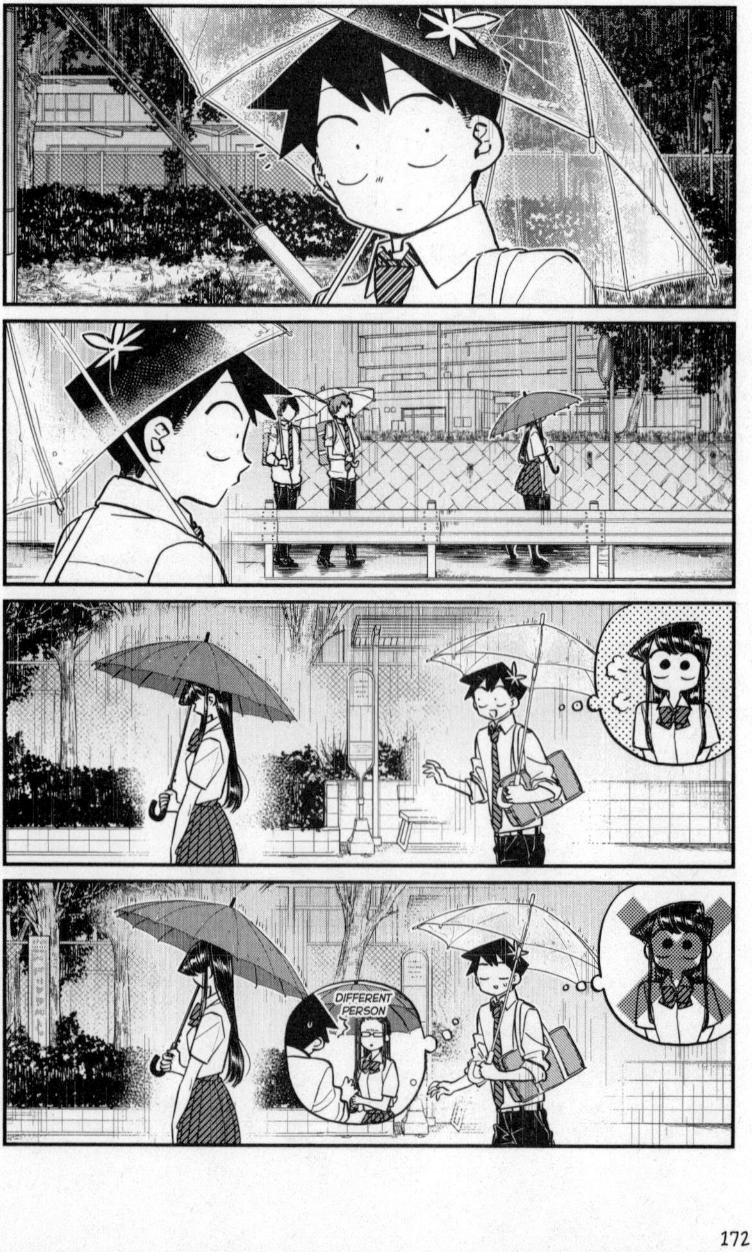
DIFFERENT PERSON

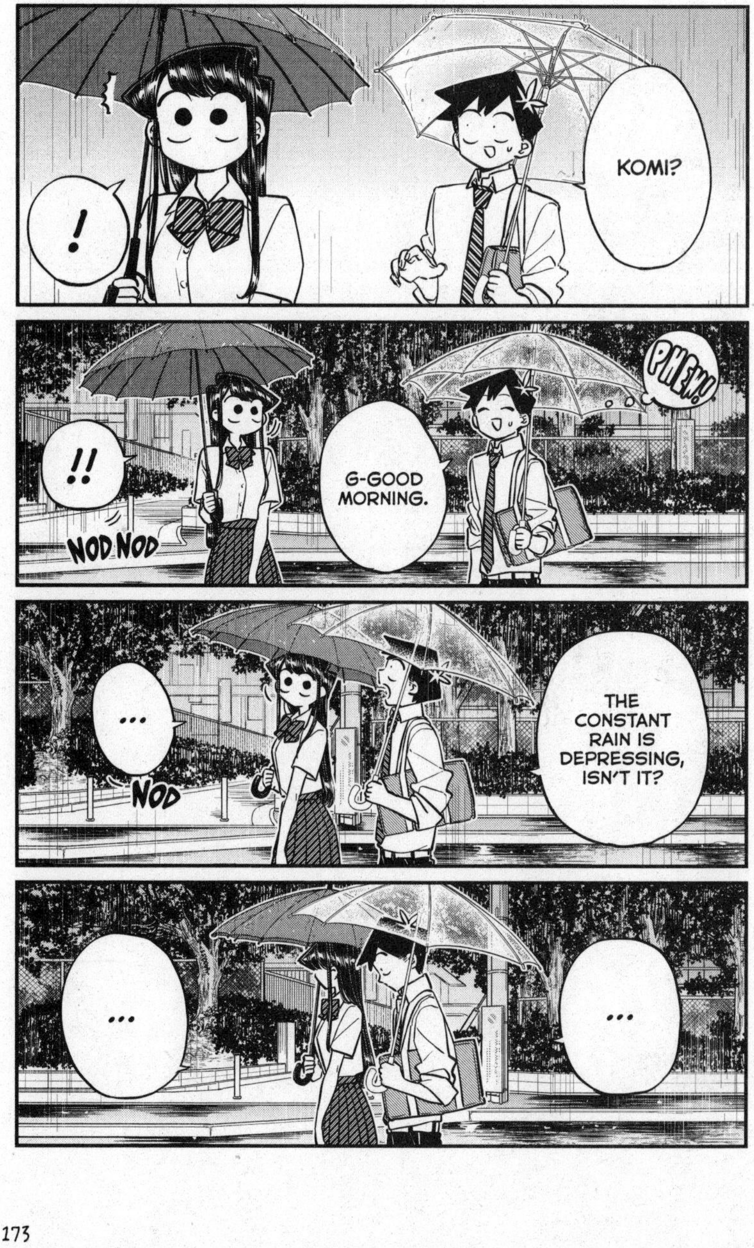
KOMI?
!
PHEW!
G-GOOD MORNING.
!!
NOD NOD
THE CONSTANT RAIN IS DEPRESSING, ISN'T IT?
...
NOD
...
...

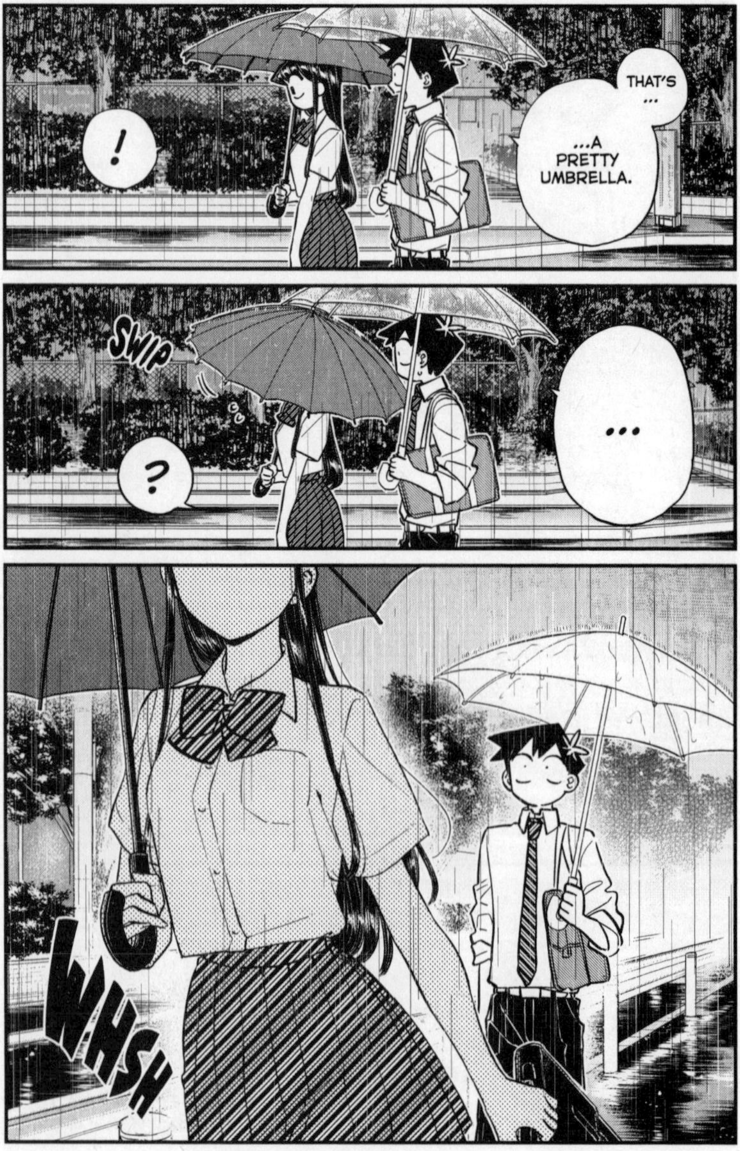
THAT'S ...
...A PRETTY UMBRELLA.
!
...
SWIP
?
WHSH

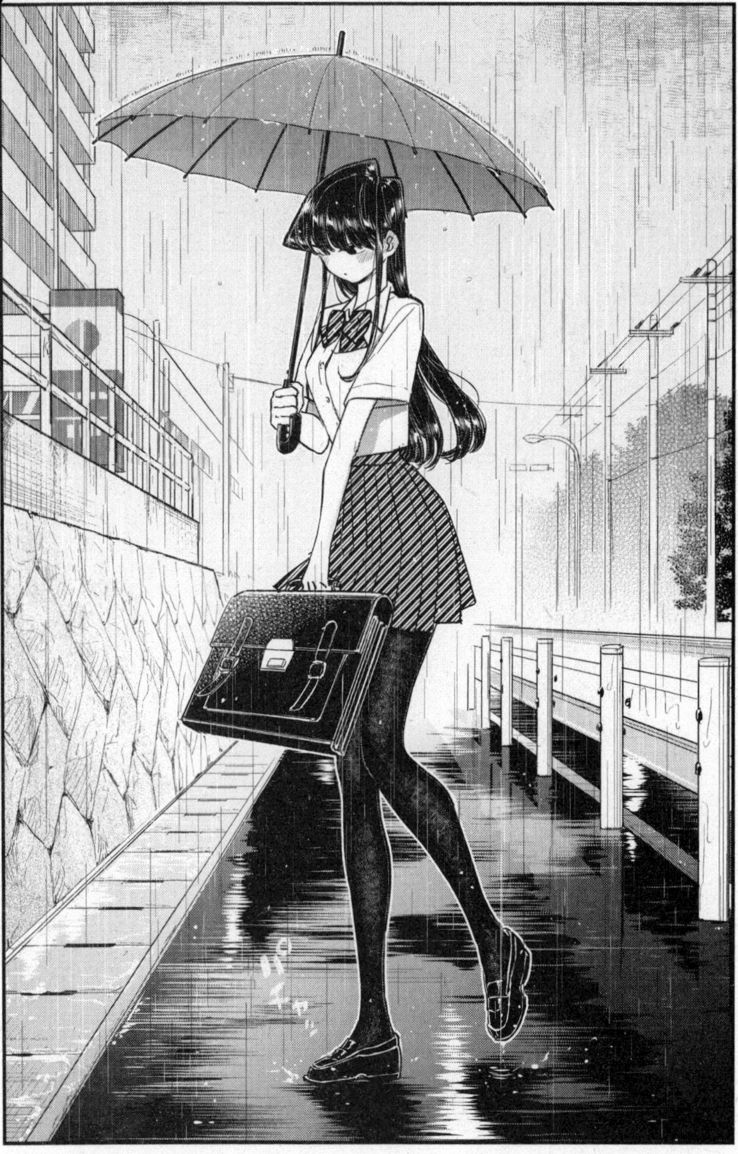
パチャッ

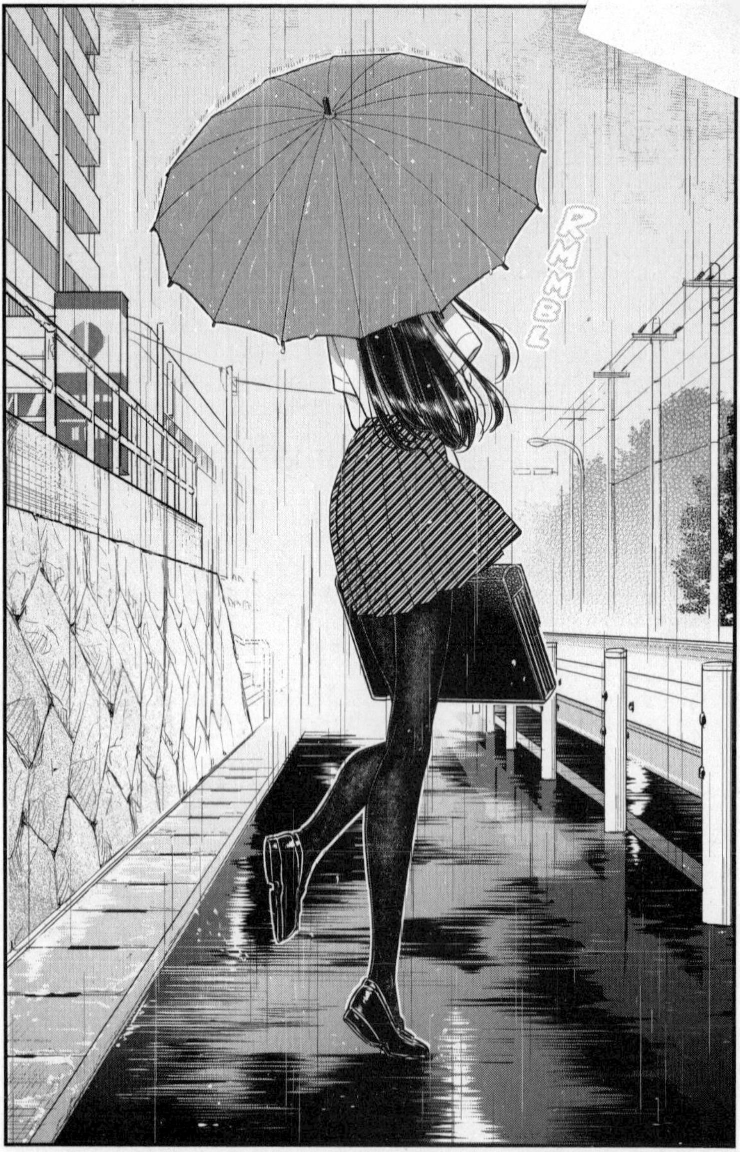
RMMMBL

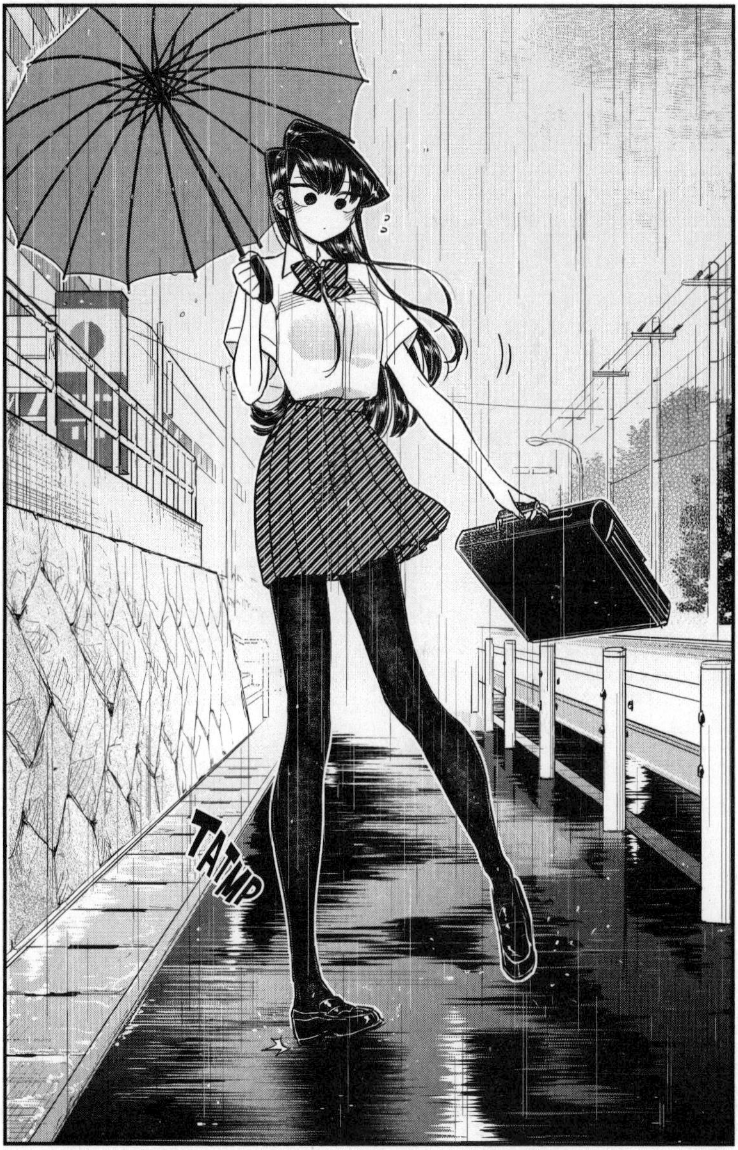
TATMP

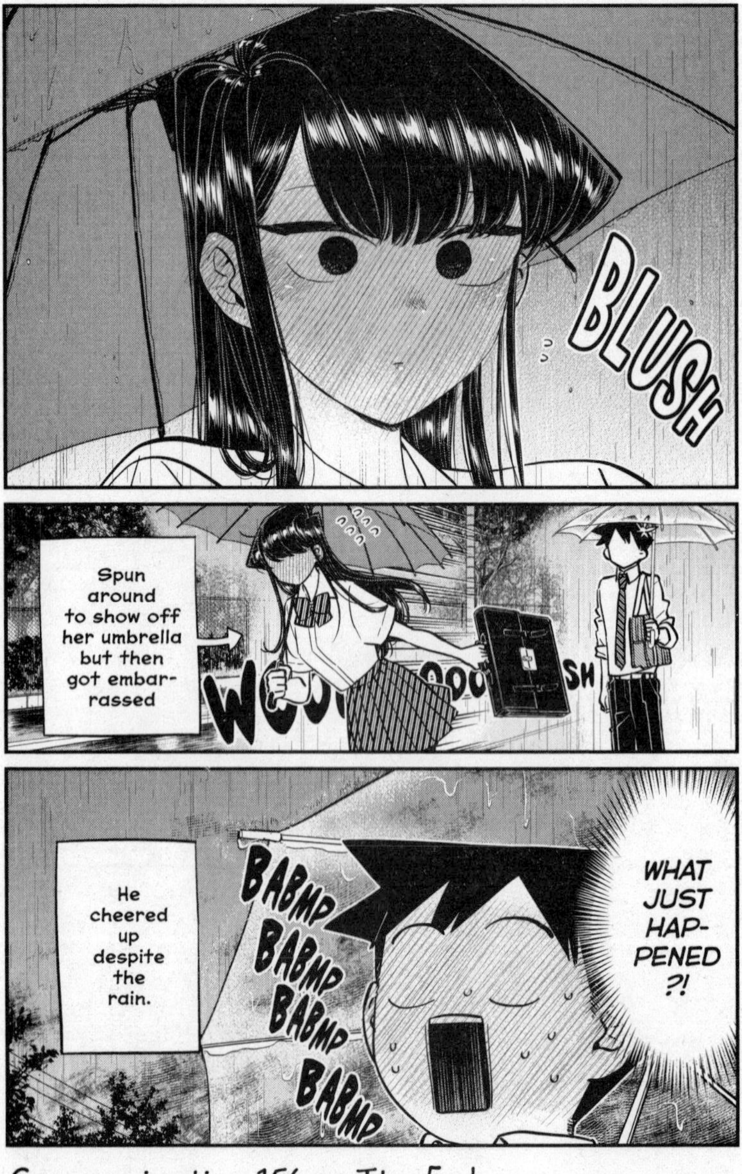
BLUSH
Spun around to show off her umbrella but then got embarrassed
WHAT JUST HAP-PENED?!
BABMP BABMP BABMP BABMP BABMP
He cheered up despite the rain.

Communication 156 — The End

Komi Can't Communicate

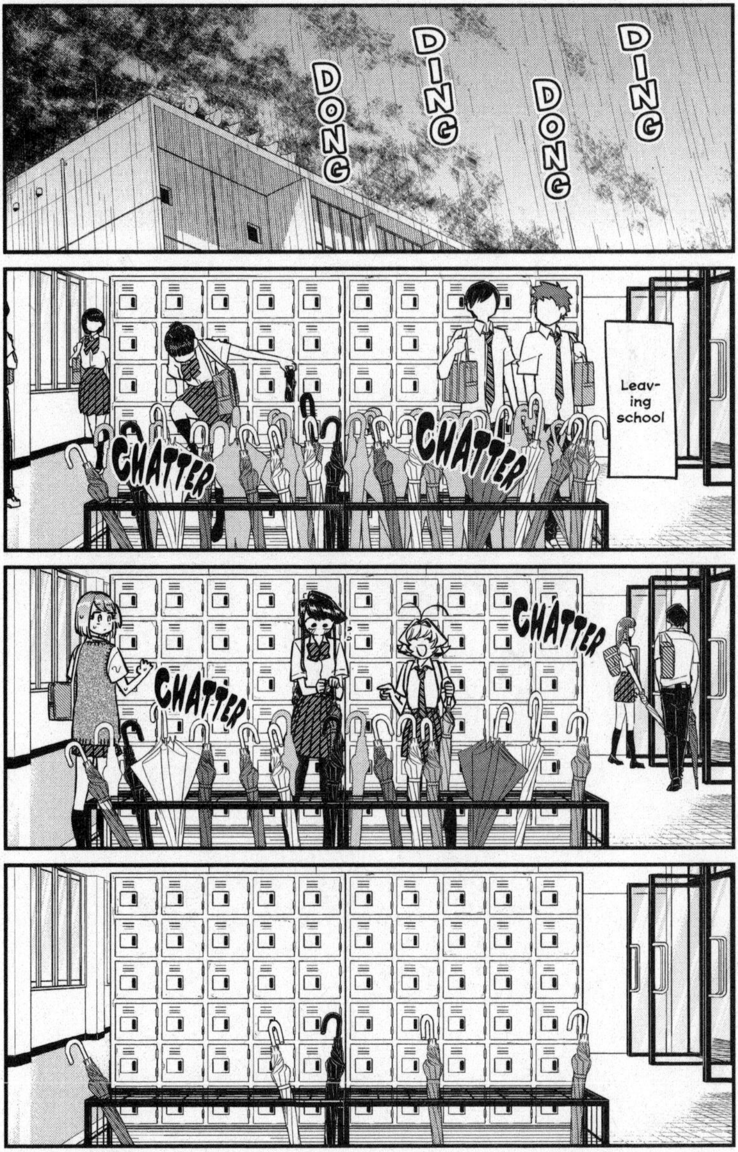
DING
DONG
DING
DONG
Leav-ing school
CHATTER
CHATTER
CHATTER
CHATTER

Communication 157: Rainy Season, Part 2

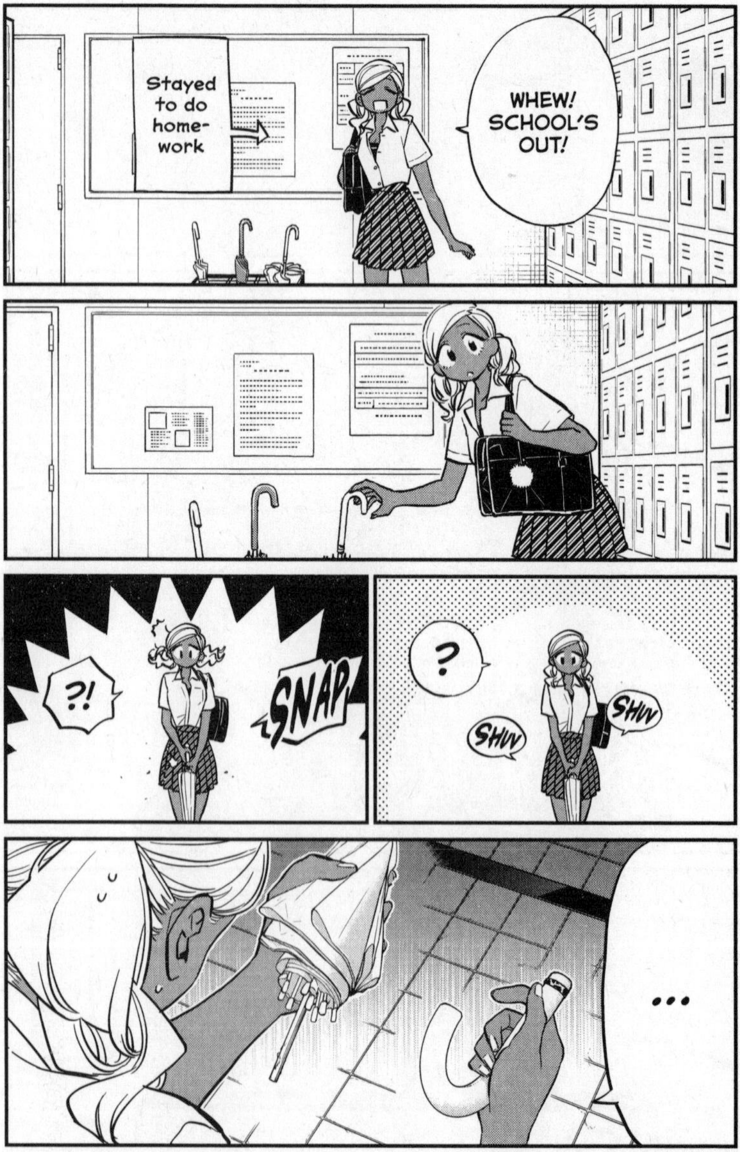
WHEW! SCHOOL'S OUT!
Stayed to do home-work
?
SHUV
SHUV
SNAP
?!
...

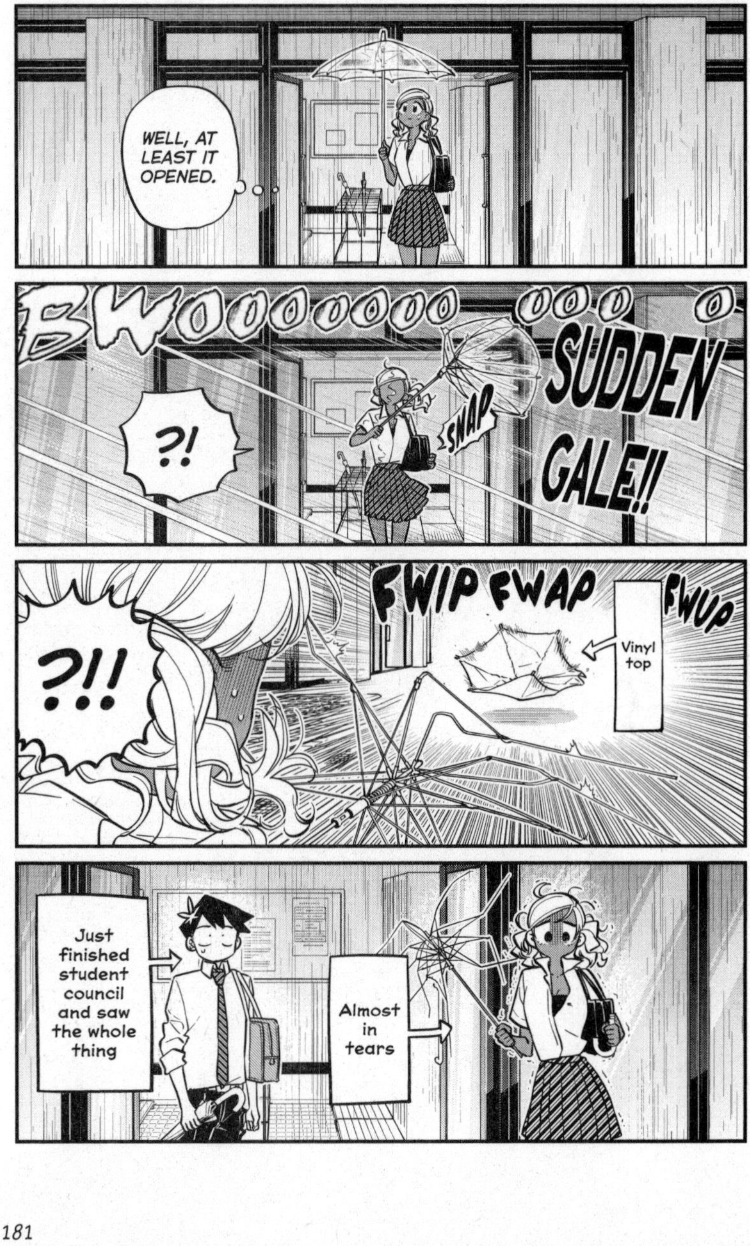
WELL, AT LEAST IT OPENED.
BWOOOOOOO OOO O
SUDDEN GALE!!
SNAP
?!
FWUP
FWIP FWAP
Vinyl top
?!!
Almost in tears
Just finished student council and saw the whole thing

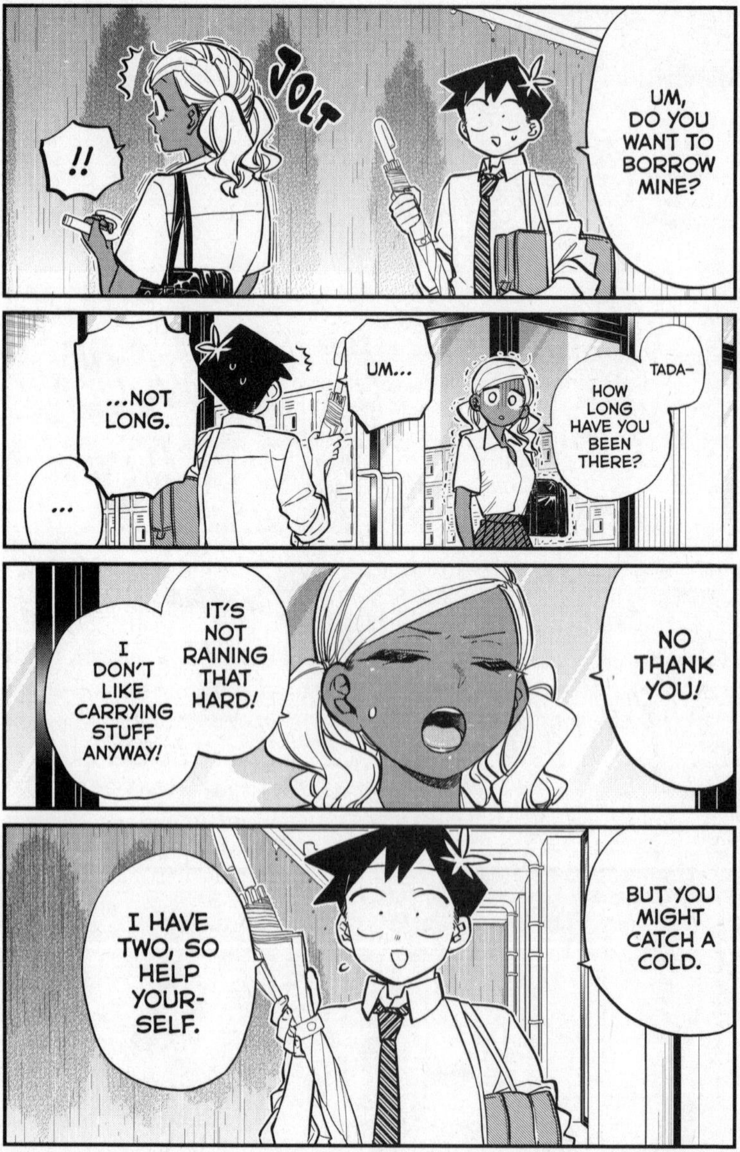
UM, DO YOU WANT TO BORROW MINE?
JOLT
!!
TADA—
HOW LONG HAVE YOU BEEN THERE?
UM...
...NOT LONG.
...
NO THANK YOU!
IT'S NOT RAINING THAT HARD!
I DON'T LIKE CARRYING STUFF ANYWAY!
BUT YOU MIGHT CATCH A COLD.
I HAVE TWO, SO HELP YOUR-SELF.

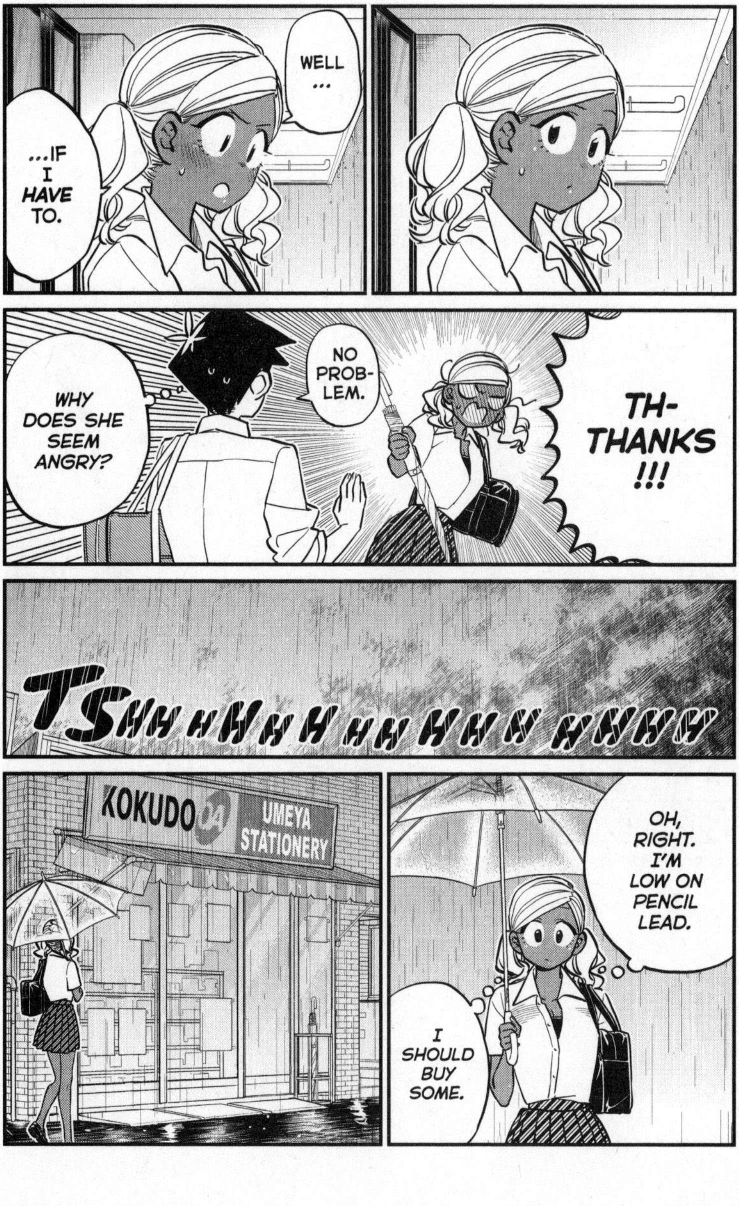
WELL ...
...IF I HAVE TO.
TH-THANKS!!!
NO PROB-LEM.
WHY DOES SHE SEEM ANGRY?
TSHHHHHHHHHHHHHHHHHHH
OH, RIGHT. I'M LOW ON PENCIL LEAD.
I SHOULD BUY SOME.
KOKUDO 04
UMEYA STATIONERY

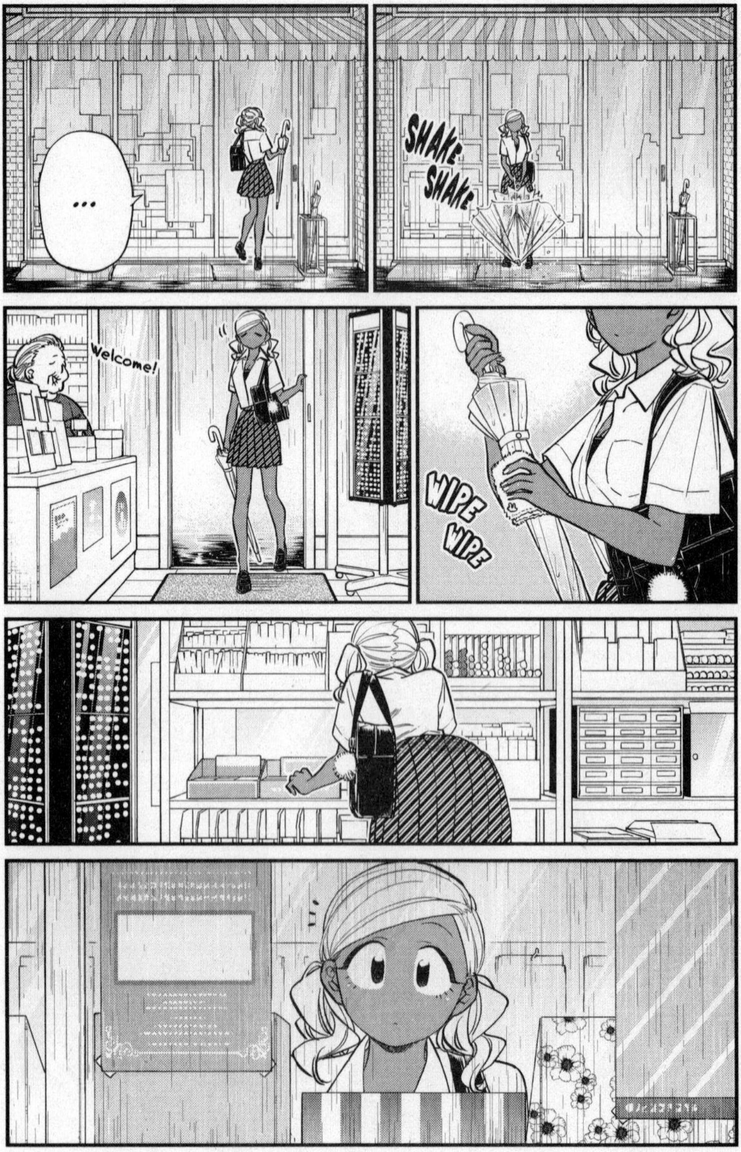
SHAKE SHAKE
...
WIPE WIPE
Welcome!

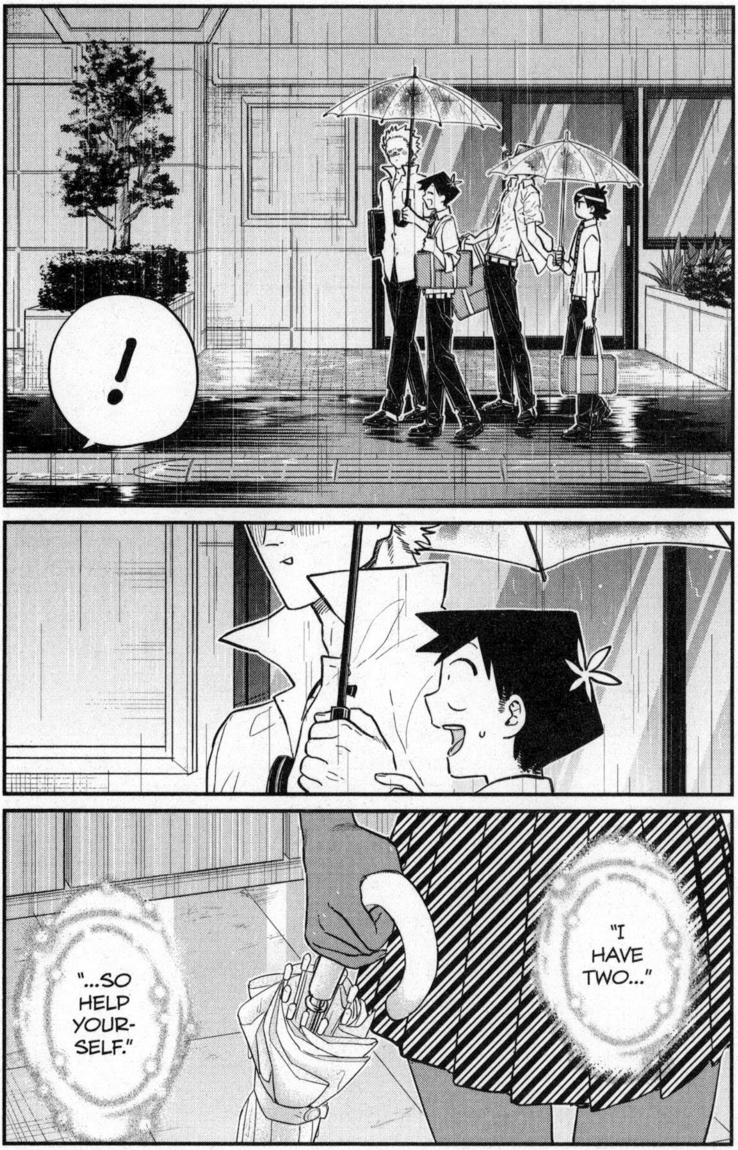
!
"I HAVE TWO..."
"...SO HELP YOUR-SELF."

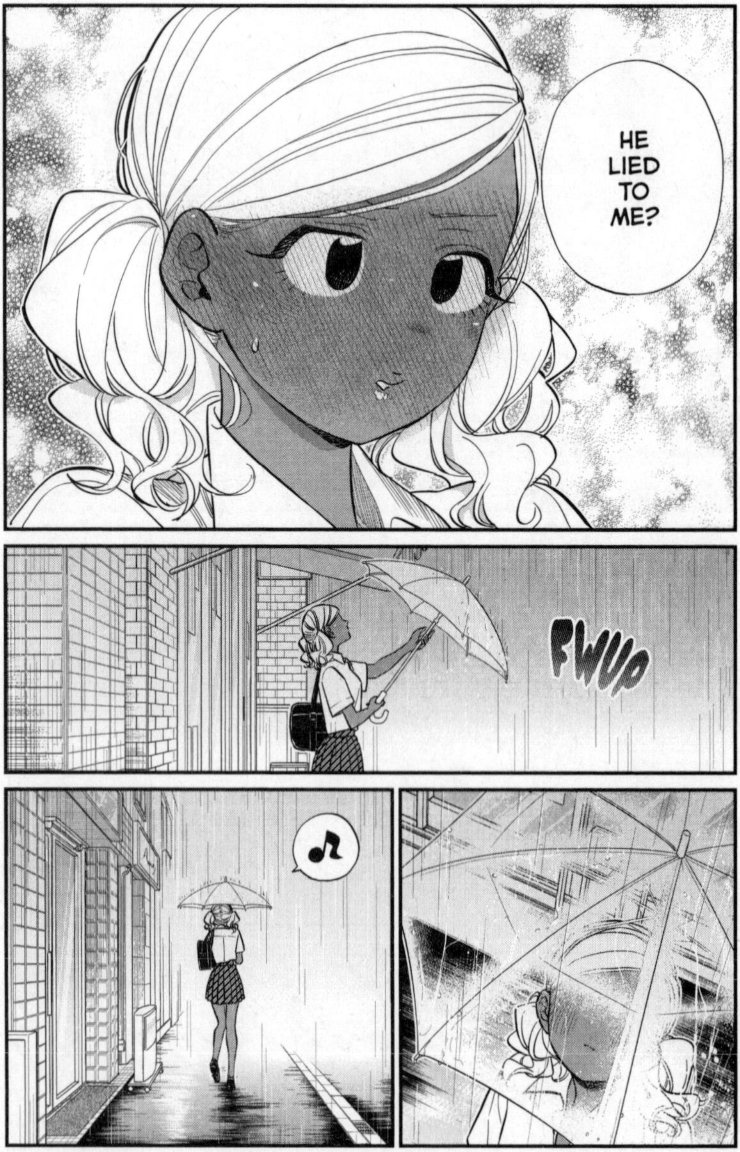
HE LIED TO ME?
FWUP
♪

Communication 157 — The End

Komi Can't
Communicate

Komi Can't Communicate Bonus

That Day Yo-Yo Hannya Appeared Wearing a Kimono!

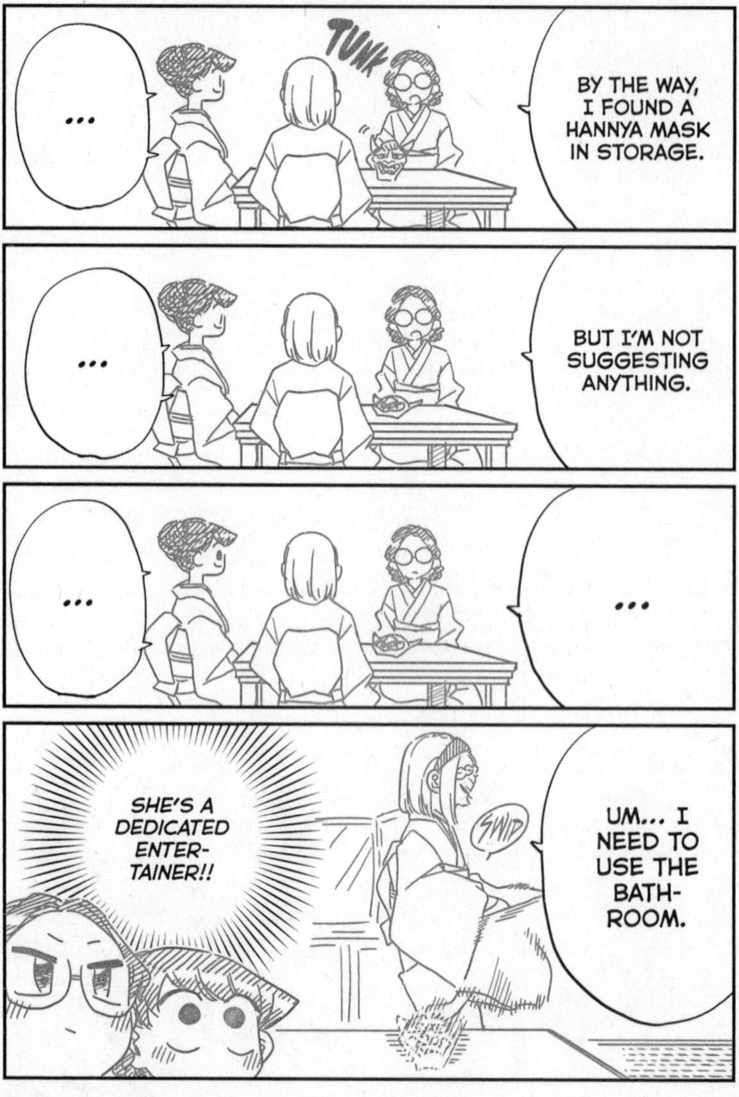
BY THE WAY, I FOUND A HANNYA MASK IN STORAGE.
TUNK
...
BUT I'M NOT SUGGESTING ANYTHING.
...
...
...
UM... I NEED TO USE THE BATH-ROOM.
SWD
SHE'S A DEDICATED ENTER-TAINER!!

Komi Can't Communicate Bonus

Can Komi Make 100 Friends? The Girl Who Sweats at Even 30 Degrees Below

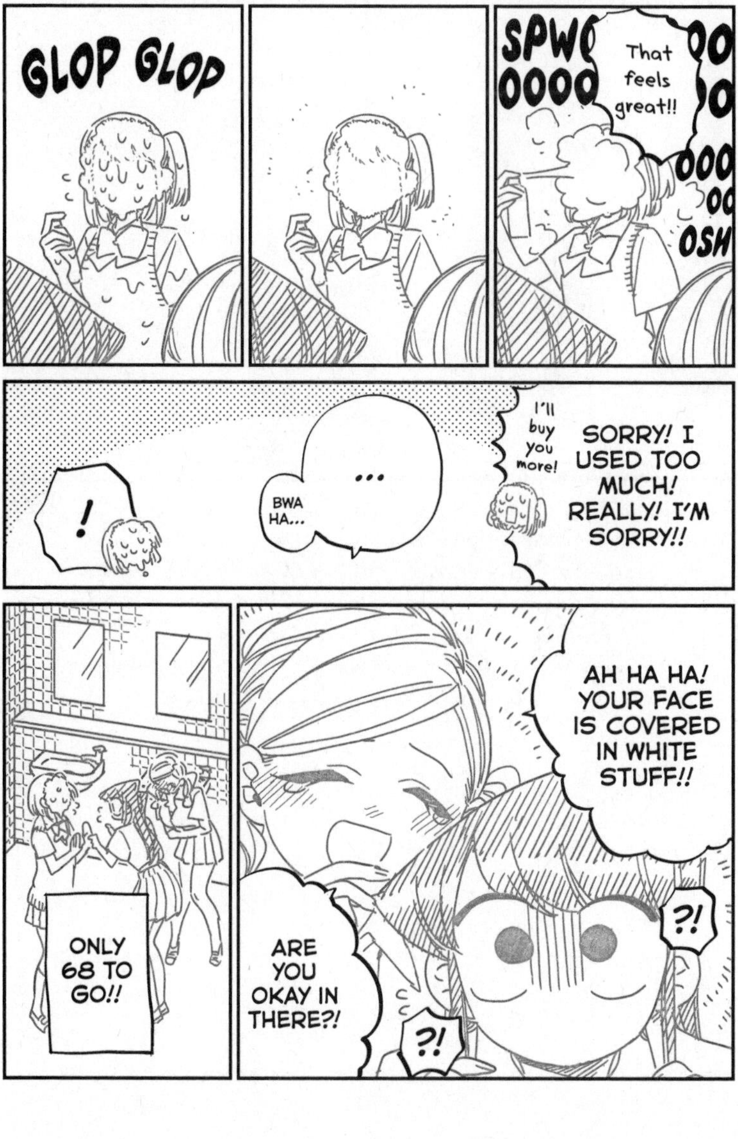

SPWOOOOOOOOOOOOOSH
That feels great!!
GLOP GLOP
SORRY! I USED TOO MUCH! REALLY! I'M SORRY!!
I'll buy you more!
...
BWA HA...
!
AH HA HA! YOUR FACE IS COVERED IN WHITE STUFF!!
?!
ARE YOU OKAY IN THERE?!
?!
ONLY 68 TO GO!!

Tomohito Oda won the grand prize for *World Worst One* in the 70th Shogakukan New Comic Artist Awards in 2012. Oda's series *Digicon*, about a tough high school girl who finds herself in control of an alien with plans for world domination, ran from 2014 to 2015. In 2015, *Komi Can't Communicate* debuted as a one-shot in *Weekly Shonen Sunday* and was picked up as a full series by the same magazine in 2016.

Komi Can't Communicate

VOL. 11
Shonen Sunday Edition

Story and Art by Tomohito Oda

English Translation & Adaptation/John Werry
Touch-Up Art & Lettering/Eve Grandt
Design/Julian [JR] Robinson
Editor/Pancha Diaz

COMI-SAN WA, COMYUSHO DESU. Vol. 11
by Tomohito ODA
© 2016 Tomohito ODA
All rights reserved.
Original Japanese edition published by SHOGAKUKAN.
English translation rights in the United States of America, Canada, the United
Kingdom, Ireland, Australia and New Zealand arranged with SHOGAKUKAN.

Original Cover Design/Masato ISHIZAWA + Bay Bridge Studio

Printed in the U.S.A.

Published by VIZ Media, LLC
P.O. Box 77010
San Francisco, CA 94107

10 9 8 7 6 5 4 3 2
First printing, February 2021
Second printing, August 2021

viz.com

shonensunday.com

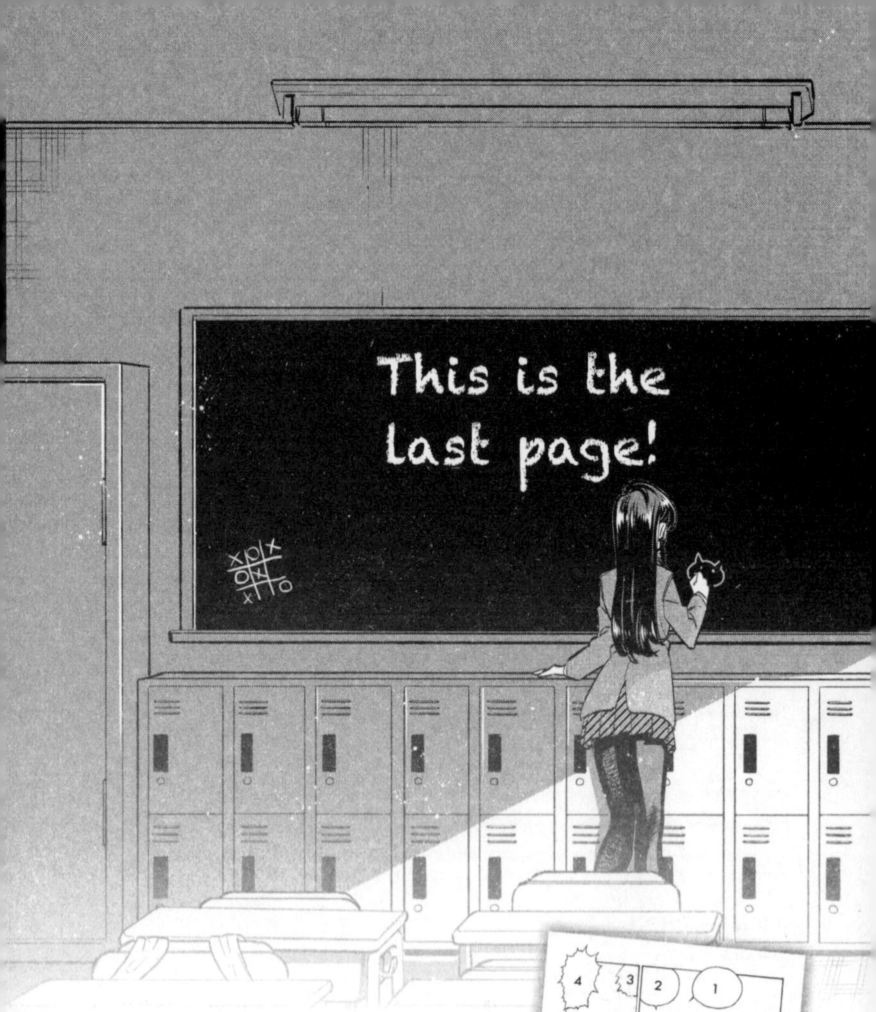
This is the last page!

Komi Can't Communicate has been printed in the original Japanese format to preserve the orientation of the artwork.

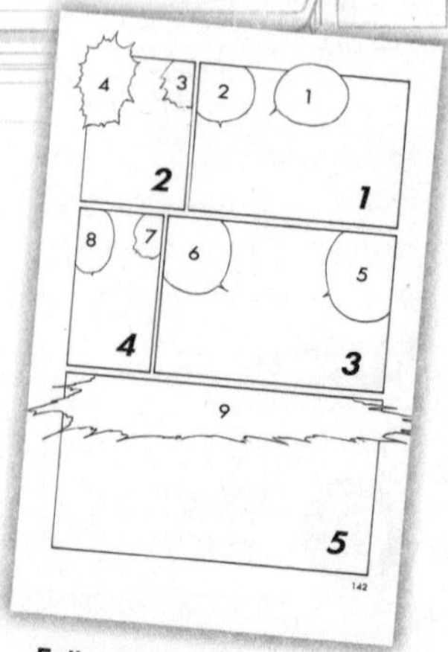

Follow the action this way.